Thaddeus Norris

American Fish-Culture

Embracing all the Details of Artificial Breeding and Rearing of Trout

Thaddeus Norris

American Fish-Culture
Embracing all the Details of Artificial Breeding and Rearing of Trout

ISBN/EAN: 9783337140243

Printed in Europe, USA, Canada, Australia, Japan

Cover: Foto ©Lupo / pixelio.de

More available books at **www.hansebooks.com**

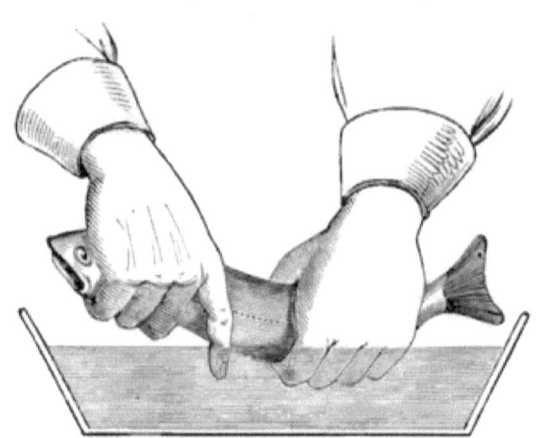

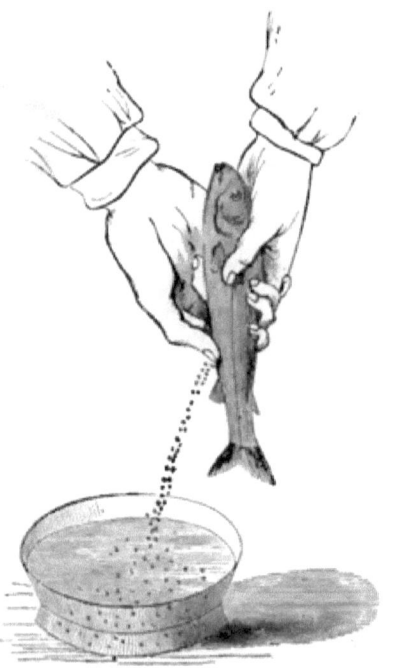

AMERICAN

FISH-CULTURE,

EMBRACING ALL THE DETAILS OF

ARTIFICIAL BREEDING AND REARING OF TROUT;
THE CULTURE OF SALMON, SHAD AND OTHER

FISHES.

BY THADDEUS NORRIS,

AUTHOR OF "THE AMERICAN ANGLER'S BOOK."

ILLUSTRATED.

PHILADELPHIA:
PORTER & COATES.
LONDON: SAMPSON LOW, SON & CO.
1868.

MEARS & DUSENBERY, STEREOTYPERS.   SHERMAN & CO., PRINTERS.

This Book

IS RESPECTFULLY DEDICATED

TO

STEPHEN H. AINSWORTH, Esq.,

IN APPRECIATION

OF

HIS PRAISEWORTHY EFFORTS TO ESTABLISH

Fish Culture

AS A BRANCH OF NATIONAL INDUSTRY.

PREFACE.

THE numerous essays and articles on Fish Culture which from time to time, have appeared in periodicals and newspapers, clearly demonstrate the increasing importance of this branch of industry, and have promoted a spirit of curiosity and inquiry amongst intelligent people. Some of the first minds amongst our countrymen are giving serious thought as to the means of arresting the gradual extinction of valuable fishes, and restoring our failing and exhausted rivers to their former fruitfulness; and are becoming convinced that the culture of water as well as of land, can be made to contribute largely to the supply of food required for our rapidly increasing population.

Many of the short essays with their illustrations, which appear in periodicals, claim the admiration and excite the curiosity of readers. But most of them, with their few and imperfect directions as to the mode of procedure, are calculated to mislead rather than direct the inquirer. With these facts before us, the writer, as well as other practical fish culturists, have declined many solicitations to contribute essays of limited space and matter to agricultural and other periodicals; being impressed with the impossibility of doing the subject justice if thus abridged. In the mean time, those who have engaged in it and have a knowledge of the art, are applied to for information

(5)

so frequently, that much time and some pains are required to put the inquirer on the right road to success. The two little essays which have appeared in the American Angler's Book, and the fact of my having engaged in the business since its publication, has made me the recipient of numerous letters and caused a voluminous correspondence. This has also been the case with my friend Stephen H. Ainsworth, who informs me that the aggregate time employed by him in answering letters and writing essays since he commenced his experiments, would amount almost to a year.

For want of directions as to the details of breeding and rearing trout, inexperienced persons who have commenced it have met with difficulties; which has discouraged others who were anxious to engage in the business. With the pushing disposition and impatience of many of our countrymen, they frequently ignore the fact that in experiments we learn as much from errors as success. In view of these facts bearing adversely on this new branch of industry, and with a wish to promote it, I have, at the solicitation of several friends who sympathize in the desire to foster it, given all the necessary details to insure success in the culture of our brook trout; being assisted, as the reader will find, by one who is as well versed in the art as any of those whose names have become prominent in this respect in France. I have also, as the reader will find in the following pages, drawn largely on my experience at the establishment I inaugurated in Warren county, New Jersey.

The artificial propagation of migratory fishes which enter our rivers, is destined to be the principal means by which we are to restock our exhausted streams, and restore those that are rapidly declining, to their former fecundity; as well as in naturalizing valuable species in waters where they have hitherto not **been known.** On this branch of the subject, I have brought to bear many years of close observation, and study of the instincts and habits of such fishes ; and have availed myself of all the knowledge of others that has come within my **reach.** That my observations and directions may be intelligable to general readers, in laying such information before them, I have used as few technicalities as I consistently could.

It will be seen that I have quoted largely from the great amount of useful knowledge elicited by the enterprising Commissioners of Fisheries for the New England States. One of the reasons for laying such information before my readers is, that many interested persons outside of those states may not be able to avail themselves of the important facts which have been brought to light, as the reports alluded **to** are published only for their own citizens, **or** those who may apply for them **to the Commissioners. As I have duly credited** the various sources from **which I have received** information bearing on fish culture, I will make **no** further mention of them here, than acknowledge my indebtedness to Mr. Bertram's work, "The Harvest of the Sea," and Mr. Francis's **book on** Fish Culture.

Although some statistics respecting salmon, **and the con-**sumption of crustacea, will be found in this book, I have **deemed** that any account of **fish** that inhabit the sea exclu-**sively, would be** irrelevant to my subject.

The publisher of an agricultural paper has urged my **compliance** with his request, to contribute a series of articles **on** trout culture, "if there were no state secrets." **I might here** suggest, **that** my starting a trout-breeding establishment **for one of the subscribers to** his paper (as I did for others, and that without remuneration), before I entertained an idea of writing this **book,** is an evidence that I have never **had any**

"state secrets" on the subject. I have a poor opinion of the man whose narrow mind and heart would prompt him to withhold any knowledge that would benefit those who should engage in the business. The proprietors of a similar periodical, who offered to pay liberally for like contributions, and who must be aware of the small remuneration I shall receive for the labor bestowed on this book, I hope, will allow that such reward has been but a small inducement; and that the reason assigned, that I could not treat the subject properly in the space allowed in their columns, is a substantial one. In conclusion of this preface, I can truly say that I have undertaken the task from a love of it, and a desire to diffuse a knowledge of the art.

THADDEUS NORRIS.

Philadelphia, July 1868

CONTENTS.

(9)

CHAPTER III.—Trout Breeding.

Incubation and Treatment of Fry.

CHAPTER IV.—Trout Breeding.

General Remarks, Food for Adults, Profits and Statistics.

CHAPTER VIII.—CULTURE OF EELS.

CHAPTER IX.—CULTURE OF OYSTERS.

APPENDIX.

AMERICAN FISH CULTURE.

CHAPTER I.

INTRODUCTORY REMARKS ON FISH CULTURE.

What it is.—Its advantages over natural propagation.—Time occupied in hatching.—Number of ova of different species.—Consequences of all the ova producing fish that would come to maturity. —Object of Fish Culture.—Its antiquity.—Practised by the Chinese and Romans.—Artificial propagation discovered by Dom Pinchon. —Rediscovered by M. Jacobi.—Subsequent discovery of Joseph Remy.—Alleged discoverers.—Experiments of Shaw and Young.— Patronage of the French government.—Its effects on Scotch and Irish rivers.—Its use as an adjunct in restoring American rivers to their former fecundity.—Commissioners of fisheries appointed by the New England States, and the States of New York and Pennsylvania.—Experiment in artificial propagation and hatching at Holyoke on the Connecticut.—Experiments in trout breeding by Stephen H. Ainsworth.—Progress in trout culture.—Fish culture in France.

It may be asked, what is Fish Culture. The reply is, that it is the propagation of fish by artificial means, and the

2   (13)

protection of the young from the dangers to which they are exposed in their natural haunts; assisting and in a great degree improving on nature. It may still be asked, can you assist or improve on nature? To this I respond, that if the fish culturist has the impregnated spawn under his own protection and supervision, it will be subjected to none of the casualties to which it is exposed in the stream where the parent fish deposits it. That no flood will sweep it away or cover it with dirt, sawdust, or tanbark. That no fish of its own or other species, sailing around like pirate craft, will devour it as it is ejected. That no eel or lamprey will burrow into the gravel-covered nest to make a dainty meal of its contents. That no duck, wild or tame, or long-legged wading-bird will gobble it up. That no water-rat, muskrat, mink, or other predacious quadruped will feed upon it. I would now in return ask my interrogator, if ten out of a hundred eggs should escape all these adverse contingencies and produce ten infant fish, if he supposes their own father and mother or other fish would hesitate for an instant to pouch them, or that aquatic birds which would have gobbled them up in embryo would spare them now? Does he think that three out of the ten infants would arrive at mature fishhood? Close observers think not, especially if they were ten infant trout or salmon, each weighed down with the umbilical sac of aliment which it carries under its belly for forty or fifty days. But if the fish culturist puts the eggs of salmon or trout into his hatching-trough, he will likely get eighty or ninety young fish from a hundred. If trout, seventy or eighty of the fry may be **grown** to **weigh** a **pound or** more, in three years, and are **worth seventy-five cents or a** dollar a pound **in** market.

If my querist reads scientific journals, he will see **that** Dr. Daniell, of Savannah, transported the fecundated spawn **of shad across the country to a** tributary **of the Alabama,** ten years **ago, and hatched** them out and stocked that noble **river and its branches with this** favorite fish. **If he only reads the newspapers, he must** have found **out that Seth Green sends trout spawn by** thousands **to all parts of the** Northern and Middle **States. That Dr.** Fletcher has brought salmon eggs **from the British province of New Brunswick to** stock **the** salmonless **rivers of** New England, **and that** salmon spawn has **even been sent from** England to Australia **to** introduce **that noble fish there. That barren** salmon **rivers of Ireland and Scotland have by** means of fish culture **been** restored to their former fecundity; **and** rivers, and **even** brooks, that **before had no salmon, have been made fruitful of them.**

There is scarcely a month in **the calendar in which fish of some** genus or other **do** not spawn. **Some** deposit their **eggs on stones, brush, or** aquatic plants, the ova adhering by a glutinous substance which surrounds them. Others, **as** the salmon family, **excavate their nests** on gravelly beds in running water, cover their spawn and leave it to the care of mother nature. Some, such as the stickleback, **the** sunfish, the black-bass, and others of the perch family, build nests and stand guard over them. Others, including some species of Siluridæ, known as **catfish, have a parental**

care for their young, and lead them about as a hen does her chickens.

The time occupied in hatching the spawn also varies. That of the salmon requires from forty to over two hundred days, according to the temperature of the water; while the spawn of the shad in water at 75° hatches in fifty-two to sixty hours.

The number of eggs produced by different species vary as wide as the time of incubation. A salmon of ten pounds only gives ten thousand eggs, or a thousand to each pound of its weight; while a good-sized codfish gives a million, a herring forty or fifty thousand, and a five-pound shad a hundred thousand. But a small percentage of ova produce fish, as it is food for fishes and other aquatic animals. If all the fish eggs produced were hatched and the fry arrived at mature age, the seas would be so full that they could not be navigated, and rivers and lakes would be plethoric. The object of fish culture is to profit by knowledge of the facts I have mentioned, and to turn a portion of the waste of piscine life to human account.

As far back as our knowledge of the Chinese extends, we find that fecundated fish spawn with them has been an article of traffic. The manner of procuring it is by placing fagots on frames permanently fixed in waters where fish are accustomed to spawn. At the proper time the fagots are collected with the spawn adhering, and the ova either hatched out by those who collect it, or is sold and transported in water. The flooded rice-fields are frequently used for raising the young fish. I would here remark that this spawn must necessarily be mostly of species belonging to the carp family, which abound in China. By this mode of culture, fish are made so abundant and cheap there that they are the chief food of the people.

The Romans, vying with each other in the splendor of their feasts, left no means unemployed of spreading their tables with the best fish their climate afforded, and fish culture was brought into requisition to a great extent to supply this demand. M. Jourdier, a French writer on this subject, says of Lucullus, " at his house at Tusculum, on the shores of the Gulf of Naples, he dug canals from his fish-ponds to the sea. Into these canals freshwater streams were led, and pure running water thus kept up. Sea-fish that breed in fresh water passed through the canals into his ponds, and stocked them with their young. When they attempted to return to sea, flood-gates barred their egress at the mouths of the canals, and while their progeny were growing the parent fish supplied the market." The value of the fish kept in these ponds, it is stated, amounted to a sum which in our money would be equal to two hundred and fifty thousand dollars.

Fish culture appears to have fallen into disuse after the fall of the Roman republic, as we find no mention of it until the fourteenth century, when, according to M. Jourard, Dom Pinchon, a monk of the Abbey of Réome, discovered the art of breeding fish in wooden boxes, the ends being of wicker work and the bottoms covered with sand, in which excavations were made and the ova deposited. The art was rediscovered about the year 1763 by Jacobi a German.

Bertram, in his " Harvest of the Seas," says : " Jacobi, who practised the art for thirty years, was not satisfied with the mere discovery, but at once turned what he had discovered to practical account ; and in the time of Jacobi great attention was devoted to pisciculture by various gentlemen of scientific eminence.   Count Goldstein, a savan of that period, also wrote on the subject.   The Journal of Hanover had papers on this art, and an account of Jacobi's proceedings was also enrolled in the Memoirs of the Royal Academy of Berlin . . . . . The results arrived at by Jacobi were of vast importance, and obtained not only the recognition of his government, but also the more solid reward of a pension."

It is strange that so important a discovery should not have produced more permanent results, and that it should not have been followed up at that time with the same success which has attended the after-discovery of Joseph Remy-Jacobi's mode of hatching the ova of salmon and trout, was the same as that of his predecessor, Dom Pinchon, using gravel, however, instead of sand in his hatching-boxes. Dom Pinchon is the first of whom it is recorded that he expressed the ova and fecundated it with the milt of the male fish ; the Chinese and Romans had not arrived at this point in their pisciculture.

In the early part of the present century there was considerable controversy amongst naturalists and fishermen in Great Britain, concerning a little fish known as the parr; whether it was a distinct species or the young of the salmon.   Also, whether the young salmon arrived at its *smolt* state and made its first migration to sea the second or third summer of its existence. To decide these points of dispute, Mr. Shaw, of Drumlanrig, and Mr. **Andrew Young**, of Invershin, Scotland, **about** the year 1834 bred salmon artificially in wooden boxes. It is likely they were aware of the plan pursued by Jacobi and followed his example, as their mode was not heralded as a discovery, and was not different in any essential point from that of Jacobi. I will here say **that the result** of their experiments proved the parr to be the young of the salmon, and that the contestants were both right as to the period of its first migration to sea, as **it** has been clearly ascertained that a portion of them, **even of** the same brood, will migrate **the second summer, and another portion defer their journey** until the following year. It is stated also, that pisciculture was practised in Norway previous to the experiments made by Shaw and Young, and that James Hogg, the Ettrick Shepherd, was one of its discoverers.

It is useless to dwell on facts that the most obtuse have not failed to notice. I allude to the gradual extinction and banishment from **our rivers of the** more valuable species, and **the** consequent enhanced value of such fish in our markets, rendering them almost unattainable by persons of **moderate** means. The **old** countries of Europe, though more provident, have suffered, more **or less, in the same way, and fish as food has become** a question of vast importance. The French government has fostered fish culture chiefly **for** this reason, and to such purpose that in a few years there will scarcely be an acre of barren water in the empire.   Not only fish but oysters, crayfish, and other crustacea are being multiplied by this new science.

The discovery of Joseph Remy has produced practical results which did not follow those of his predecessors. This French peasant, who gained a livelihood from the Moselle, its tributaries, and other streams of his native district, La Bresse, lamenting the sure extinction of the finer kinds of fish; by long and anxious vigils became convinced of the outer impregnation of the spawn and all the adverse vicissitudes to which it and the young fry were exposed.   His experiments based on these observations were successful beyond his anticipations, and in 1849, when his doings and those of his companion Gehin were brought to the knowledge of M. Coste, professor of Biology in the College of France, improvements were made in the manner of hatching the ova, the patronage of the government was secured, and the present establishment at Huningue, and subsequently its branches, were inaugurated.   The effects of liberal and judicious government patronage have not only been spread over France, but its benefits have reached all parts of enlightened Europe; and our own country is now resorting to this new science to restock its exhausted rivers, and adopting it as a branch of industry.

In a chapter devoted to the salmon I shall endeavor to give a summary of what has been done in Scotland and Ireland in cultivating that valuable fish.

In this country, our utter disregard for the bounties of nature so wonderfully lavished upon us, and our inordinate rage for internal improvements, have caused our state governments rather to legislate for the extinction than the protection and continuance of the finer species of migratory fishes. Individuals have been allowed, and companies have been chartered, to construct impassable dams, driving back salmon and shad from their spawning-beds; and not only above, but below such barriers most of our rivers have become as barren of such fish as if they had never resorted to them. These are not the natural consequences of civilization and progress, as some would urge, but rather of barbarism and reckless improvidence; and at last, when a shad or a pound of salmon is sold for twenty times the price it brought when we ceased to be colonies of Great Britain, our legislators have set seriously to work to regain for us the liberal provisions of nature which they have thrown away.

Our separate interests as states, it is to be feared, will defer or prevent the restoration of many rivers to their former fruitfulness, as many of them form the boundaries between, or flow through, several states. The New England States, notwithstanding, have at length set to work with a will, and, from all we can gather from the reports of their fish commissioners, there is much good feeling and concert of action. The joint commission have defined the part to be taken by each state. Those to whose territory the spawning-beds of the long rivers are confined, have agreed to stock them with shad and salmon, and are using the fecundated spawn of these fish to do it the more speedily. The enormous number of forty millions of young shad were hatched out by Seth Green at Holyoke on the Connecticut last summer and turned into the river. The intermediate states are to construct efficient fishways for the passage of the fish to their spawning-grounds. Those owning the mouths of the rivers are to provide against destructive fishing, and give a free passage to the upper waters. All the states referred to have enacted laws, or revived those that were obsolete, to promote the object in view. It is devoutly to be hoped that a liberal spirit will prevail, and that the energy which now characterizes the commissioners will continue until the much-desired end is attained. I shall have occasion to refer to the reports of the commissioners of each state; that of Maine is lengthy, and contains much of interest to the friends of the enterprise; the Vermont report is also interesting, and that of Massachusetts instructive, practical, and spirited.

The state of New York has also appointed fish commissioners. It is to be regretted that Stephen H. Ainsworth is not of the number. Still, from the reputed energy of Mr. R. B. Roosevelt and the known experience and skill of Mr. Seth Green,* we may expect favorable results. If the latter should go to Canada or New Brunswick to manipulate the salmon, and then have charge of the hatching, there is no fear that the Hudson and the streams flowing into the St. Lawrence and the Lakes will be without salmon for many years after the fry are produced. Of course fishways are to be constructed, and laws for the protection of the fish and

---

* Since writing the above I have been informed that Ex-Governor Seymour, who, it is said, takes much interest in the matter, has been added to the commission.

fry rigidly enforced, or no permanent good will come from merely stocking the rivers.

Pennsylvania, on the 30th of March 1866, passed a law making it incumbent on the owners of dams on the Susquehanna and its tributaries, whether companies or individuals, to erect efficient fishways over such dams by the first of December of that year, and a competent engineer was appointed to see the law enforced. The companies who had bought the different internal improvements from the state, contended that they were purchased without encumbrance, and resist the law, as some other companies also do, and it is now a matter of litigation. One, however, the Susquehanna Canal Company, acquiesced and constructed a fishway under the supervision of the engineer appointed. The report of this gentleman to the legislature shows that shad in numbers and of large size ascended the fishways in the spring and summer of 1867, and were taken as high up as New Port on the Juniata; the number being variously estimated from ten thousand to eighteen thousand. Numerous fry were also seen in the river during the latter part of the summer, as well as some bodies of Shad that had died, as they frequently do, from the exhausting effects of spawning. This proves conclusively that shad will ascend rivers to new spawning-beds if suitable fishways are provided. To introduce them into tributaries which they may not enter, or to repopulate the Susquehanna the more speedily, artificial propagation must of course be resorted to. If it should be decided that the Act of March 30th 1866 is not constitutional, it remains for the state to defray

the cost of restoring to the people who dwell on the river
in question and its tributaries, the privileges of which it
unjustly deprived them in constructing internal improvements, or granted away to corporate companies. This the
New England States have already done, and when appropriations have fallen short in effecting some desired object,
commissioners have footed the bill, trusting to the liberality
of their state to refund the difference.

Although our state governments have been tardy in avail-
ing themselves of the benefit to be obtained from this new
science, individual curiosity and enterprise have not been
idle.   From a lack of knowledge of the requirements and
mode of procedure, however, success in most cases has been
small or unsatisfactory, and experiments have been almost
or entirely confined to breeding trout.   Our most zealous
and able fish culturist, Stephen H. Ainsworth, commenced
ten years ago with whatever light he could get on the subject from newspapers and periodicals, generally accounts of
what was doing in France.   With a supply of water that
does not fill an inch auger hole, and of exceedingly variable temperature, it may be said, he has taught himself this
science, discovering many of its hidden truths not recorded
by French fish culturists, and is now our chief authority on
all matters pertaining to it.   He imparts the knowledge
he has gained by years of unwearied observation, to all
inquirers, and has done much by his letters and newspaper
contributions to create an interest in the art.   He has been
my preceptor; all that I shall endeavor to teach in a chapter on trout breeding are lessons which I have learned of

him, or from my own experience which grew out of his teachings. I will give a brief description of his establishment and that of his neighbor, Seth Green, in a subsequent chapter.

Breeding and raising trout for private use and to supply our markets is destined to become a national branch of industry, and many who possess the requisite natural advantages are now turning their attention to it. I shall notice the efforts of many of those who have commenced it, under its appropriate head.

I have alluded on a former page to the fact that the French government is making every effort to extend this branch of industry, so that waste waters which were entirely barren, are now beginning to be more productive than the same area of cultivated land. The fish ponds of Doombes extend over thirty thousand acres. Under the advisement of proficient persons appointed by the government, all kinds of waters are stocked with fish suitable to them : carp, perch, eels and pike for sluggish streams, lakes and ponds; trout for the bounding cool brook, and the salmon for the clear swift river. France being a Roman Catholic country, with its many fast days, fish are more requisite than where Protestantism prevails; therefore, fish of the cheaper kinds are more in demand than with us, and are used where meats would be bought in our markets. The cultivation of oysters, as well as crustacea, is fostered by the government; so, also, is that of sea-fish. Experiments are even being made on the sea coasts, in the propagation and rearing of the finer kinds of turtles.

3

CHAPTER II.

TROUT BREEDING.

THE TROUT, TROUT PONDS, ETC.

The Trout.—Its adaptability to **culture.**—**Season** of spawning.—
Spawning grounds.—Appearance of **the sexes** at spawning time,
habits and condition.—Subsequent recuperation.—Water-supply.—
Effect of the temperature of water **on the** time of **hatching.**—
Spring water necessary for incubation. *Series of Ponds.*—Their
shape.—Method of shading them. *Raceways.*—Their **construction.**
—Protection of **them** from muskrats.—Screens.—Depth **and size**
of ponds.—**Transfer of** fish from one pond to another.—Estimate **of**
number of trout for a given supply of water.—Jeremiah **Comfort's**
ponds.—Stocking ponds.—Procuring **and transporting brood trout.**

THE artificial hatching and **raising of** fish, as I have
already intimated, has, with few exceptions, been confined
in this country to brook trout. **These are not** only fish of
the rarest beauty **and most delicate flavor,** but **they also**
command the highest price in market and afford the greatest sport to **the angler.** Moreover, their **spawn is more**
easily procured and can be hatched in a manner more resembling that of nature, than **the** ova of any **other fresh-**
water fish.

The season of spawning **with** trout extends from the
latter **part of October** to the middle of December; and in
some cases where **the** water does not freeze, as in Caledonia

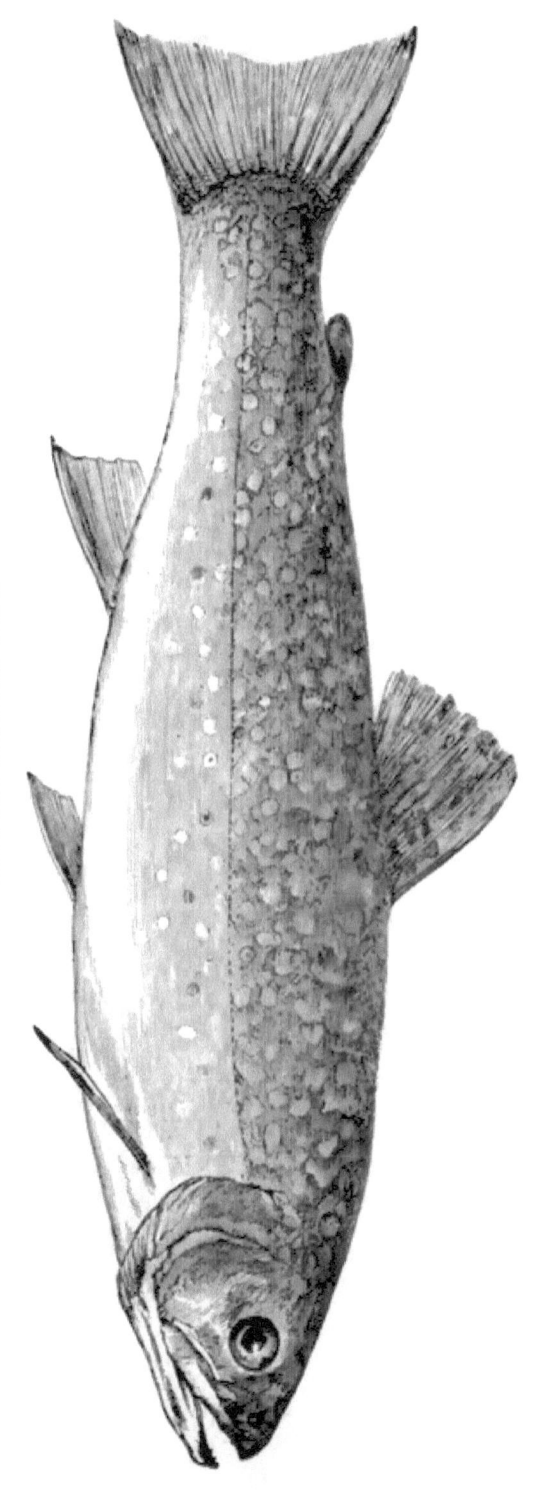

THE BROOK TROUT.

creek, in New York, to the middle of March.* When they have a choice of spawning-grounds, trout will seek shallow water of gentle current, with pebbly bottom, or the lower end of a ripple where the water is almost still. To occupy such places, they will run out of deeper water either up or down stream, leaping over an obstructing log, or wriggling through water half the depth of their bodies, the males preceding the females some days. At this season the

---

* About the 1st of May (of this year) I visited Mr. A. J. Beaumont, near New Hope, Pa., for the purpose of inaugurating a trout-breeding establishment. He has a spring which supplies the power for a paper and grist mill, the water flowing in a raceway about five hundred yards to the mill site. This race is well stocked with trout, and the water is of such unvarying temperature that the fish know no summer or winter. On taking a few fish with the fly I found that more than half of the females presented the slender body and peculiar appearance of fish that had lately spawned. When I mentioned the circumstance to Mr. Beaumont he informed me that only three days before, while cutting water cresses at the spring, his son removed a stone that lay at a slight angle with the bottom, and found beneath it a large number of trout spawn. On examining the ova he could not detect, with the naked eye, any formation of the young fish. The conclusion to be deduced from this and similar facts which have come under my observation, is that the more equable the temperature of the water, the longer will the time of spawning extend into the spring of the year, and that trout taken from cold forest streams, where they spawn only in the fall, and placed in unvarying spring water ponds, will, in successive generations, breed later and later, until they take on the habit, in this respect, that prevails with the trout in Mr. Beaumont's raceway and in Caledonia creek.

sexes are easily distinguished, the males putting on a decidedly orange tint, their fins brilliantly red, with the first
two or three rays of the ventrals and anal vividly white;
while the females are of a sober silver gray. Their forms
also differ at spawning time—the males deep-bodied, slab-
sided, and long-headed; the females with the usual small
head, and the looked-for rotundity and protuberance of
abdomen. The males show all the ardor of quadrupeds
on such occasions, and in their contests for the favors of
the shy spawners the result is sometimes fatal. I have
picked up males at the outlet of my pond whose scarred
and gashed sides left no doubt as to the cause of their
death. A greater part of the time of the male is occupied
in driving off rivals, and fish that wait at hand to devour
the eggs as they are dropped.

A male may have milt enough for several females of his
own size, consequently, his milting extends over a period
of a week or ten days; during which time he may have
two, or three mates in succession. A female when she is
mated and her spawn matured, deposits it all in a day or
two, or in three days at most; if her mate is so small that
his milt is exhausted before she is done spawning, she
seeks another companion.

As the time for spawning approaches, the fish fall off in
flesh and flavor, which they do not generally regain until
late in the following spring. When they have access to
brackish and salt water, as on Long Island, where they
find shrimp and small fry, this may be in March. In fresh-
water ponds where there is much feed, as the larva of flies,

worms on certain weeds, and **minute crustacea, or when**
they are bountifully fed, they are edible in April. In the
streams of the forest **however,** they are seldom in season
before the 10th **of May.** The peculiar habits, appearance,
and condition of trout at spawning time can be observed in
clear ponds where they are kept for breeding, as well, or
perhaps better, than in their wild haunts.

Water Supply.—Spring water, whether hard or soft, if
not impregnated to any great extent with mineral, is best,
not only for hatching but also for **supplying ponds.** The
warmer the water the more rapid the incubation, though a
low temperature conduces to **the** healthy condition of **the**
ova during this process, as **well as to** that of the young **fish**
until the umbilical **sac is absorbed, as** it is not **favorable to**
the growth of byssus and confervia. In proof of this I
would instance the small percentage of eggs lost in incuba-
tion by Mr. Ainsworth; though much of his success in
hatching is to be attributed to his experience in expressing
the spawn and milt, as well as the care he bestows on the
ova after taking them. A spring with a deep source will
furnish water of almost unvarying temperature, and will
indicate the mean of the atmosphere in its locality. In the
neighborhood of Philadelphia, this **is about 51°** or 52°
For hatching, the water should never be above 54°; 46°
or **47° is.** perhaps **the** best temperature. Spring water is
almost indispensable in hatching, as few or no brooks are
uniformly clear, or have not more or less dirt or vegetable
fibre carried along **by the** current.

It is to be **supposed** that the beginner has a spring of

3 *

certain flow for hatching, and perhaps a cold brook which he can also use in supplying his ponds. He will therefore wish to know the size his ponds should be, and the best form. Before I give any directions on incubation and its appliances I will treat of ponds, remarking by the way, that if one uses brook water to increase his supply, he should **not** introduce it, if avoidable, into his first pond where the small fry are kept, and should make some contrivance for shutting off the brook or confining it to its usual volume in time of heavy rains. He should do this, not only that he may keep the water in the first pond **at its** usual temperature, but also to prevent dirt from **being** washed in, which will soon foul the bottom with mud.

The plan usually pursued with those who raise trout as a " **crop,**" is to have a series of ponds connected by raceways, the latter being **used** as spawning-grounds for the fish. At least three ponds are required. The first for the young fish from the time they are taken from the hatching-trough or nursery, until they attain the age of eighteen or twenty months. The second **pond** for the same brood for the next twelve months, at the **end of which time they will** be thirty or thirty-two months old. **The third** pond for the **same fish** from the age last mentioned, until they are three years and a half old. From the last pond it is supposed they are to be taken for sale or the proprietor's table. **It** will be observed, that when the last pond is vacated the trout from the second pond will occupy it, that the second will be occupied by the fish from the first, and the first pond **by the new brood from the nursery.**

It requires careful forethought, that the size of the ponds may be in accordance with the supply and temperature of the water. The cause of failure in most cases **has been** where persons have attempted to supply large ponds with a diminutive stream; thus exposing a large area to the heat of a summer atmosphere and the rays of the sun. The shape also of the ponds has much to do with the temperature of the water; an oblong is preferable to a circle; if the width of the pond is one-tenth of its length, so much the better, as the water passes through quicker, and retains its coldness to a greater degree. Trees, though they may shade and serve to beautify, cause much annoyance, as the leaves falling or being blown into the water, sink and accumulate on the bottom, or are carried by the current against and clog the wire screens which are placed in the outlets to keep the fish in the ponds allotted to them. A cheap and efficient method of diminishing the surface exposed to the sun is with floats or platforms made of rough boards, moored in the ponds; these also make an acceptable shade and hiding-place for the fish.

The race-ways, which, as I have before remarked. **are** the spawning grounds of the fish, should be five **or six** inches deep, from two to three and a half feet wide, and from twenty to sixty feet long, according to the size of the ponds and the supply of water. The bottoms of the raceways should be covered to the depth of three inches **or** more with fine gravel for the trout to make their nests in. The sides should be of boards an inch thick and twelve inches wide. If the slope of the ground is such that there

will be much fall between the ponds, the water should discharge at each outlet into a box or pool, and flow through
the race below in a gentle current. The water is thus
aerated without creating a rapid, which is unfavorable to a
spawning-ground. When the supply is small, the water
in a pond may back half way up the race which feeds it.
At the end of each raceway strips should be nailed perpendicularly against the board sides, one set on each side at
the entrance into the pond, and another set three or four
feet above, so that wire gratings can be slipped in to secure
the spawners when they are driven from the race above.

I would here impress on the beginner the necessity of
not allowing too rapid a stream in the raceways, or having
the water shallow, or gravel in the ponds where they enter.
If he does, the trout may find a more acceptable spawning-
place in the upper part of the pond, even in broad sunshine, than in the covered race above; and if he attempts
to secure his spawners at the head of the pond with a seine,
he will frighten back into deep water those that might,
perhaps, enter the raceway.

If the sides of the raceways are lined with boards, it
will not only secure them from the effects of frost and
prevent dirt from falling in, but will also be a protection
against muskrats. A hundred feet of hemlock or third
quality pine will cost but a trifle, and will line a raceway
fifty feet long. This is also the most effectual way of protecting the sides of ponds from these pests. On perfectly
level ground, however, if the water comes within a few
inches or a foot of the top of the bank, there is no harbor

for them, as they **burrow under** water only where the bank is high enough above it **to allow** them room for their nests. In severe weather, when **the ground is covered with snow, muskrats** are driven by hunger to feed on grass, **which** may even then be found on the margin of spring water, or they may **come into** it for the warmth it **affords.** When they nib the **grass, much** of it is set adrift and clogs the wire **screens, at least I have found** it so in my experience. On this account it **would be well to have the** margin of the raceways and ponds gravelled. A great inconvenience is experienced **in** keeping the screens **at the** outlets from becoming clogged with leaves and floating trash. There should therefore be **a coarser screen** to act as a leaf **catcher, placed** before each of those **intended to keep the fish in their** respective ponds. **Seth** Green, at Caledonia creek, that he may prevent the fish in his ponds from running up into the mill-pond that supplies them, has a water-wheel turned **by** the current at the head of the raceway, the edges of the buckets or paddles coming so close to the **concavity of the frame** in which it revolves, as to keep the fish from ascending, while those from above can descend **between the** buckets. Floating grass and leaves also **pass** without **obstruction.** This contrivance, however, **although it will keep the large fish in the** last pond, will not prevent those of pond No. 1 from **running down into No. 2,** and the fish **of both** from getting into pond No. 3, where the yearlings would be devoured.

Pond No. 1 being for **the** small fry, from the time they leave the hatching-troughs or nursery, until they are some-

c

thing over eighteen months old, the water in it should not be more than six inches deep at the upper, and two feet deep at the lower end. Young trout delight in shallow water, and will therefore be found mostly where the race-way enters; as they grow larger they will seek the deeper water at the lower end of the pond. The bottom of **this** pond should be covered to the depth of two or three inches with coarse gravel.

POND NO. 2.—The fish, when they are old enough to enter this pond, will **require** deeper water and more room. It may therefore be a third or a half longer, two or three feet wider, and have an average depth of three feet; **thus** containing four or five times as many cubic feet of water as pond **No. 1.** The depth may be more uniform; care being **taken to have a** good depth and no gravel where the race **enters, so as to offer no** inducement for the fish to spawn in the pond. The trout, spawning for the first time a few months after entering this pond, and being still small, and giving not over three hundred eggs to each spawner, it **is** not requisite that the raceway supplying it should be as long or as wide as that leading into the next pond below.

POND NO. 3 should contain double or three times the number of cubic feet of water of the preceding, and have **an** average depth of five feet. This, as well as the other ponds, if it can be so arranged, should have **a** flume in the bottom, **so** that it **can** be entirely drained if sufficient mud **should** accumulate to make it desirable. The fish entering this pond when somewhat over two and a half years old, will give double or thrice as many ova as they did the preeeding autumn. On recovering condition the following spring they will average about a pound, and are then fit for the market or one's own use. **If any are left they will likely** prey on the smaller of those from pond No. 2 **when** transferred to this. For it must be borne in mind that some are of slow growth from the egg, and will not be half the size of others of the same age when driven into this pond, or one-fourth the size of some a year older that may remain in it. It is therefore better to clear it of all its occupants **before those from No. 2 are admitted,** as it is not safe to calculate that trout of a pound, or it may be a pound and a quarter, will not swallow those of four ounces ; I have had ocular proof that they will. **How many of the latter size** were devoured by the **larger at night, or when I** was not **observing them, it is hard to tell. If,** therefore, one should wish to keep trout beyond the age of three and a half years, it would be better to have a fourth pond and transfer them to it. The water having answered the purpose of hatching **and** supplying **the** stock ponds, where the fish are, **I** might say, stall fed, may now be used for a miniature lake if ·**not too** large, where the fish would find their own **feed, and** where **the** owner might indulge his taste for the pic- **turesque and have a** fly cast for himself and friends.

The proper time for transferring the fish from one pond to another is the latter part of August. Pond No. 3, as I have already remarked, **by** that time will have been vacated and can be occupied by those **from No. 2 ; pond No. 2 by** those from No. 1 ; **and No. 1** by the new brood from **the** nursery. After the 1st of September trout should not be eaten, as they are then getting out of season. If transferred about this time or a little earlier they are not so heavy with spawn as to be affected by change of habitat, and will become accustomed to their new home by spawning time.

In the proportions I have given for ponds, the fish are more under the control of the owner and can be fed with greater certainty and regularity than in those which approach a square or circle in shape, and the ponds can be easily dragged with a seine so as to secure every fish if necessary to clear it.

As the fish in pond No. 1 do not spawn at the age they inhabit it, a raceway with the requisites for breeding is not necessary. The water should be led in through two or more shallow rills from a foot to two or three feet wide, according to the supply. If bulkheads made by setting narrow boards edgewise, put out from each side alternately, nearly to the middle of the rills, they will create a zigzag current and form eddies for the fry. These bulkheads may be set from four to eight feet apart, the distance apart being proportioned to the length of the races. The bottom of the race, though, should also be covered with gravel.

This question of course will present itself to the reader: How many trout will a supply of given volume and temperature keep in healthy condition? In reply, I will cite a case on which I have in a great degree based my estimate; I have already referred to it in "The American Anglers' Book."—Owen Desh, at Hellertown, Penna., has a spring in his garden, the temperature of which we will suppose to be 51°, and the volume one and a half inches square; it flows through a trough about twenty-four feet long and two feet wide, at a depth of eighteen inches, which gives seventy-two cubic feet of water. His usual supply of trout in it is, or was, eight hundred, although at times he has kept twelve hundred, varying in size from nine to thirteen inches. If we take seven hundred and twenty fish as the minimum, it gives ten trout to each cubic foot. These trout were kept in thriving condition on one or two quarts of curd fed to them on alternate days, and not over a dozen died during the summer. If the reader takes this as a basis he can make his own calculations, remembering that it is not the quantity of water a fish has to live in, so much as its life-giving qualities. If Mr. Desh's supply had been spread out over an acre at a depth of three feet and exposed to the rays of the sun and a summer atmosphere, it is doubtful whether the water would have been sufficiently oxygenated to sustain trout at all. Therefore, if trout are to be grown as a crop, the fish culturist should be careful how he indulges his fancy for the ornate in making his ponds. It would be practicable for any farmer having a spring of low summer temperature, flowing a full square inch, to have a series of three small ponds, to keep fifteen hundred yearlings in the first, a thousand two year old in the second, and six or seven hundred three year old in the third.

My friend Jeremiah Comfort, near Spring Mills, on the Norristown Railroad, has a supply of sixteen square inches (not sixteen inches square). In laying off his ponds last fall I gave the sizes as follows: Pond No. 1; sixty feet long, eight feet wide, four inches of water at the upper, and

4

twenty inches at the lower end, contents, four hundred and eighty cubic feet, to sustain nine thousand six hundred young fry, or twenty to each cubic foot of water, from the time they leave the nursury until they are eighteen or twenty months old. Pond No 2; thinking that the water would increase from one to one and a half degrees in temperature in passing through pond No. 1, we estimated that a cubic foot in this would sustain three trout from the time they were twenty until they were thirty-two months old, and allowing for loss or sales, reduced the estimated number for this to eight thousand one hundred. We accordingly laid it off ninety feet long, ten feet wide, and intend filling it to the average depth of three feet, which gives twenty-seven hundred cubic feet as its contents, and three fish to each cubic foot. Pond No. 3; assuming that the summer temperature of the water in this would seldom rise above 56° or 58°, we thought that a cubic foot would sustain one trout, and again making allowance for losses or sales, reduced the estimated number to six thousand four hundred and eighty, and so staked off the pond one hundred and twenty feet long, twelve feet wide, and allowed for an average depth of four and a half feet. I would here remark that Mr. Comfort has a spring branch rising three hundred yards away, flowing at right angles and joining that already described, the supply being double of that just given. This he intends using as accessory in filling his third pond. The united streams flow also through an ice pond below, which he will stock with trout.

If one is desirous of having ponds of the largest capacity

a diminutive stream will supply, he should deepen them rather than increase the area. The deeper the water the cooler it will be at the bottom in summer and the warmer in winter.

Stocking-Ponds.—The best time to procure brood trout, of course, is when the streams are low, and the nearer the time of spawning the more easily they are captured. If on the spawn-beds, this is easily done in the small streams they generally seek for that purpose. Last November I was present when P. H. Christie, at the head of Fishkill creek, in Dutchess county, New York, with only one assistant, took one hundred and twenty in an hour and a half; we manipulated those that were ready to spawn the same afternoon, and got five thousand eggs from them. Two weeks before, Mr. Christie, in going over the same length of the stream, had taken four hundred before noon. The best kind of net for the purpose, is what is termed a set or stir-net. It has a straight strip about four feet long which rests on the bottom, and a bow of ash or white oak, the ends being inserted in the strip. The bag of the net should be of coarse gunny cloth, to avoid injuring the gills of the fish, as they are apt to stick their heads through the meshes of the ordinary net, and so injure themselves in that vital part. If taken with artificial flies of moderate size, they are seldom hooked so as to injure them.

Transporting Adult Trout.—A barrel is a good impromptu vessel for this purpose; a piece four or five inches square being sawed out of the head, and a strip nailed across the piece, so that it can be replaced without a chance of its falling in; large gimlet holes are also to be bored in it, so as to afford air to the fish when it is in its place. The water should be renewed as opportunity offers, and the state of the weather demands, and may be oxygenated by dipping some out and pouring it back, elevating the vessel from which it is poured as much as possible for that purpose. The usual place for a barrel when so used in carrying trout by railroad, is the baggage car, and as the barrel is necessarily wet outside from jolting (and the more jolting it gets the better), it should be set near the side door of the car, where there is a draft of air, which tends largely to keep the water inside cool. In moderate weather in June, I have thus taken a hundred and fifty trout in a forty gallon barrel two-thirds full of water, sixty miles without replenishing it. When ice can be had, a piece may be dropped in occasionally to keep the water cool. Too great a degree of cold, however, is injurious. I have had trout to die in my ponds some days after transporting them as I thought safely, from the effects of what I considered too lavish a supply of ice. Pump water should never be used in replenishing; I have seen fifty trout turn on their sides as soon as it was poured into a barrel. A bellows may be used for aerating the water, by inserting the nozzle the whole depth and blowing. A zinc vessel on this principle is used in England, the air being pumped through a tube opening into the bottom of the vessel. The same principle was applied, though differently arranged, by Barnum, at his old Museum, for aerating the water in the aquaria in which he kept trout. When taking them in a wagon, the barrel or vessel should be rocked to and fro, while stopping, so as to oxygenate the water. For a small number of fish a bucket or pail can be used. Mr. Christie uses ordinary milk cans holding about twenty gallons in transporting trout in a wagon, carrying from fifty to a hundred in a can.

When trout cannot be procured for stocking ponds, and one is willing to wait a few years, much trouble and expense can be saved by hatching the spawn. This can be procured at about ten dollars per thousand of Seth Green, Mumford, Monroe County, New York; or of Stephen H. Ainsworth, West Bloomfield, New York; or P. H. Christie, Clove, Dutchess County, New York; or Dr. J. H. Slack, whose post-office is Bethlehem, Hunterdon County, New Jersey.

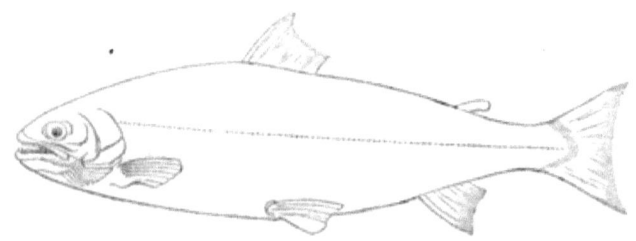

CHAPTER III.

TROUT BREEDING.

INCUBATION, AND TREATMENT OF FRY.

Hatching apparatus.—French and American plans.—Supply of water for a given number of eggs. *Hatching-house.*—Illustration with explanations.—Filterer.—Troughs.—Nursery.—Management of filterer.—Washing gravel for troughs.—Implements. *Taking the spawn.*—Action of the female when about to spawn.—Method of catching the fish on the spawning-beds.—Indications of the maturity of the eggs.—Manipulation.—Placing the ova in the troughs. —Packing and transportation of **eggs.—Manner of taking a large number of** eggs for transportation from a trough.—How to examine **them.—Illustration with explanations of the appearance of ova at** different stages **during incubation.—Table showing progress of incu-**bation with water **at** different degrees of temperature.—Hatching out and progress in growth and activity **of** fry. *Treatment of fry.* —Their food, and manner of feeding them.—Their disposition to escape.—Transferring them to the nurseries.—Their admission into the first pond.—Transportation of fry.

Hatching Apparatus.—Since **the** early experiments **of** Remy, a great many **improvements have been made in** hatching fish spawn. At Huningue, trays or **troughs of** earthenware about **twenty-five inches long, five inches wide, and four** inches deep, **are** used. The eggs are placed on a *grille,* made by arranging small parallel cross-bars in a **wooden** frame, which rests on projections on each side of the tray, a little below the surface of the water. The bars of the grille are near enough together to hold the eggs; while any floating dirt falls between to the bottom of the tray, and can be removed by drawing the water off through a hole which is kept **corked** at one end in the bottom. The young fish, **as they are** hatched out, also drop between the bars, and are removed through the same aperture **and** placed in other troughs or apartments. **These trays can** even be scrubbed and replaced, by moving the grille (which may safely be done after the young fish are developed in the ova), **to** a spare tray kept **for the** purpose. The trays are placed in shallow vessels or cisterns, elevated **to the** height of a man's waist; each cistern, which is **thirty or** forty feet long, containing a proportionate number of trays. It is not deemed advisable, however, that a jet of water from the supply pipes should flow through more than six **trays.**

Another mode in France, is to have a series of troughs arranged like steps, one slightly above the other, as shown in illustration at end of next chapter. The water pouring through a hole in a little jet at one end **of the upper** trough, and running the length of that below, discharges in the same way, and runs the length of the next trough. This plan has the advantage of aerating the water as it enters each, and can be placed in any spare room of proper temperature in one's dwelling.

In this country a much more simple, though not as effectual, mode of getting rid of sediment and suppressing the growth of byssus is pursued. A wooden trough, twelve or fifteen inches wide, and four inches deep, is divided into

nests or apartments from sixteen to eighteen inches long, by placing strips across; over these strips the water flows in a slight ripple, and the force of the current is thereby **broken.**   The bottom of the trough is covered **with clean gravel,** to the depth of an inch or so, to receive **the eggs, over which** the water, an inch deep, flows in a **gentle current.**   This plan has generally been discarded in France, but here, by using pure spring water after passing it through three or four flannel screens and a small heap of fine gravel, **it is perhaps as** efficacious as the **French** mode.   Our largest fish culturist, Seth Green, has by these simple means **hatched out** ninety per cent., and Stephen H. Ainsworth as high as ninety-eight per cent. of the ova. In my first experiment, which was with filtered Schuylkill water, a thousand eggs produced nearly seven hundred fish.

A floating **box for hatching is also used.**   It is made of boards generally **a** half inch thick ; the bottom is covered with fine wire gauze, which should be painted ; on this the eggs are distributed.   If the box does not set deep enough to allow the water to cover the eggs an inch **or** an inch and a half, sufficient weight should be placed on the cover to sink it to that depth.   If the bottom of the box is made of boards and gravel strewed **over** it, two or three rows of large gimlet holes should be bored in each end below the **water line.**   These boxes are usually two feet long, eighteen inches wide, and about six inches deep, and are tied to a strip extending across the raceway and allowed to float in **the** current.   **A box of this** kind can also be placed in a spring, its size corresponding with the area.   By this mode of hatching, the advantage of filtration must be dispensed with. The first essay of **P. H. Christie in** hatching, was by depositing the eggs on gravel in the bottom of a corn-popper, and placing it **on a stone in his spring.** I mention **this to show how simple a thing** the hatching **of trout spawn** can be made.

Many persons in France and England, for amusement, or the novelty of the thing, have miniature hatching appara-tus in their houses. Any spare room where the thermome-ter does not mark over 55° will answer, and the smallest dribble from a tank of twenty to a hundred gallons can be used. No class of our countrymen are more favorably situated for hatching trout spawn **than farmers.** Many of them bring the water into their houses **from** springs of greater elevation ; and, without occupying much space, and by incurring but slight expense, might hatch thousands of ova to stock streams and ponds on their own premises, **or** to supply waters in their neighborhood.

I have already remarked, that success in hatching de-pends much on the puri**ty of** the water, and even the purest must be **filtered.** As to the quantity for a **given** number of eggs ; a square inch divided into four jets and flowing through the same number of troughs, will **suffice** for three or four hundred thousand ; but double or even four times the supply will **be required** to sustain the same number of young fish for any great length of time in the nursery. An additional supply must therefore be provided for the fry after they have absorbed the umbilical sac, say a square inch to each hundred thousand.

It is better for many reasons, that the supply should flow through earthen pipes or glazed tile; there is some risk in conducting it through leaden pipe, as the action of certain limestone waters on lead is injurious, unless the pipe is coated with zinc.

Although a trough for hatching a few thousand eggs may be placed in the open air if kept covered, it is necessary that a number of them should be under the cover of a building of some kind, that the ova may be protected from the weather and the depredations of rats and other animals that would eat them, as well as for the comfort of those who attend to them. A house of rough boards will answer the purpose. A stove is not necessary in the hatching-house unless the water is very cold. Where the water is as high as 48° or 50° the temperature of the air inside of a close board house will be almost the same, and comfortably warm. The windows, or the greater number of them, should be on the north side, if it can be so arranged, so as to admit the light with as little sunshine as possible. In a length of forty-eight feet, three windows are enough, the panes may be eight by ten inches, and the sash two panes high and four panes wide, and may slide horizontally in opening them. Each window should have a curtain or sliding shutter to exclude the light when it is deemed expedient to do so.

On the opposite page is a ground plan for a hatching house. Scale, one-sixteenth of an inch to the foot.

A is the filterer, four feet long, two feet wide, and eighteen inches deep. The three transverse lines repre-

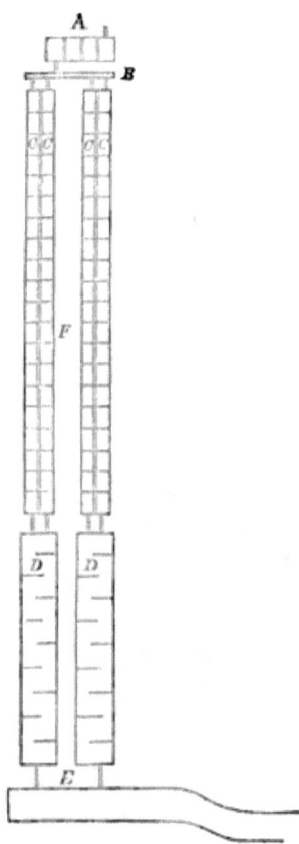

sent the flannel screens; if there were four it would be better. The water entering the first apartment on the right, passes through the screens and flows into the distributing trough B, which by four jets supplies the troughs c c c c.

The troughs are thirty-two feet long, fourteen inches wide, and four inches deep, inside measurement. Each trough is divided into twenty nests eighteen inches long, besides having an apartment two feet long at the upper end, which is filled with fine gravel, through which the water is again filtered as it passes into each trough. F is a gravelled walk two feet wide. There should also be a gravelled space of the same width between the troughs and the sides of the building.

D D are the nurseries, three feet wide, and half the length of the hatching-troughs. The lines which extend alternately from each side beyond to the middle, represent small bulkheads or strips, so placed for the purpose of breaking the force of the current when an additional supply of water is let in for the young fish, and to form eddies where they find shelter from its force if they require it. The latter is an improvement of the Rev. Livingston Stone, of Charleston, New Hampshire, and was suggested for this book by Theodore Lyman, Esq., one of the Massachusetts Commissioners of Fisheries. The bottoms of the nurseries should be of boards, and should be gravelled. The depth should not be much, if any, over an inch at the upper end, and four inches at the lower end. E is a channel leading from the nurseries into the first pond.

These four troughs will hatch from three to four hundred thousand eggs. By increasing the supply of water and lengthening the distributing trough, two or even four additional hatching-troughs can be used.

The screens of the filterer are made by stretching and tacking flannel to frames, which are slipped into grooves made by nailing strips on the insides of the filterer, either perpendicularly or at an angle inclining towards the outlet. The flannel on the screen nearest the entrance of the supply, should be of stout but open fabric; the second, not so coarse; the third, medium, and the fourth, closely woven. A duplicate set should be provided, as the purest water, to all appearances, in which one cannot detect the most minute particle, will, in the course of four or five days or a week, so clog the screens as almost to stop the flow. At intervals of a few days the screens should therefore be slipped out and a clean set put in. The flannel is cleansed by allowing it to dry, and then brushing the dust off with a whisk broom, or better, by rubbing the screens with a stiff hair-brush while wet. The filterer and supply trough should both be kept covered.

There should not be more than two inches fall from the upper to the lower end of a trough of thirty-two feet, if the aperture through which the water enters is a half inch square. If the supply be doubled, the fall should not be more than an inch. This will give a ripple about the sixteenth of an inch deep over the strips dividing the trough into nests. The bottom of the trough should be perfectly true, and the strips fit neatly, so that the water may not

5   D

flow beneath but over the top of the strips. The strips
should also be exactly the same width, so that the ripples
over them may be uniform. They should be made of half-
inch pine, and should slip out or in so that they can be
removed at one's option. The gravel should be about the
size of peas, and if possible of some uniformly dark tint,
that the eggs lying on it may be the more easily examined
It should be thoroughly washed, by shaking and turning it
in a basket in clear running water, and again, by stirring
it after placing it in the hatching-trough, commencing at
the upper end of the trough and stirring it in each successive nest until the water runs clear. Mr. Ainsworth is
so careful as to boil the gravel, that he may destroy the
eggs or larvæ of insects that may possibly remain after the
gravel is merely washed. When there is sufficient fall
from the spring to admit of it, it is better to have the
hatching-troughs elevated about three feet, so as to allow
of an easier examination of the eggs, as it is no small labor
to attend to them on the ground if one has four troughs to
go over daily during the incubation.

A few simple instruments are required by the fish culturist. For examining the eggs a small vial, two or three
inches long and a half-inch in diameter, is used. The eggs
are taken up with a small pair of pliers and dropped into
the vial nearly filled with water, which, after replacing the
cork, is held horizontally before the light and turned so as
to present different views of the eggs. The pliers can be
made either of single or double wire; if of the latter, a small
bowl can be formed at the end of each prong by bending

the wire into the required shape for clasping the egg. My friend Christie, of Dutchess county, New York, with a little instrument made by bending a thin brass wire into the shape of a miniature spoon and lashing it to a small wooden handle, removes the addled ova from his troughs, he says, three times as fast as he can with pliers. For dipping up young fish in the troughs, a small net is made by bending a stout piece of wire into the shape of the letter D for the frame, the ends of the wire being twisted together on the convex side for the handle. The material used is bobinett, or some light fabric sufficiently open. The net need not be larger than an ordinary tea cup, and is used by moving the straight side along the bottom of the trough.

Taking the Spawn.—In autumn when the fish work up towards the heads of the ponds, and some of them enter the raceways, it is time that the latter should be covered with loose boards, and that persons should show themselves as little as possible to the fish in that vicinity; they can be observed through the cracks between the boards. It will be seen that the females only prepare the nests. This is done by laying their sides against the bottom and rapidly flapping their tails to displace the gravel, the males in the mean while being engaged in a defensive war with rivals and fish that are ready at hand to devour the spawn. The peculiar motion of the female when she is about to spawn, or has commenced, is a long, slow, sideway undulation of the body from head to tail, resembling the moving of a snake along the ground, although she does not progress, her vent being down in the excavation she has made, and her abdomen pressed on the gravel to help the emission of the ova. When this is observed it is certain that the trout have commenced spawning. The lower grating or wire screen should then be slipped into its place at the end of the raceway, and the box or trap which I have already described should be covered with a platform made for that purpose. The boards covering the raceway nearest the trap should then be removed, when the fish will run down and find cover under the platform; the upper screen is then quietly slipped into its place and the fish enclosed. On removing the platform the fish are dipped out with a net made of gunny cloth or sea grass skirting, attached to a square frame, which should be as wide as the trap; it should also be tied at the bottom so that the string can be removed and the fish dropped into a tub of water. As the fish are manipulated they are returned to the pond or placed in another tub, which is to be emptied into the pond after the spawn and milt are expressed. A milk pan of the ordinary shape, holding about six quarts, and filled a fourth or a third full of clear water, is also provided for the spawn and milt.

It is better that the water should be fecundated first, so that the eggs may be brought into contact with the atoms of milt as soon as they are expressed. The manipulation should be quickly and carefully performed. Putting the hand into the tub and approaching a male, close on him gently and lift him out; then grasping him with as little violence as possible, with the right hand by the head and shoulders, his head towards the wrist and the left hand

holding the tail, as represented in the figure in the front
of this book; hold the vent of the fish beneath the
surface of the water in the pan, bending the head and tail
slightly upwards. If the milt is well matured, and he does
not struggle or hold it back, a small portion will be emitted;
then with the forefinger of the right hand, the other three
still encircling the head and shoulders, rub the abdomen
gently towards the vent, extracting all the milt he will
give, and stir the water with his tail. If the fish are pas-
sive, as they generally are during the operation, the hold
on the head and shoulders may be relaxed, and the right
hand passed along the body below the head, pressing
the milt or the ova towards the vent. The female is
handled in the same manner, the eggs flowing in a pale
yellow stream from the vent; if she is fully ripe all the
eggs should be taken from her; if she is large and struggles,
and the same remark applies of course to the males, an
assistant should hold the tail. The mere bending of the
head and tail, as illustrated, will frequently cause the eggs
to flow if the fish is fully ripe. The indications of ripeness
when taken in the hand are, firstly, a pale sickly yellow
tinge; secondly, she is very soft and flabby; thirdly, the
vent is exceedingly protuberant and of a dark purple color;
fourthly, the eggs are loose in the ovary, and fall towards
the vent when she is held with the head up, and towards
the head if held by the tail, and will flow, as I have
just remarked, without pressure, by bending the vent well
down. If the eggs are not ripe enough to be extruded,
they will be felt like shot or small peas in the belly. The

5 *

water should be stirred gently, now and then, as each fish
is operated upon, and the fish (males or females) may be
handled as they come to hand. When enough eggs have
been taken to cover the bottom of the pan, and enough
milt to give the water a milky appearance,* the pan may be
covered and set aside; the water of the pond surrounding
it, if the weather is cold, or it may be placed in an unoc-
cupied nest of one of the hatching-troughs. The eggs, in
a few minutes after receiving the milt, will adhere to the
bottom of the pan, and should not be disturbed until they
are loose, which will be in the course of fifteen or thirty
minutes. During this time impregnation takes place, and

---

* About the middle of May, this year, I met Mr. Ainsworth by
appointment in Elk county, Pa., to enjoy a few days fly-fishing.
In our conversation on the impregnation of ova, he narrated the
following occurrence. Last fall, near the end of the spawning season, when the males had mostly cast their milt, he one day had
taken enough eggs to cover the bottom of the pan, and could only
procure a single male. From this he expressed not more than a
good sized drop of milt, not enough to tinge the water. He, nevertheless, set the pan away, giving the ova and this slightly sperm-
atized water the usual time, and then placed the eggs in a separate
nest in his hatching-trough, and was agreeably surprised in a few
days to find them all impregnated. In due time they hatched, but
few eggs being lost in incubation. Will any biologist give us the
result of his speculations as to the number of spermatozoa in this
drop of milt? Although we cannot but admire this wonderful provision of nature, I cannot advise my readers to be as trustful of a
single drop of milt imparting its fecundating quality to two or three
quarts of water, unless it be for mere experiment.

as soon as possible after they should be placed in the hatching-trough.

When all the fish in the trap have been handled, it may be set again, and the boards towards the upper part of the raceway removed. Fish that are not disposed **to leave the race should** be driven down, and in doing so, although a pole or stick may be used, it is better not to disturb the bottom of the race; as it is possible that very rough usage may deter them from entering again, and induce them to seek a spawning-place in the pond, where the eggs or the young fry at all events would be devoured. The disposition with the breeding fish to enter the race again, however, **is** very strong. **I have** seen scores **of them that had been** handled and not quite **ripe,** on being returned to the **pond, waiting for the grating to be removed, and** would run **up as soon as it was** lifted.

If there are many ripe fish running up the race, they may **be** taken and manipulated once or twice a day. When there **are fewer spawners, it may be as well to take them** only on alternate days.

After the eggs **have** remained in the fecundated water for twenty minutes or a half hour, **or until they are loose** from **the** bottom of the pan, they should **be washed; a** board extending across the **race, or the platform** of the trap being **a** convenient place for doing so. The edge of the pan should be lowered **gently** beneath the surface that the fresh **water** may **enter. It is then poured off,** allowing enough **to remain to keep the eggs well covered.** After **repeating this several times, until the** water is clear, the eggs are ready to be placed in the hatching-trough. Although they will be whirled **about** by the influx of the water in washing, they are so much heavier, that they will remain at the bottom of the pan. The washing should be done with an effort to give them **no** more motion than is required in the operation.

There are sometimes four or five times as many males as there are spawners taken in the trap, particularly at the first of the season. An additional tub should therefore be provided, and the excess of males placed in it for the time, so that their milt may be used or not, as may be required.

The plan pursued in France of holding the fish pendent by the head, as is illustrated in the lower figure in the frontispiece, and allowing the spawn to fall into the pan of water **below, is** not practised in this country by experienced fish **culturists. By the improved** method of holding the vent beneath the water, the unnatural falling of the eggs from a height, and bringing them in contact with the air before they are impregnated, is avoided. It is obvious also that **the** new mode is more in accordance with the natural way of the parent fish.

Before depositing the eggs **in** the trough, an extra strip an inch and a half, or two inches wide, if a notch is cut out of the upper side, is placed above the strip at the lower end of the nest, to dam the water and increase the depth. The edge of the pan is then gently lowered beneath the surface that some of the water of the trough may enter, and the eggs poured slowly out, distributing them as evenly as possible over the nest. A more equal distribution should after-

wards be made by using the soft side of a stout feather.
A nest fourteen inches wide and eighteen inches long, will
suffice for four thousand eggs without their lying on top
of each other. When the strip used for the temporary
damming of the water is removed, it should be done gradually, that the eggs may not be disturbed, as they would be
if it was lifted suddenly. The eggs first placed in a trough,
should be in the lower nest, and then in each successive
nest towards the head, so that the fry below, hatching out
before those above, can have access to the nursery, when
old enough, without passing over and disturbing the un-
hatched ova, or the young fish that have not absorbed the
umbilical sac.

A trout, the second autumn, when twenty-one or twenty-
two months old, will give from two hundred to three hundred eggs. The third autumn, from four to six hundred.
The fourth, from a thousand to twelve hundred. The fifth,
from two to three thousand, according to its size.

The fish culturist will not be able to procure all the eggs
that his spawners have, for his hatching-troughs. A good
portion of the ova will be deposited at night, or between
the times of driving them into the trap. Much of it will
be devoured as soon as it is emitted, or will be thrown out
by repeated nest-making on the same bed of gravel, and
then eaten by the fish. Notwithstanding all this, he will
find through the winter a goodly number of young fish in
his raceway and at the heads of his ponds, that have come
from eggs which have escaped these dangers. It would,
therefore, be as well to exclude the fish from the raceways

at the close of the spawning-season, and prevent the fry
that may be hatched out from coming down into the ponds.
This can be done by putting in a fine wire screen at the
lower end of the trap, and a coarse one to catch the leaves
and drift at the upper end.   The race will thus be turned
into an out-door nursery, and the young fish can be taken
at the trap and turned into the first pond, when those from
the nursery under roof are transferred.

Packing and transporting ova.—As soon as the first formation of the young fish can be seen, eggs may be sent off,
although some persons think that the eyes should be plainly
visible before transportation.   The plan now pursued at
Huningue, is to pack them in short wide-mouthed glass
jars.   In this country shallow tin boxes are generally used.
Both here and in France they are packed in damp moss,
the top and bottom of the jar or box being perforated so
as to admit some air.   The bottom of the box is covered
with moss, well washed and water pressed out, but still quite
moist ; on this the eggs are spread so as not to overlie each
other.   A layer of moss an inch thick is then placed on the
eggs.   Then comes another layer of eggs, and so on until
three or four alternate layers fill the box.   The tin boxes are
securely closed and packed with saw-dust between, in a
wooden box, a layer of saw-dust two or three inches thick
protecting the top, bottom, and sides, from exposure to
extremes of heat or cold.   A tin box six inches in diameter
and three inches deep will, with the moss, contain easily
three thousand eggs.   At a temperature from five to
fifteen degrees above freezing point, a box of ova, if care-

fully handled, may be two weeks on the way without injury. Seth Green, to test their vitality, has kept eggs packed in moss, in his hatching-house, for more than six weeks, and then placed them in his troughs, where, in due course of time, they hatched out. P. H. Christie, of Dutchess county, New York, sent me last fall in an old tin tobacco box as large as my three fingers, one hundred and twenty eggs by mail; which from delay by snow-storm and otherwise, were a week on the way. On opening them they were all in good condition but one, which had been mashed. A few thousand eggs, if on the way but two or three days, of course require less exterior protection after packing them in moss than I have recommended above. If the moss becomes dry, the eggs will undoubtedly perish.

In manipulating fish by the side of the stream, if at a distance from the troughs, the ova is necessarily carried in water. Care should, therefore, be had that the vessel is perfectly clean and free from any taint or odor that might affect the eggs. Mr. Ainsworth informed me that he once lost two or three thousand by carrying them in a new cedar bucket, and Mr. Robinson, of Meredith Village, New Hampshire, had many thousand lake trout ova spoiled from the jolting they received in a rough wagon.

On arrival at its place of destination, the box containing ova should be carefully unpacked, the tin boxes or jars taken out and set in the water of the hatching-house, or in a cool cellar where they will not freeze. Each box or jar, after removing the cover and taking off the top layer of moss, should be immersed in a vessel of clear water and turned bottom up. The moss should then be gently shaken and picked out that the eggs may fall to the bottom; whatever moss cannot be conveniently picked out with the fingers can be floated and poured off by two or three washings, as is done after taking the eggs from a trout, and before depositing them in the trough.

Mr. Ainsworth says: "The best contrivance for taking the eggs from the trough in numbers, is a piece of fine wire cloth six or seven inches square, turned up at the sides and at one end like a dust-pan. In using it, place it on the bottom of the nest and gently brush the eggs into the open end with a feather or wing, then put the wire pan into a dish of water and allow them to slide off. In this manner they can be removed with ease and rapidity. The best thing to examine a large number of eggs on, and see at once all the imperfect and unimpregnated spawn, is a pane of window glass with a tight wooden frame around it. Set this with a half inch of water on it, in the light of a window, shading the side towards the window, so as to allow the light to come up through the bottom of the pane, and you can see every imperfect egg and pick them out.

In counting them, a four-sided tin dish with sloping sides, holding forty in a line lengthwise and twenty-five across, can be used. Six eggs laid in a line measure a little over or under an inch. If, therefore, the bottom of the vessel used for counting is six and two-third inches long, by four and one-sixth inches wide, it will take about a thousand eggs to cover it.

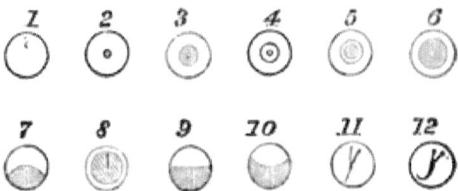

The plate above, was drawn for this book, by my esteemed friend Ainsworth, to whom I have so often alluded.
The following explanations of the different figures are his
own words.

"In a few hours after the spawn is taken, there is a
small light brown spot to be seen on the top of the egg
whether it is impregnated or not. Turn the egg over any
way, in many ways, and as often as you please, this speck
will soon rise to the top. This is the germ where impregnation takes place. Whether it is between the two membranes of the ova,* or under the inner membrane, I am not
able to say; but it is certain it revolves within the outer
membrane to the top. This speck, when the egg is held
before the light in a small vial, looks to be about the size
of the head of a small pin elongated upwards, as shown in

---

* There are two membranes to the eggs of fishes, or at least to
those whose young come forth with an umbilical sac. That part
contained within the inner membrane, it may be said, is somewhat
analogous to the yolk in the egg of a fowl, and is the umbilical sac
when the fish is hatched out. Hence, it is asserted by some, that
the young fish emerges from the egg with the yolk attached.

6

figure 1. Looking down on the egg, the speck is seen in the centre, apparently on top, as in figure 2.

" Seven days after the ova is taken, (the water at 47°), a small circle is seen around the speck, whether the egg be impregnated or not, and the two are so much alike at this stage, that it is difficult to know which are the fecundated, and which are not, and yet a very close examination will show a difference. The fecundated egg has a clearer speck in the centre, and the ring around the speck is larger, as will be seen by referring to figure 3. The unimpregnated is illustrated by figure 4.

" When nine days old, the circle in the impregnated egg has enlarged, a slight brownish or bluish gray tinge pervading the interior; the germ having spread over a sixth part of the egg, presenting the appearance of figure 5; while the unimpregnated still remains as pictured in figure 4. The latter never change after the ninth day, unless to become opaque, which they continue to do during the incubation of the fecundated ova, and are as easily distinguished from them in the hatching-troughs as a few white beads would be if scattered amongst those of transparent glass.

" On the eleventh day, the first formation of the fish can be seen; a brown line extending from the circumference towards the centre of the circle, which now covers one-third of the egg. The appearance of the egg at this time is exhibited, up by figure 6, and sideways by figure 7.

" When twelve days old the circle will be seen to cover one-half of the egg. Front view shown by figure 8, side view by figure 9.

"On the thirteenth day the circle has passed three-fourths round the egg, a side view being represented by figure 10.

"On the fourteenth day the circle has passed entirely over the egg and the young trout is formed, as shown in figure 11.

"On the twenty-fifth day, the eyes, heart, arteries, red blood, circulation of blood and motion will be observed. The egg and young fish at this stage is pictured in figure 12. About the fiftieth day the young trout will begin to come out of the shell, and continue to do so for some days or a week."

I have some notes and memoranda of my own on incubation, but the foregoing is so brief, and yet so comprehensive, that I have preferred giving it. In referring to the little plate of figures, Mr. Ainsworth, in a recent letter, says: "It would have been a great advantage to me in the beginning of my experiments, and I hope it will be of much benefit to those who attempt the artificial propagation of trout, as they will see at a glance what has taken me nine years to learn."

Mr. Ainsworth has also arranged the following table, giving the temperature of the water from 37° to 54°, showing the progress of development, the time of incubation, and at what time the young fish will commence feeding. This table is made from memoranda he has kept of all the spawn he has taken for four years; he says: "I have estimated a little in the higher and lower figures as to the time of hatching, as my water did not hold at these degrees long enough to hatch the ova."

Average tempera- ture of water.	No. of days to first forma- tion of trout.	No. of days to formation of eyes and red blood.	No. of days to hatching.	No. of days af- ter hatching to feeding.
37°	43	81	165	
38½°	29	64	135	77
39°	28	62	121	
40½°	27	54	109	60
41°	21	49	103	
42½°	19	42	96	
43½°	17	37	89	46
44°	16	34	81	
45½°	15	31	73	
46½°	13	29	65	
48°	11	26	56	
50°	10	23	47	30
52°	8	18	38	
54°	7	15	32	
Appearance of spawn as fig. 3.	as figure 7.	as figure 12.		

By comparing the top with the bottom line of this table, the reader will observe the large difference in the development of the embryo and fetus, and the term of incubation of water at 37° and at 54°, as well as the difference in the time occupied by the young fish in absorbing the umbilical sac and beginning to take food. The time of incubation is five times as long at 37° as it is at 54°.

During the time of hatching the fish culturist should examine his troughs daily, removing the addled eggs, which can be easily detected from their being perfectly white and opaque. A record of the estimated number of eggs deposited should be kept, and the number of bad eggs taken out also noted, so that the percentage of loss in incubation can be arrived at after that process is completed. Every precaution should be taken **to** exclude vermin from the hatching-house, the light should be modified with shutters or curtains to the windows, and the sunshine which promotes the growth of byssus, should not be allowed **to** fall on the eggs. Byssus, which is a fungous growth, is perhaps the greatest enemy; with its long filaments it closes upon and destroys the vitality of the egg; when one **is destroyed** the dead egg promotes its growth for the destruction of others, **until a** score may be clasped by its long fingers. The eggs should be disturbed as little as possible during incubation. An accumulation of sediment in one place can be removed by a glass syphon or syringe to some extent, but no dependence should be placed on such remedies, as the perfect filtration of the water **is the main** reliance.

There are few things more interesting than the observation of the gradual development of embryo and life in the egg of a trout. When the time of its deliverance approaches, the young fish is restive in its little prison. **A** gleam of sunshine, or the warmth imparted by the hand **to** the vial containing the ova when examining it, incites **it to** vigorous struggles for liberty. At **last the** shell is broken, **the** head appears, then the pectoral fins, then the tail; it comes forth and its house floats away. Although helpless, it is not needy; an umbilical sac three times **the bulk of** its body is provided. Apparently exhausted by its late efforts, and weighed down with **its** bag of provisions, it lies on it, or **rests on** its side, or stands on its head; any position suits it; its eyes, unless closely inspected, the only part visible. Its body three-eighths of an inch long, and not

larger than a "wiggle tail" in a barrel of stale rain-water.
Poor helpless pigmy! will it ever rise to the angler's fly, a
monster of four pounds, and give him a half-hour's hard
fight, or smash his tackle? Not one chance in a hundred
if born in some pebbly brush-covered rill. How many such
would its own father or mother, a foot long, devour at a
single meal? five hundred? yes a thousand! If such was
not the law of nature, trout would be as thick in our streams
as mosquitoes or midges sometimes are in the air above
them. They would be dirt cheap in our markets—they
would be a nuisance. Therefore, He who made nature's laws
is all wise. Shall we thwart these laws or violate them?
Did we do so when we made a Newton pippin of the
crab apple of the forest? or produced the cabbage, that
grows tons to the acre, from a trifling plant found on the
sea-shore?

In a week or two, the troutlings begin to move about,
then to flit through the mimic brook in the hatching-trough
as you cast your shadow over it, and, true to instinct, stick
their heads under pebbles, or hide under the fall made
below the strip **at the head** of the nest. They become
more agile as the sac is absorbed, and **at last, when the**
whole stock of pabulum is exhausted, they begin to seek
their own living, darting through the water after microscopic insects, groping in the gravel for larvæ; or rising
at some minute gnat, or at atoms of blood or curdled milk
or yolk of egg, that are fed to them.

As soon as the first brood appears in a trough, a fine wire
cloth screen should be placed across the lower end. **When**

they begin to move about, wire screens should also be placed across every fourth or fifth nest, to confine them in apartments, so that they may not be over-crowded in any one part of the trough. The water should also be deepened, by placing additional strips an inch wide on top of those where the screens are placed; and an additional supply, but not enough to wash them in numbers against the screens, should be let on. If there are too many in one apartment, a portion may be removed into another where there are not so many, by lifting them out with the little net already described.

Some of the fry, as I have before remarked, will be puny, and others large and vigorous *ab ova*. The latter, when two months or ten weeks old, will not hesitate in their efforts to swallow those that are just hatched out, and will generally succeed in doing so. Therefore, if a month or two should elapse in planting the whole length of a trough with eggs, it is necessary to protect the late from the early comers. When the fry become lively, the bottom of the trough can be cleansed by washing the gravel, commencing above and stirring it in each successive nest towards the lower end. The young fish will move out of the way and resume their places as the water becomes clear.

Treatment of the Fry.—When the sac has nearly disappeared, a little food should be offered to the fry at intervals of two or three days; when they begin to take it readily it should be supplied to them twice every day. They will rise with avidity for the particles that float, and seize those that are carried along beneath the surface.

This is a critical time with the fry, and some, perhaps many, will die from no ascertainable cause. Great care should be taken that they are not washed by the current in numbers against the screens, as many are too weak to disengage themselves, the stream pressing them against the wire cloth until they die. It would be well, therefore, to place something in each nest to make an eddy for those that require still water, or have two short bulkheads, as pictured in plan of the nursery. Four or five different kinds of food have been recommended. Liver or lean meat boiled hard and grated; the yolks of eggs boiled hard and reduced almost to a powder; raw liver chopped fine with a long sharp knife; fresh or coagulated blood; fresh shad or herring roe, raw or boiled; thick milk or bonny-clabber, and curds. The best way of feeding bonny-clabber, is to dip out two or three spoonfuls from the pan in which it has thickened, into the small net used for transferring the fry from one apartment to another. The net is held in the water, and the clabber, by breaking and stirring with a spoon, is reduced to fine particles, while the whey is carried off by the current. By shaking the net and canting it, the atoms float out and are borne along mostly on top, when the fry will rise eagerly at them, and also take those beneath the surface, as well as the particles that after awhile sink to the bottom. This is the lightest, and, I think, the most suitable thing for fry when they first begin to feed. Curd, which may be fed to them a few weeks or a month later, should be made from milk which has turned in the pan; it is not so hard, but lighter and more digestible than that made over the fire. I have fed fifty thousand fry with curd for more than two months, the time occupied at each feeding, not exceeding a half-hour. For feeding so large a number two or three quart bowls should be provided, and a lump of curd as large as one's forefinger dropped into each, half-full of water. The curd in each bowl is then triturated successively, and the milky water poured off after the particles settle to the bottom. Two or three triturations reduce it to atoms sufficiently small. In feeding it to the fry, the rim of the bowl is placed beneath the surface; the influx of the water suspends and whirls the light particles around, when the bowl is canted and a portion distributed in different parts of each nest. Four lumps of curd each as large as one's forefinger, fed in this way, suffices for forty thousand fry when they commence feeding; as they grow, the quantity should be gradually increased; but double this quantity is enough as long as they remain in the hatching-troughs. When they are let into the nursery the quantity may be again increased, but not enough to foul the bottom. An hour or two after feeding, if the gravel is stirred lightly, the particles of food that have settled to the bottom are set adrift, when the fish will take it again. If too much of this food is given it will make a mouldy covering over the gravel, and emit an unpleasant odor. As often as this occurs, the gravel in the troughs should be washed as already directed.

A strip four or five inches wide should now be placed

above the wire screen at the end of each trough, as the fry will leap over the top if it is only an inch or so above the surface, and thus make their escape. When, from their numbers and size, the hatching-troughs become too small to accommodate them all comfortably, they may be lifted out with the small net and placed below. It is well, also, to keep the bed of gravel at the top of each trough an inch or two above the surface, as they have a disposition to wriggle over, if it is even the eighth of an inch in depth, and run up the little jet from **the** supply-trough, then into the filterer, and even into the supply-pipe. Concerning their disposition to escape from the nursery, Mr. Ainsworth informed me he once missed many of his fry, and found them in a pond where he kept his large fish. After many days' search for the place of exit, he found that one of the planks **had** a hole the size of a quill in it, eaten by a wood-worm before it was placed there; through this, an earth-worm which had found it, made its way, and then through a bank of clay five or six feet to the large pond; the fry had escaped along this narrow channel. I had a like experience at **the** establishment which I started in Warren county, New Jersey; many thousand of the fry escaping through a crack in the mason-work, not more than wide enough to thrust the blade of a stout breakfast-knife in. These little matters of experience I jot down to show the necessity of having the sides and ends of the nursery of sound plank, and of providing against every chance of escape.

A month or six weeks after the fry commence feeding,

they will grow to a size which will cause the troughs to be overcrowded. When this occurs, those in the lower nests, being the older, should be lifted out as I have already advised. After those in the upper nests have been feeding for three weeks or a month, the screen at the lower end of the trough may be removed, and as many as are inclined, or all of them, should be allowed to run down into the nursery, or, as some call it, the "rearing-trough." It will be observed by the plan ·that a nursery is provided for each pair of hatching-troughs, and that the width of the latter scarcely exceeds that of the two troughs. The reason for this is that the fry may be the more easily fed, and that they are more under control than if a single nursery the whole width of the hatching-house was used for four or six troughs. I have found the latter hard to keep clean; much of the food thrown into it is not eaten, and it remains only to foul the bottom; besides, it has no current and little eddies, which the fry are so partial to. The feeding in the nurseries is the same as in the troughs.

After all the eggs in the house have hatched out, the curtains to the windows should be removed so as to admit the light, and the windows and doors left open when the weather is fine. Part of the roof on each side over the nursery should be put on in sections, say three planks of a foot wide forming a slab. Two of these slabs on each side are enough. Each slab may be removed, or may turn on hinges to admit the sun. Young trout delight sometimes in basking in the sunshine, on shallows where the water does not cover the gravel to more than the depth of an inch, and such contrivance (which I adopted at my place in Warren county, New Jersey) will meet the case.

Transportation of Fry.—A large number of young fish may be transported in a few cubic feet of water. A short time after they commence feeding, I have no doubt that a thousand or fifteen hundred might be sent off in twenty gallons, if care is taken to renew the water, as I have remarked on transporting adult fish. A hundred might be taken in a jar holding a gallon, if the water is kept cool and aerated. On one of the plates of the Massachusetts Fish Commissioners' Report for 1867, is figured a tank a-fourth wider at the bottom than at the top, with a pump inside for oxygenating the water. It is an excellent contrivance for conveying either young or old fish. Care should be taken that the vessel in which the fry are carried is free from any strong taint. A new red-cedar bucket for instance might prove fatal to them.*

According to the system of rotation in occupying the ponds as already given, pond No. 1 will be vacated by the latter part of summer. The fry should then be admitted from the nursery, care being taken that none remain behind. If any should linger they will become attenuated and ill-favored from lack of food, and may, if they survive, be hungry devourers of the fry next season.

---

* I this day (May 28th 1868) noted a great disparity in the size of the fry in Mr. Comfort's troughs and nursery, the largest being at least four times the size of the smallest. Mr. C. assured me he has seen within a few days, the larger endeavor to swallow their smaller brethren of the same brood, and supposes they have succeeded in their efforts in some instances.

CHAPTER IV.

TROUT BREEDING

GENERAL REMARKS, FOOD FOR ADULTS, PROFITS AND STATISTICS.

Food of adult Trout.—Curd, liver, maggots.—Maggot-factory.—
Allowance of food for a given number.—Natural food.—Stall
feeding and its advantages.—Trout culture a branch of farming.—
Facilities possessed by farmers.—Will fish culture pay?—Instances
of its being profitable.—Estimate of cost of feeding on curd.—
Proposed trout breeding at Ingham Spring.—Growth of trout.—
Description of Huningue, and M. de Galbert's establishment, in
France.—Heidelberg.—Fish cultural enterprise in Switzerland.—
Trout culture in the United States.—Notice of Mr. Ainsworth's
establishment.—Description of Seth Green's.

Food for the Fish in the Ponds.—Trout are carnivorous
and can hardly be driven to eat vegetable food. I have
known them in winter to linger around the entrance of a
spring branch where kitchen pots and pans were scraped;
attracted no doubt by the small portion of animal mixed
with the vegetable food, which the brook carried into the
pond. When the weather became warm enough, however,
to bring flies on the water and to set the minnows in motion,
the mouth of the branch was deserted. The nearest ap‑
proach to purely animal food is curd, and on this, with what‑
ever fresh animal offal may come from the kitchen, the
farmer or one who grows trout for his own use must chiefly
depend. If sea-fish or liver can be obtained in quantities

7

at moderate rates, it is the cheapest strictly animal food for a large number of fish.

When trout are raised in ponds of the dimensions I have given, it is evident that little or no dependence is to be placed on natural feed, such as flies and their larvæ. Hence, the necessity of providing curds, or liver and lungs of animals at prices that will not cause too great an expenditure for the value of the crop. I have found that the curd from the milk of one cow which gave fourteen quarts, would feed bountifully a thousand or twelve hundred trout, averaging five-eighths or three-quarters of a pound; the smallest being seven inches long, and the largest from two to three pounds in weight. The food should be chopped or crumbled to the size of peas.

In feeding, a good plan is to have a piece of timber extending over the pond; the person giving the food standing on it, thus familiarizes the fish with their presence. They soon become acquainted with sounds or objects on the bank which indicate an approaching meal. The sight of a person with a basin or crock, or the sound of the chopping hatchet, causes a great commotion in the finny community; when a handful is thrown in, heads, tails, and bodies immerge in an upward shower. When they are fed from the cross-timber, they soon become so tame as to take the food from one's fingers—with risk to the feeder, however, of receiving some severe scratches or bites from their sharp teeth.

The larvæ of the common green fly, known as maggots, are hatched in putrid flesh or animal offal from May to

December, and are more nutritious as well as more natural food, than any I have mentioned. It is true, that many persons would be disgusted at the idea of eating so beautiful and delicious a fish as a trout, fed on maggots. Does it ever occur to us what a hog eats, when we have sausages or broiled ham for breakfast? or what trout feed on in their natural haunts? An inventory of a trout's stomach, I have often found, would exhibit rather a heterogeneous assortment,—not omitting a few green caterpillars, and numberless maggots hatched from the eggs of such flies as deposit them for incubation in waters that are natural homes for trout. If these diminutive larvæ give growth and flavor to trout in wild streams, what would the plump offspring of green flies do, if fed to them in stock ponds? I have found them to be taken with as much gusto as green turtle was taken by London aldermen in olden times, and they no doubt produce the same aldermanic proportions. From my own experience, I would say that ten pounds of beef's liver produces more than that weight of maggots. If boxes are provided, with bottoms of woven wire sufficiently open to allow the larvæ to drop through when shaken, and sliding board bottoms to detain them as they are hatched out, these boxes may be kept as worm-producers in some out-of-the-way place, and taken to the pond and shaken, after removing the sliding bottom. Seth Green finds the head of a beef productive in this way, dipping it in the water and shaking the larvæ off to his fish, and setting it away in a box to produce more. An old friend, who takes an interest in all that pertains to trout-breeding, discourses on this wise, on maggots as trout food : "The City of London contains about three and a half millions of people ; its citizens are great egg-eaters, consuming more than a million daily. To supply this demand in part, egg-producing communities have grown up on the opposite side of the British Channel, in France and Belgium. A man, or a family, may own a thousand or more hens; little or no vegetable food is given to them, but they are fed on maggots, which stimulate the laying of eggs. This food is obtained in great quantity by digging trenches or pits three or four feet wide and as many deep. The bottom of the pit is strewed with fresh horse manure, and into it is thrown all manner of animal offal; a dead cat or dog, or any animal that has died naturally, is eagerly sought after. The maggots, which are produced in great numbers, are raked out and fed to the hens." As the matter of food is one of importance to those who intend breeding trout in large numbers, an experiment of this kind is well worth the trial.

In ponds of large area, much natural food is found on aquatic weeds and other plants. The long green silk-like growth, as fine as human hair, which we observe in some waters, and generally in the spring of the year, we find filled with little red coiled up worms; young periwinkles and snails abound on certain weeds. The larvæ of flies are also found on weeds, as well as on decaying brush and logs. Minnows, and the small fry of harmless and worthless species, can also be grown as trout food. It follows, then, that when fish have more range, less food is required to be given them. But in such ponds they are less under control, and resort must be had to the net, or the uncertain hook and line in taking them. Besides, if such ponds are overstocked there is a lack of food. In such as I have recommended, it is provided for them. In the former they are at pasture, in the latter, stall fed, under control, and ready for market when wanted.

Fish Culture a branch of Farming.—In the beginning of this chapter I have alluded to the facilities which most farmers have for hatching trout spawn. Taking them as a class, they are far more favorably situated and circumstanced for the whole routine of breeding and growing trout than persons of any other occupation. As regards the first requisite, most of them have springs of more or less volume and of the proper temperature on their premises, and generally near their dwellings. Labor with them is cheap, and much can be done at different seasons of the year without interfering with their ordinary farm work, or hiring extra help. The employment of horses, carts, wagons, and men, which they keep of necessity, would, therefore, cause no expenditure, and fill up their leisure time. The little mechanism necessary, could be done by any one of them having an eye for a straight line, and an aptness with square, mallet, chisel, saw, hammer, and jack-plane. The only outlay would be for lumber, and trout or spawn to commence with. Four men, with a span of horses, a plough, roadscraper, shovels, and hoes, would excavate and construct ponds of the size I have described, if the ground is not over stony, in less than ten days. If the farmer has no mechanical skill, a country carpenter, with the assistance of two

7 *

farm hands, would put up a large hatching-house in a week. The time between corn planting and the first ploughing, might be put in to advantage. After hay and oat harvest, another turn at the ponds might be taken, and the lull after the crops are in would suffice to finish them. Winter, in which the farmer has but little to do, would be pleasantly and profitably employed in attending to the hatching. He would have a certain supply of fish food from curds, and an occasional one from the animals he would kill. Using milk does not rob the butter jar or the pig pen, as it can be turned into curd after skimming, and the whey can go to the slop barrel. A friend in an adjoining county keeps forty cows to supply milk dealers in town. He has embarked in trout breeding, and says if his hopes are realized, and the matter of food should require it, he will make butter instead of selling milk, and turn all the latter, after skimming, into curds.

Farmers, taking them as a body, are slow in receiving a new idea or adopting new theories. Wheat and corn, which they know all about, are pretty certain, although they require much labor, and some outlay in their production. But here is a branch of industry which can be grafted on, aquæculture an adjunct to agriculture. It can be made as much of an accessary as keeping bees or poultry, and with no more labor. Trout are much less mischievous than the latter, they do not invade the garden or a newly sown or planted field, and can always be found within their circumscribed bounds. "But," says the farmer, "folks will steal my trout," a town or manufacturing village within a short distance suggesting the fear. This is true; but they may also steal **your poultry or** your pigs, and what is crime in one case is crime in the other, and **there is** a penalty **for both.** " **Well, but a fellow who would not** rob a pig-pen **or a hen roost will rob a fish-pond ; he wouldn't** think **that so much** harm." **Wouldn't he! Only keep** a sharp lookout after the one as **you would after** the other, and let the culprit take **the consequences, and** an example of the punishment **of** one fish thief would have a wonderful effect through the neighborhood, and **even through the county.**

The question asked **by many is, will fish culture pay?** It will certainly pay **in stocking barren rivers, as was de-** monstrated at Holyoke **last summer,** when forty millions **of** young shad **were hatched out.** But will **breeding** and **raising trout for market pay?** In answering this question, **I will give a brief summary of** what *has been* **done,** and **then** endeavor **to show what** *can be* done.

A few years since, Seth Green, after seeing what Ste- phen H. Ainsworth was doing, and learning **whatever he** could from his little **fish** cultural establishment, bought an **old** saw-mill **site** on Caledonia creek, **for two** thousand **dollars.** The creek abounded in trout, **and** by erecting **divisions, and** barriers to their escape in the old forebay and raceway, he soon **had** an abundant supply of **breeding fish.** He had scarcely commenced artificial propagation, **when a** partner was admitted **by** paying down six thousand dollars **for a half interest ;** the place, which was bought for two **thousand, being valued** at twelve thousand. From what I **can learn, his** profits **in 1866 were about a thousand dollars,**

in 1867 five thousand. This year he sells three hundred thousand spawn at from eight to ten dollars per thousand; and two hundred thousand young fry at from thirty to forty dollars per thousand; the sales amounting perhaps to ten thousand dollars from spawn and small fry, to say nothing of the larger trout which he sells from his ponds.

Mr. Ainsworth experimented in fish culture for recreation, with a desire to diffuse a knowledge of the art, and to introduce it as a new industry, and does not follow it for any profit it affords. Still, with his small supply of an inch of variable water, he assures me he could have sold five hundred dollars worth of spawn and small fry every year, if he had applied himself with that object. He has generally refused to sell spawn, unless the object of promoting fish culture induced him. So his sales have varied from a hundred to five hundred dollars per annum. In the mean time, in a quiet way, he has stocked streams and ponds without remuneration. From his largest pond, which contains about fifteen hundred trout of various sizes, he has this spring taken two or three messes every week— enough for his family, and a dozen men who are employed in his nurseries. He takes them all (from three-quarters to a pound and a half), with the artificial fly. When feeding them, they are so tame that they will allow a lady, who is his neighbor, to lift them from the water, and appear to like to be fondled. I have just returned (May 20th) from a fishing excursion, where I met him by appointment, and he gave me these items verbally.

In the town of Spring Water (I think, in Ontario

county), New York, a few years since, a farmer owning the sources of a fine spring brook, made three dams on the stream at small expense, and sold the property, which cost him two or three thousand dollars, for ten thousand. So wonderfully had the trout increased by natural propagation in a few years, that the place, otherwise of little value, commanded this price for its fish.

On Long Island, near the city of New York, a person cultivates trout and allows anglers to fish his pond at a price per day. His income from this source is about twenty-five hundred dollars per annum, so I am informed. The amount of his sales from young fish for stocking the ponds of gentlemen, who keep these preserves for fly fishing, I am not aware of. An advertisement in the New York Tribune, reads: " 10,000 Live Trout.—Ponds on Long Island, or near New York City, stocked with live Brook Trout of one year's growth. Address Wm. Nichol Islip, New York." I would say that trout of one year generally command from ten to twelve dollars per hundred, and are in demand amongst New Yorkers owning ponds on Long Island.

Mr. Ainsworth, in a letter to the Vermont Fish Commissioners, gives an estimate of the profits which may be derived from hatching and growing trout on a large scale. As his figures have connection with the description of the ponds, and both would occupy several pages, I must omit them; his showing is, that large profits will accrue from it.

The following is an estimate of my own, based on my experience in feeding curds. The number of trout is the

F

same as those intended to be raised in the ponds of my
friend Comfort, described on a preceding page, using round
numbers.

Food—Curd for one Year.

Pond No. 1—10,000 yearling,   3 quarts per day.
Pond No. 2— 8,000 two year old,   6   "   "   "
Pond No. 3— 7,000 three year old, 12   "   "   "

21 × 4c. per quart = 84c. × 365 = $306.60
Attendant's wages   .   ·   400.00
                                       ————
                                       $706.60

Annual Sales after the Third Year.

7000 trout from pond No. 3, 1 lb. each, 7000 lbs. 75c. per lb., $5250.00
Sales of small fry, 3,000 yearlings 10c.,   .   300.00
                    3,000 three or four months old 5c.,   150.00
                    50,000 eggs, $8 per 1000,   400 00
                                                               ———————
                                                               6100.00
Deduct food and attendance as above,   706.60
                                                               ————————
                                                               $5393.40

An intelligent lad of fourteen, under the direction of an
experienced person, can manage hatching-house and ponds,
and not occupy more than half of his time. Such a lad
can generally be found amongst the sons or lads employed
by a farmer. In addition to the curd, the offal of the kitchen, and livers and lungs of animals killed on the farm, as
I have before said, can be used to hasten the growth.

The foreman of a tannery near Lehigh Gap, on the
Lehigh Valley Railroad, last summer sold to a fish dealer a
number of large trout, which he had kept in a rapidly
growing condition by feeding them on the fleshings of
hides.

I give these few instances of fish culture paying, as they
have come under my observation, or as they have been

told to me by others, and this is all I can do, as it is yet a branch of industry, which I might say, is " in embryo;" but I am so well convinced of the profitableness of a large and well-organized system, that I am about engaging in it again, with Mr. A. J. Beaumont, near New Hope, Bucks county, Penna. Mr. Beaumont has a spring on his property known as the Ingham Spring, which flows about, or over, three thousand gallons per minute. I have alluded to it in a note at the bottom of a preceding page. He has ample room and favorable ground for the ponds, and I do not think it at all unlikely with such advantages, that twenty-five or thirty thousand trout, averaging a pound, can be taken from the third, or it may be a fourth pond, after the enterprise has been in operation three or four years. Of course, the question of food is the most important. In this connection, I would remark, that Mr. Ainsworth told me a few days ago, that he kept an account of the expense of feeding his fifteen hundred fish on beef's liver for one year, and that the amount so expended was only seven dollars and a half. But in his neighborhood, he can buy a beef's liver for ten cents. He fed his trout two livers per week as a general rule, chopping up a quart or so for each meal, but in extremely warm weather and in winter he gave it to them but sparingly.

Growth of Trout.—I have already said, or intimated, that trout kept in ponds will average a pound, when a few months over three years old, if well fed. I am confident from my own experience, that the allowance of curd just given, for the different ages, will produce that weight.

Still, they are like pigs in more respects than in greediness in their disposition to eat offal, for their increase in flesh will be in proportion to the amount of food given. A respectable old gentleman, who, I think, would not "fib," tells me he has had them of four pounds, when as many years old; but they had the run of the spring-house, receiving many a spoonful of cream thrown to them in removing moats, much curd, many worms which his boys fed to them, and the whole population of many a big catterpillar's nest cut from a limb in his orchard; as well as young wasps and hornets. Per contra to this, a trout will live in the bottom of a well, or in a spring, without being fed, for years, and show no growth. In stocking my ponds in New Jersey, several of my trout received unmistakable marks, which they never got rid of; two of these, which were not over eight or nine inches long, and not over five or six ounces in weight, grew, on the amount of curd already mentioned, to thirteen inches in length before they had been in their adopted home a year. They were very stout, and doubtless weighed a pound. Here the weight was more than doubled in a year. **Mr. Ainsworth** stocked a pond near West Bloomfield, New York, with fry as soon as the umbilical sac was absorbed, and three years after caught them, weighing two pounds. In stocking a pond for angling, on Long Island, a friend of the writer bought yearling trout not over five inches long; the following spring, say in twelve months, they were about eleven inches long, weighing a full half-pound; in twelve months more, they had grown to average fourteen ounces, some of them weighed more than a pound. As a fish increases in size, its propensity for further growth also increases. A young salmon at a year, or sometimes even at two years old, does not weigh three ounces ; it goes.to sea and frequently returns in six weeks, or at least the following summer, a fish from three to eight pounds. The abundant and nutritious food obtained at sea causes this wonderful growth ; if it is prevented from going to sea, it does not grow to more than twelve inches, or three-quarters of a pound, in a year from the time it weighs three ounces. Thus an abundance of food causes a rapid growth.

The enemies of larger trout in stock ponds, **are fish**-hawks and night-herons. Water-frogs, snakes, and ducks, may also be destructive to the fry when first turned out of the nursery. In a confined space, the water-snake first muddies the water, and then finds its victim. A duck also **has** the same cunning. A frog, in solemn silence, waits for their approach to shallow water amongst grass or weeds, and pounces upon them. The little king-fisher may also capture some. But the foe which it is the most difficult to protect the fish from, is the species of heron alluded to. Though not numerous, these wading birds, when they have found a feeding place so well stocked, may come for many successive evenings, and prey upon the trout. Other enemies are more easily provided against.

Huningue.—The following description of this celebrated establishment, where fish culture, it might be said, was inaugurated, is from Bertram's " Harvest of the Seas."

" The series of buildings erected at Huningue, are

admirably adapted to the purpose for which they were designed. The group forms a square, the entrance portion of
which—two lodges—is devoted to the *corps de garde*, and
the centre has been laid out as a kind of shrubbery, and is
relieved with two little ponds containing fish. The whole
establishment, ponds and buildings, occupies a space of
eighty acres. The suite of buildings comprise at the side,
two great hatching-galleries, 60 metres in length, and 9
metres broad, containing a plentiful supply of tanks and
egg-boxes; and in the back of the square are the library,
laboratory, and the residence of the officers. Having
minutely inspected the whole apparatus, I particularly
admired the aptitude by which the means to a certain end
had been carried out. The egg-boxes are raised in pyra-
mids, the water flowing from the one on the top, into those
immediately below. The grand agent in the hatching of
fish-eggs being water, I was naturally enough rather particular in making inquiry into the water-supplies of Huningue, and these I found are very ample; they are derived
from three sources—the springs on the private grounds of
the establishment, the Rhine, and the Augraben stream.
The water of the higher springs is directed towards the
building through an underground conduit, while those
rising at a lower level are used only in small basins and
trenches, for the experiments in rearing fish outside.
Being uncovered, however, they are easily frozen, and
besides, are frequently muddy and troubled. As a general
rule, fish are not bred at Huningue, the chief business ac-
complished there, being the collection and distribution of

their eggs; but there is a large supply of tanks or troughs, for the purpose of experimenting with such fish as may be kept in the place. The waters of the Rhine being at a higher level than the springs, can be employed in the *appareils* and basins. The waters of the Augraben stream which cross the ground, are of little use. Nearly dry in summer, rapid and muddy after rain, they have only hitherto served to supply some small exterior basins. Of course, different qualities of water are quite necessary for the success of experiments in acclimatization carried on so zealously at this establishment. Some fish delight in a clear running stream, while others prefer to pass their life in sluggish and fat waters. The engineering of the different water-supplies, all of them at different levels, has been effectually accomplished by M. Coomes, the engineer of this department of the Rhine, who, in conjunction with Professor Coste, planned the buildings at Huningue; indeed the machinery of all kinds is as nearly as possible, perfect.

" The course of business at Huningue is as follows: The eggs are brought chiefly from Switzerland and Germany, and embrace those of the various kinds of trout, the Danube and Rhine salmon, and the tender ombre chevalier.* People are appointed to capture gravid fish of these various kinds, and having done so, to communicate with the authorities at Huningue, who at once send an expert to deprive the fishes of their spawn and bring it to the breeding or store boxes, when it is carefully tended and daily

---

* An exceedingly fine species of large lake charr, one of tho genus *salmo.*

watched till it is ready to be despatched to some district in want of it."

After describing the manipulation of fish to procure the ova, and discussing the probabilities of exhausting the streams of Germany and Switzerland by receiving such large supplies of fish-eggs from them, this writer continues :—

"It would scarcely pay to breed the commoner fishes of the rivers, as carp, pike, and perch. The commonest fish bred at Huningue is the *fera*,* whilst the most expensive is the beautiful ombre chevalier, the eggs of which cost about a penny each before they are in the water as fish. The general calculation, however, appertaining to the operations carried on at Huningue, gives twelve living fish for a penny. The fera is very prolific, yielding its eggs in thousands; it is called the herring of the lakes, and the young, when first born, are so small as scarcely to be perceptible . . . . I inquired particularly as to the Danube salmon, but found that it was very difficult to hatch, especially at first, great numbers of the eggs, as many sometimes as 60 or 70 per cent., being destroyed; but now the manipulators are getting better acquainted with the *modus operandi*, and it is expected, by and by, that the assistants at Huningue will be as successful with this fish as they are with all others. . . ."

"Up to the season of 1863–64, the total number of fresh-water fish-eggs distributed from Huningue, was far above 110,000,000, and nearly half of these were of the finer kinds of fish; there being no less than 41,000,000 of the

---

* A species of *Coregonus*, similar to our small Whitefish.

eggs of salmon and trout. Subjoined is a tabular statement of the fish-eggs collected and distributed at Huningue
for the season of 1861–2.

Species.	Time of operations.	Ova provided.	Loss.	Quantity despatched from the establishment	Retained for experiments at Huningue
Common Trout Great Lake Trout Rhine Salmon Ombre Chevalier	Oct. 24 to March 7 135 days.	6,382,900	2,602,400	3,360,000	420,500
Fera	Nov. 16 to Dec. 25, 30 days.	11,995,000	12,000	9,519,000	2,464,000
Total................. ..	....	18,377,900	2,614,400	12,879,000	2,884,500

The establishment of M. de Galbert on the Isere, at
Buisse, in the Canton Voiron, is one of importance. He
has a hatching-house and a series of ponds; selling ova and
young fry, as well as adult fish. Five years ago, he could
sell 50,000 young fry every spring or summer, without
interfering with his crop of mature fish.

Many of our countrymen on their return from Europe,
speak of the trout-ponds at Heidelberg. The following
is by Prof. A. D. Hager, one of the Vermont Fish Commissioners.

"In Europe the experiment of raising fish in artificial
ponds has been successfully made in many instances. One
of the great attractions at Heidelberg, in Baden, is the fish
pond where the fish are trained to take their food from a
person's hand.

"Near Neufchatel, in Switzerland, Prof. Vouga has been
employed by his government for the past six years in pro-

8 *

pagating trout artificially. When hatched and of suitable
size they are turned into Lake Neufchatel and the streams
emptying into it. At the time of our visit to his establishment, he was greatly enlarging and improving his ponds,
hatching-boxes, &c. The result of his experiments had
satisfied the people of his canton, that the project of stocking the lake (a body of water twenty-eight miles long and
seven miles wide), was a feasible one, and would richly pay
for the expense incurred in rearing the young fry and
turning them into the waters, notwithstanding the people
of the cantons of Freyburg and Vaud, that joined upon
the lake, would also get a considerable share of the mature
fish.

"When we witnessed the outlay of money to fit up the
hatching establishment at Prof. Vouga's, and realized that
it was done by a people numbering less than 80,000 persons, and in a territory of less than three hundred square
miles, we could but contrast that people with those of New
England."

The first experiment in fish culture in this country, from
all I can learn, was made by Dr. Garlick and a friend, at
Cleveland, Ohio. Owing to the death of one of them, the
enterprise was abandoned after a season or two. Mr. Kel-
logg of Hartford, Conn., Mr. Pell of Esopus, and Mr. Ainsworth of West Bloomfield, New York, commenced a few
years later. Following these, came Seth Green of Mumford, New York; Mr. Vail, of Long Island; the writer, near
Asbury, New Jersey; Rev. Livingston Stone, Charlestown,
N. H.; Benjamin Kilburne, Littleton, N. H.; D. G.

Bridgman, Bellows Falls, Vt.; J. S. Robinson, Meredith, N. H.; Judge Tilden, Lockport, N. Y.; P. H. Christie, Clove, Dutchess county, N. Y.; Jeremiah Comfort, near Spring Mills, Montgomery county, Pa., and others.

Mr. Ainsworth commenced nine years ago, with a diminutive supply of water collected from a dozen or so of small springs in his nursery of fruit trees. Leading these through glazed tiles underground to a reservoir, he obtained scarcely water enough to fill a hole an inch in diameter, and that, of exceedingly variable temperature; in winter, only a few degrees above freezing point, and in summer, quite warm. Mr. A.'s mind is particularly constituted for experiment and analysis; with this imperfect supply of water, he has unweariedly pursued his object of making fish culture a branch of national industry, and may be considered the father of the science in this country. The following notice, taken from the Rochester Democrat of May, 1862, shows what progress he had made at that time, and gives a tolerably accurate account of his little establishment.

"*An Attraction in the Country—Visit to a Trout Pond.* —We were not aware, until a few days since, that within twenty miles of this city there is a trout-pond in which sport hundreds of the speckled beauties, fed every day by the generous and enterprising proprietor with as much regularity and care, as he feeds his horses and cattle. Having been posted upon the subject, and, moreover, having been summoned by a polite but pressing invitation, we took a drive on Wednesday, in company with Louis Chapin, Esq., to the village of West Bloomfield, and without delay reported ourselves to the Hon. Stephen H. Ainsworth, whom we found at his hospitable mansion, in the quiet and pleasant village aforesaid. Mr. Ainsworth is by no means a novice in anything pertaining to the tastes or the wants of the disciples of Isaac Walton. Hence, while appreciating the **anxiety of** his visitors to hasten to his trout-pond, he was thoughtful enough to feed his guests before he did his fishes, and we can testify that he does both with a liberality which always characterizes the large-hearted man. And while **waiting a few moments** for the coming demonstration of hospitality, there was just time to look at a small part of Mr. Ainsworth's horticultural **department.** He has over one hundred varieties of grapes—among them, the choicest to be procured anywhere—pears, peaches, and all other fruits grown in this region, in the greatest variety **and profusion.** And we are pleased to know, that within a few years, his industry and enterprise have been generously rewarded, by returns which consti**tute a** fortune, which we hope he and his amiable family may long enjoy.

"The inner man refreshed, **it was quick work to** prepare for a visit to **the trout-pond, situated a short distance from** Mr. Ainsworth's **residence.** Besides the usual food for the trout, Mr. Ainsworth produced **a fly and a** bait rod, reels and lines, **with** permission to do what **he** had scarcely before done **for himself—take enough** trout for a generous **mess.** The pond **covers** something over sixty rods of ground, **and is** filled **by** conducting the water from thirteen different springs in tile **laid under** ground, and brought into pools a short distance above the pond. From thence it flows over a prepared bed of gravel to the pond. Perhaps one man in a million might have thought that a fish-pond, and above all, a place for speckled trout, could have been made in the spot where this is located. The water is fourteen feet deep in the main pond, and this depth has been secured by excavation—the original depression being very slight, although the spot was swampy and of little value. As a means of saving every drop of the small supply of water, two parallel walls have been built around the pond, sunk into the blue clay, and the space between them grouted, so that not a drop is wasted except by solar evaporation. At the bottom, large stones are placed in positions to afford hiding-places for the trout whenever they choose to retire from the hot sun. In this respect, Mr. Ainsworth has studied the habits of his finny stock, and as far as he could, compensated them for removing them from their native streams in Victor, Springwater, and other places, where they were captured. The walls around the pond are carried to the height it is intended the water shall reach, and then a sufficient quantity of earth placed over them to sustain shade trees, a large number of which are in a thrifty condition. The water comes into and passes from the pond through fine sieves, through which nothing but the water can pass.

"Inside of the parallel walls there is a slope wall, and from the top the ground recedes in all directions, so that no surface water is washed into the pond. In places where it is likely to stand too long it is carried off by tiling.

Altogether, it is a perfect gem. Nothing has been neglected, and those who have the facilities, the good taste, and the enterprise to follow Mr. Ainsworth's example, would be greatly aided by paying him a visit. He will, we run no risk in assuming, take great pleasure in giving them the benefit of his experience.

" It is, so far as we are advised, an unsettled matter how many fish can live in a given quantity of water. Mr. Ainsworth has placed nearly eleven hundred trout in his pond, and some additions have been made by the process of artificial fecundation; and this process he will continue to follow until his pond is sufficiently stocked. If it were possible to protect all the spawn deposited by the small number of trout now left in our streams, we should quickly see them restocked to their full capacity. But it is known that even under the most favorable circumstances, only a few of the eggs hatch, and of those which do, much of the product is devoured by snakes, water-fowl, and the larger fish. It would be a very easy matter to resort to artificial fecundation, by which an immense quantity of the most beautiful and delicate fish known in American waters could be raised.

" But to the sport. Both bait and fly were taken the instant they touched the water, and had a hundred hooks been upon each line, each one would have had its victim. They were of various sizes when put into the pond two years ago. Those of three years, are now plump pounders. A majority are of three-fourths and half a pound. Mr. Ainsworth knows their ages as well as he does those of his

colts and cattle. In swift running water, however, they
do not grow as rapidly—they are longer and less plump.
There are a few two and three pounders, but here as in
other waters, these seldom honor the angler's hook with a
nibble. Of course we could not think of following up the
sport for only a few minutes—just long enough to try the
game of the ten noble fellows which were seen in the show
window of the Arcade House yesterday. And they were
game. Every one of them made the rod bend and tremble.
The females were invariably returned to the water. But
more exciting sport remained. The food for their evening
repast was now dealt out by spoonfuls at a time, and the
moment it struck the water, dozens of great fellows darted
for it. They knocked against one another under the water
and above the water, and a person standing close to the
edge would, in five minutes, be well ' spattered' from head
to feet. The ' whipping' had made them a little more
shy than usual, but they will feed from the hand of their
owner, and leap from the water when shown their food
upon a spoon !

"Mr. Ainsworth is a public benefactor in what he has
done. While constructing and filling a pond, at a large
expenditure, for his own amusement and gratification, he
has demonstrated the fact that, under circumstances more
favorable as regards water and places for making ponds,
immense quantities of the most delicious food can be raised
at almost a nominal cost. When this country becomes as
populous as France, such advantages as we possess for the
propagation of fish will be appreciated and improved.

Until then, we can only hope to see here and there a liberal and public-spirited citizen like Mr. Ainsworth set the example.

"We will only add, that an evening pleasantly spent in the family of our friend, a refreshing sleep, an early breakfast, and a ride of twenty miles, ended this delightful excursion to the country."

The following extract from an article on fish culture, which appeared in the New York Tribune, in January 1866, is from the pen of Mr. Ainsworth, and will give the reader a general idea of Seth Green's establishment and Caledonia creek.

"The most prolific stream for trout that I have ever seen, or of which I have ever heard or read, are the Caledonia Springs, and brook from them. This celebrated trout brook rises from the rocks in the village of Caledonia, Livingston county, New York. Its whole length is but one mile, when it unites with Allen's creek, one of the tributaries of the Genesee, in the village of Mumford. The stream falls about 50 feet from the springs to its junction with Allen's creek. The country is all thickly settled, and one of the richest and best farming towns in the state. The surface of the land is quite level, with banks but little above the surface of the water.

"The stream in places is very rapid, and in others has quite a gentle current, of a mile or more per hour. The springs, as now situated, cover about six acres, being dammed slightly for milling purposes. They afford about 80 barrels of water per second, and make a creek from three to four rods wide, and from 18 inches to 6 feet deep, according to the current. The bottom is covered with small white shells and **gravel**. The water is clear, pure, and perfectly transparent, so that any object can **be seen** for three or four rods very distinctly. It is tinctured with lime and sulphur. **Its** temperature at the springs is 48° the whole year round, but down the creek, three-quarters of a mile, it rises in the hottest days in the summer to 58° by night, but it is down in the morning to 52°. In winter it settles at times to 43°, but generally keeps up to 45° or 46°. The temperature of the water to Allen's creek is very even the year round, **but very cold in** summer, and quite warm in the winter, never freezing in the coldest weather. The water through the whole **length of the** creek, as well **as every** stone, stick, weed, and blade of grass, is alive, and literally covered with numerous insects and larvæ of flies, summer and winter, so that the trout, however numerous they are, easily obtain all the food they want all times of the year.

"There is but very little surface water that makes into the creek, hence the volume of the water is very even, and seldom roily. The first settlers of the country found the creek literally filled with trout of great size and beauty, and it has remained so to this day, notwithstanding it has been almost constantly fished, night as well **as** day, from that time to this. The largest and finest trout are taken in the evening with a large artificial white or gray miller. Dark nights, the banks of the creek in spring and summer are often lined with fishermen, when they reel in the

9 G

speckled beauties, hand over hand, and often carry them off by back loads. In this way they sometimes take them that weigh four pounds each. The most ordinary pupil of Isaac Walton can take them in the evening, when in the mood of rising, with the right miller, and with a small piece of angle worm on the point of the hook, to induce them to hold on to the hook till the novice can make his twitch to hook them. But in the day-time none can succeed but the expert. The water is so clear, **and they** are so shy and so well educated, that it requires a 50 or 60 foot line, a fine 10 foot leader, and very small flies, or hackles, and those must be cast upon the water so gently and life-like, to induce them to rise and take the fly, and when they do take it they discover the deception, and spit it out so quick **that but very** few are ever able to so cast the fly and to jerk quick enough to hook them. The fishermen among the oldest inhabitants tell me that at the least calculation there are 4000 pounds of trout taken from the creek yearly, and yet they compute the number of trout to-day at 1000 to each rod of the stream, or 320,000 in the creek, of all sizes, from four or five pounds down to **five** inches in length. On the 18th of this month **I took 110 fine** trout in about three hours, with **the fly, from the creek, and put** them into one **of Mr.** Green's ponds. The day was clear, and the water so clear and transparent that I had to fish with a 60-foot line, which took the most of the time to get the line out to this length and to reel in the trout against the strong current after being hooked.

"The next day I took 85 splendid fellows **from one**

place, hardly moving from my tracks. These facts show how plenty they were, and how ready they are to take the fly in winter. These trout were as fat, active, and gamey as ever I saw them in any other stream in May or June.

"Seth Green, **Esq., the** celebrated marksman **and fly-**thrower of Rochester, bought this creek a year ago **last** fall, for the purpose of growing trout artificially as well as naturally on an extensive scale. He has since prepared ponds, races, hatching-house and hatching-boxes, and troughs for 3,000,000 of spawn, which he expects to fill during the spawning season, which is, with him, from the 1st of November to the 1st of April. Last winter his two best months for spawn were January and February, **and** he expects they will be this year.

"He has one pond, only 75 feet long, 12 feet wide and 5 feet deep, that has 9000 trout in it from 9 inches to 20 inches long, that will weigh from a quarter of a pound to three pounds each, all as fat as seals and as beautiful as **trout can** possibly be, all caught with the fly, by his **own hand,** since he bought the creek, and all can be seen now, any day, at one view, by any person who will **take the** trouble to call on him. Only think what a sight—9000 such trout all in the eye at once! What a gigantic **and** magnificent aquarium!

"I **am** certain that this is the largest and finest exhibition of trout in America, and, probably, in the whole world. This alone would well pay a journey of any lover of Walton from any part of the country to see. But this is not all. He has another pond, right by the side of this,

30 by 50 feet, which contains 20,000 beautiful trout, mostly one and two years old, from six to nine inches long, all taken by his own skill, as above. He has still another **pond,** filled with last spring's fry, from three to five inches long.

"It seems incredible at first thought that such a vast number of large trout could live in so small a space, but **it is** all accounted **for and made** plain, when **one** learns that the water **in the** ponds **is** changed **every** minute through the day by the large current constantly pouring in upon them of this cold, pure spring water.

"Some of the trout produced 6000 spawn each, and from that down to 200, according **to size.** Last year Mr. Green hatched as high **as** 98 per cent. in some instances— in others, about 80 per cent. This year he expects **to** hatch **nearly all, as he has** become master of the business, and knows the right time to take the spawn to insure perfect impregnation. I could see the young trout in almost every egg that had been taken fifteen days, with the naked eye, so that I know his success is perfect so **far. With** this continued success he will very soon be able to stock all the private streams and ponds in the country with spawn and young trout, as well **as to** furnish tons yearly for the **table of this, the most delicious and** costly of all the finny tribe."

The **culture** of trout I have conceived to be of so much importance, that I have gone much into detail in every thing bearing upon the subject. It may perhaps be tiresome to a portion of my readers, but my excuse is, that it is in these details, which are so necessary to success, that most of the essays on trout culture are deficient. As I have already remarked, it is an industry which is yet in its infancy, and although I have given all the directions which have arisen from Mr. Ainsworth's and my own experience, and much that I have learned of Seth Green, there will still be additional discoveries in the minutiæ of the art, as progress is made in it.

I deem it a branch of industry that should claim the attention of our national government. If the agricultural bureau has no discretionary power to foster it, special legislation should be directed to it, and appropriations made for the purpose of experiments, and its promotion.

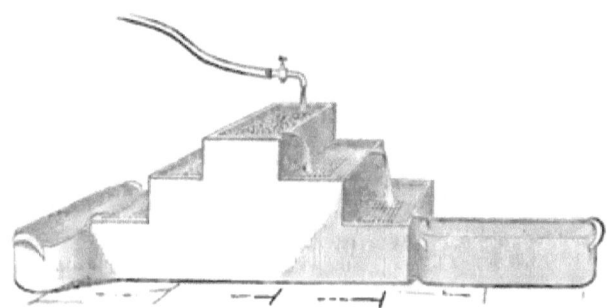

CHAPTER V.

CULTURE OF THE SALMON.

The Salmon.—Its instincts.—Difference in appearance and size
of those belonging to different rivers.—Their former abundance
and cause of decline in numbers.—Their growth and adolescence.—
Migrations.—Time of ova hatching in European and American
rivers.—Growth of the fry, with illustrations.—Early fecundity of
the males.—Attempts at artificial propagation in the United States.
—Their naturalization.—Fishways, with illustrations. *Salmon
breeding.*—At Stormontfield.—On the Dee.—On the Galway.—On
the Doohulla.—At Ballisodare.—In Australia.—Salmon statistics.

AN intimate knowledge of the instinctive habits of this
fish is required in repopulating rivers from which it has
been expelled, or naturalizing it in others. The most important instinct in this connection is, that it is anadromous,*
acquiring its wonderful growth and excellent flavor at sea
and visiting its native rivers for the purpose of reproducing
its species. This it will unerringly do if no insurmountable
barrier opposes it, nor stop short of the pebbly shallow
where it emerged from the egg. Many of them will go
beyond, as was shown by their ascending the fishway at
Lowell on the Merrimack last summer, and as I have witnessed by observing their attempts to ascend impassable

---

* This term is applicable to the shad, salmon, alewife, and other
fishes that enter fresh waters to spawn. I use it to distinguish
these from the migratory genera that live entirely in salt water.

THE SALMON.

falls, in my salmon-fishing excursions. To this infallible instinct* it is owing that Mr. Ashworth has restored the Galway, in Ireland, to more than the fecundity of its palmiest days; that Mr. Cooper has established valuable salmon fisheries on the Ballisodare and its tributaries; that the Doohulla, a little stream ten or twelve feet in width, has been made a highway for salmon which now spawn in the feeders of the lake that discharge through it; that there is a large increase in the numbers of salmon in Scottish rivers; and on this instinct, with the aid of fishways and fish culture, the New England states now depend for restocking their salmonless streams. If an impassable dam prevent salmon from going as high as their native spawning-ground and no favorable place be found below, or in a tributary entering below, they will desert the river for some other. Thus a few stray salmon driven off by such obstruction or by some natural enemy may enter some other than their native stream, as they have been known to enter the Delaware. Even those that went up the fishway at Lowell (if there are no spawning-grounds below on the Merrimack), may have been natives of some other river.

---

* "The Earl of Dunmore caught on his property in the Isle of Harris, in the Hebrides, some twenty or thirty salmon; these he marked and carried alive in his yacht to the opposite side of the island, where they were all turned into a lake. In the course of the same season in which they were transported, it was ascertained that some of these very fish had come back again, all the way home, a circuit of forty miles at least, through the pathless waters of the great Atlantic, passing several rivers in their journey, up which they might have gone had they not preferred their native stream."

In seeking the mouths of their native streams, the salmon of two or more rivers may pass a point in **bay or** estuary where a net extends from the shore, and the catch may embrace a portion of each. When this occurs, as it frequently does on the Bay of Chaleurs, one of the habitans, **who may be standing** by, can easily point out the fish of **each river :** this, he will say, belongs to the Ristigouche, **and that** to the Nipissiguit. The difference is as clear to him, **as the** dissimilarity between a Durham **and an** Alderney cow would be to one of **our farmers.** There is a peculiarity in the formation and general appearance **of the** salmon of a river which is transmitted to their progeny; therefore, if we are successful, as we will no doubt be, in introducing the salmon in our waters, the fish of the Connecticut, in the course of some generations, will differ from **those** of the Delaware. Those **of one** river may be short and thick-set, while those of the other may be long of body and twice the average size of the former.

Salmon at one time, north of the Hudson, were not exclusively for the opulent, they **were** as much or more the food of the **poor, because** they were cheap. Even **now,** when in season, on the coast and in the rivers of the British Provinces **they can be bought for four or five cents** a pound ; **and the angler from the States, as he** takes his **hook from the mouth of a pretty ten-pounder, on a** stream **of the Bay of Chaleurs or the north** shore of the St. Lawrence, **turns the** fish over with **the toe of his** boot and mentally says : "Well, it is only worth fifty cents, now that I have landed **it.**" He would **give five, or even ten dollars,** if he could lay it, bright and silvery as it is, on the table of some friend at home.

Hendrick Hudson, **when he** sailed up the river that bears his name, wrote in his journal: " Many salmon, mullets,* and rays very great." When he got beyond **the** Highlands he wrote again, " Great stores of salmon in **the river."** Alas! where are they now, or those that swarmed in the lakes and streams of New York which connect with the St. Lawrence? But it is useless now to rail at internal **improvements, chartered companies,** and enterprising indi- viduals who have been instrumental in banishing them; our object, at present, is **to induce them to return.**

Salmon commence **to make in towards the rivers from** which **they migrated at rather a later period than shad. Of course those of a more** southern latitude are earlier comers. **On the Bay of Fundy, for instance, at** St. John, **N. B.,** some are taken in May, in June **they are** abundant. **If they are** introduced in the Hudson and Connecticut they might, doubtless, be taken in **Long Island Sound** and in the lower bay **in April. They continue to come in** schools and ascend the rivers all **summer,** the earlier comers **being the earlier spawners, while the late** spawners fre- quently remain in **the river all winter, and go to sea in** the spring. The latter, as has been **ascertained in** Scotland, may not spawn the ensuing **fall, a period of two** years ex- piring before they reproduce. **From** the information gained in the British Provinces, **I am of** opinion that there is **only** one, and that **an annual,** migration **of the** same fish to and

---

* Most likely shad.

from sea on this side of the Atlantic. This is necessarily the case, as most of the rivers are rigidly closed with ice for some months, and many of them for half of the year. On the coast of Great Britain, where the rivers are always open, their migrations occur nearly every month; still there is a throng time when the greater number enter fresh waters. Smolts and grilse have frequently been marked and have gone to sea and returned in six or eight weeks. In Ireland there are fresh run fish in January and fair fly-fishing in February.

In the rivers of the British Provinces north of us there is also what may be termed a throng time. This is generally when the first schools come in. In some rivers they are found at the lower rapids within a week (earlier or later) of the middle of June, and in others, even of the same latitude or district of country, somewhat later. There are different "runs" up to the middle of September; the schools being influenced by easterly storms to enter the bay, and by a rise in the river to ascend. Unlike the shad, which are deterred or driven back by a freshet, salmon seem to delight in a heavy rise, after which, there is always good fishing as the water clears.

When a school of salmon, coming from sea, reaches a bay or the mouth of a river entering the sea, some weeks are occupied in working up towards the head of tide,* the fish in the mean while undergoing a change of system which fits them for their habitation in fresh water. Dur-

---

* As the season advances the time so occupied grows shorter, until only a few days are spent in tide-water.

ing this time they feed on smelts, sparlings, and other small fish as well as crustacea. After entering fresh water no food is to be found in their stomachs; notwithstanding, they will rise occasionally at a natural or artificial fly, and will sometimes take a worm bait. In their journey upwards they generally linger on the way, at the foot of many a rapid or just above, until they reach their native spawning-grounds, or go beyond. They lose the silvery brightness which they bring from sea, and continue to grow darker and fall off as the summer advances. A fish that was a twenty-pounder, when fresh run, in three weeks will be one of seventeen pounds, and so on to the time of spawning, when they have lost half of their weight and are scarcely fit for food. If their native water is some inconsiderable brook, which is frequently the case, they will wait for a rise, or wriggle over shallows scarcely the depth of their bodies. The canoemen who have attended me on my fishing excursions, have told me that at spawning time they can be captured with almost any kind of a net; no doubt persons whose object it is to hatch the ova in the States could then procure it in any quantity.

The spawn of the salmon, as all experiments have shown, can be hatched by artificial appliances as easily as the ova of our brook trout, the term of incubation being somewhat longer in water of the same temperature. I have no doubt that in spring water, uniformly at 50°, the time would not exceed fifty or sixty days. In Scotland it has extended to 130 days, and in the almost Arctic winters of the British Provinces it is likely that six months or more is required. The short time which, under favorable circumstances, would be requisite in artificial incubation in New England and in the Middle States, where the salmon could be naturalized, would produce the fry in winter, and give them such a start that nearly all would probably reach the smolt state and go to sea the second summer.

In my remarks in the "American Anglers' Book," on the time required to hatch out salmon ova in Canadian rivers, I have alluded to the fact that many of them, where the water is shallow enough, and where it affords the requisites for a spawning-bed, freezes to the bottom; and have inferred from this that the eggs do not (at least not all of them) lose their vitality. In proof of this theory, it is stated in the London "Fisherman's Magazine" that salmon ova had been kept in ice ninety days, and that half of these frozen eggs were afterwards hatched out.

When the young salmon frees itself from the shell, it is about three-fourths of an inch long, and has the same umbilical sac which we observe in the fry of brook trout. This it carries for about six weeks; during this time it refuses all food. As soon, however, as this sac is absorbed, its predacious instinct is observed, rising eagerly at the smallest insect or atom, and seizing animalculæ beneath the surface. In pisciculture the food of the fry is much the same as those of the trout; I therefore refer the reader to the directions for feeding the young of that fish.

Although the incubation of salmon ova is similar to that of the trout in breeding them artificially, the manipulation of the fish is different on account of the large size and vigor

of the salmon, requiring two and sometimes three persons
to perform the operation. If the fish is held pendent by
the head, the ova, if mature, will distend the lower portion
of the abdomen, and some of it flow without pressure; and
this, from all we can learn, is the position in which the salmon is generally held when it is being operated on. Mr.
Francis, however, gives an illustration of holding one somewhat horizontally, with the vent beneath the water of the
basin, and raising the head and tail slightly, as is done with
the trout in this country in extruding its eggs. In manipulation, Messrs. Martin and Gillone, on the river Dee, use a
box about three feet and a half long, seven inches in
breadth, and of corresponding depth. It is filled with
water, and the eggs are pressed out of the fish in the position in which it swims.

The young of the salmon, as long as it retains what are
known as the finger-marks on its sides, is called a *parr*.
When these marks are no longer visible, and it assumes a
silvery coat, it is a *smolt*, and is sufficiently advanced for its
first migration to sea. On its return, which may be after
six or eight weeks, or not until the following summer, it is
a *grilse*, its average weight being about four pounds. After
its second visit to its marine feeding-grounds, it is a *salmon*,
weighing from eight to fifteen pounds. Immediately after
spawning it is called a *kelt*, or a *black fish;* the latter
appellation is given to a fish that has spawned and remains
in the river for any length of time, which generally occurs
in the winter months.

10

The figures on this and the opposite page exhibit the growth of the young salmon *ab ovo*. No. 1 is the egg; No. 2, the fish when it casts off the shell; No. 3, after the umbilical sac is absorbed; No. 4, the size when three months old; No. 5, when five months; No. 6, when ten or eleven months old; and No. 7, when it puts on the silvery vesture of the smolt and is ready for its first migration to sea. Figures 5, 6 and 7 represent the growth under favorable circumstances, and of such as go to sea the second summer, when somewhat over a year old. Experiments in Scotland and Ireland have shown that only a portion of the fry become smolts the second summer, the remaining portion, which is about half, not arriving at that state until another year has elapsed. It was supposed at one time, by those who conducted the salmon-breeding establishment at

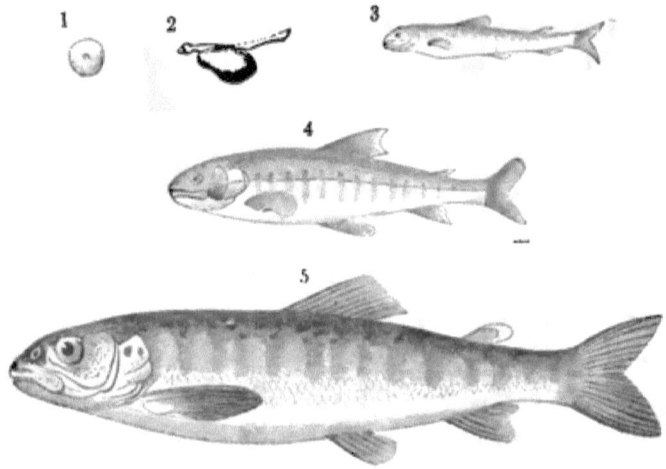

Stormontfield, that the latter might be the produce of parr with grilse, or either of these with the salmon, while the early immigrants were entirely the offspring of mature salmon. It was found, however, on impregnating the ova of the one with the milt of the other, that the produce of each of these minglings at the age of a year were about the same size, the largest of them, which was but five inches long, being from the ova of a salmon impregnated with the milt of a large smolt taken from the pond. Owing to the limited extent of the single pond at that time, however, the rearing of the young fish was done in such confined space (as in small ponds or boxes) as evidently stunted their growth, and the riddle, why a part of the fry become smolts when a little over a year old and the remaining part not until the following summer, is still unsolved.

Those who are not conversant with the natural history of this fish will no doubt be astonished to learn that the male parr in Scottish rivers has milt sufficiently mature, at the spawning season, to impregnate the ova of a grilse or full-grown salmon. Whether this be the case on this side of the Atlantic it is difficult to say; I am inclined to believe it is not. In European rivers the female grilse has also mature spawn at the proper season, while the female grilse in the waters of New Brunswick has not, although the male grilse may be found with well-developed milt. In examining a dozen or more through the summer, and as late as the 1st of September, I did not find one in which the ova was in more than a rudimentary state. Whatever may be the difference between the growth or adolesence of the salmon here, compared with Europe, the same rule holds, that the males precede the opposite sex a year in their power of reproducing.

In the supplement to the second edition of the American Anglers' Book, I have alluded to a discovery made by Mr. W. F. Whitcher, that the salmon in Canada frequently express their spawn and milt simultaneously, by bodily contact, the male and female lying partially on their sides.

I am also strongly impressed with the belief, from the long term of incubation required in the rivers of our eastern coast, that the fry do not come from the ova until the summer has set in or advanced somewhat, and that this retards their growth so much that none of them come to the smolt state the second year. In fishing from June until September I have taken many of the fry on my salmon flies. I have had them, in some pools, continually jumping at the knots on my casting-line; and at the entrance of small spring brooks, when there was a good current in the river, have taken them when fishing for trout; but all had the usual finger-marks of the parr, none the silvery garb of the smolt. Nor had any of the canoe-men I have employed at different times ever seen a young salmon with the bright vesture that is significant of its intention to make its first trip to sea. The migration of smolts, therefore, must be before the rod-fishing commences, which is in June or after the middle of September, when it is over. If they migrate in May some of them may return as grilse in August or September, but the large schools which come into the rivers in July are doubtless those that have remained at sea all winter. At Ballisodare, in Ireland, marked grilse have not returned until the expiration of sixteen or seventeen months; and the question has even been mooted whether some smolts, when they go to sea, do not remain long enough to pass through the grilse state and become salmon before they return.

After all the experiments, and the close observation of the habits of salmon, there is still much uncertainty as to its growth and its migrations. What modifications may be made in series of generations by artificial hatching and raising the young fish in ponds, remains to be seen. With water for incubation at 50°, and chopped liver, &c., fed to the fry, it may make a whole year's difference in producing mature salmon. In artificial culture in Scotland, the fry, as a general rule, are not turned into the river until they become smolts, being kept in ponds until that time, and thus protected from their natural enemies, which would prey upon them if turned out to shift for themselves as soon as the umbilical sac is absorbed. In the short account of the salmon-breeding establishment of Stormontfield, given on a succeeding page, it will be seen that a pond covering an acre, and having the average depth of four feet, is deemed sufficient for the feeding and rearing of three hundred thousand young salmon.

The salmon of the Danube,* which migrate to and from the Black Sea, are said to grow to double the size of those

* This is doubtless the "*Salmo hucho*," described by Sir Humphrey Davy in his "Salmonia."

of Northern Europe. Although their growth is much more rapid than the latter for the first year—in which time they attain the weight of a pound—their subsequent increase in size is slower. Large salmon of the Danube must therefore be fish of advanced age.

The first attempt at breeding salmon artificially in the United States, as far as I have been able to ascertain, was by James B. Johnston, Esq., of New York city. Four years since he imported the **ova of** salmon, salmon of the Danube, trout, and charr. A part of these were hatched out at the studio buildings on Tenth street, New York, in troughs similar to those at the College of France, but the Croton water was fatal to most of them. The fry which Mr. Johnston removed to Long Island were promising in confinement, he says, "but died from preventable causes when liberated."

Salmon ova which were planted in the Pemigewasset in the fall of 1866, it is thought did well, as Dr. Fletcher, of Concord, N. H., saw the fry last autumn. This gentleman, who had the matter in charge, also brought home from the Mirimichi last fall seventy thousand eggs. Half of these were placed under **charge of Mr. J. S.** Robinson, **of Meredith, N. H., and the** remaining half were put into the **hatching-troughs of** Rev. Livingston Stone, of Charlestown, N. H. The first fry hatched in sixty-two days from impregnation. In a letter to Mr. Ainsworth, dated February 6th 1867, Mr. Robinson says : " The hatching of the salmon ova has concluded and the result is very gratifying, as 99 **per cent.** have hatched and seem to be perfectly

healthy. I do not mean of all the eggs, but 99 per cent.
of all the impregnated ones, which was 12 per cent. of the
whole. One-half of the eggs were sent to Charlestown,
N. H., and are designed for the Connecticut."

There cannot be a doubt but that with experience in the
manipulation of salmon, and in the transportation of ova,
we shall be able to introduce them into our rivers as readily
as we can trout into brooks which they have not before
inhabited.

The naturalization of this fish in rivers a few parallels
south of those it once visited, would be an exceedingly
interesting experiment. The expenditure of a few thousand dollars in this way, and strict enforcement of laws,
provided for their protection, would add largely to the value
of our fish product, and make salmon cheaper than beef in
our markets. Let any one ride in the cars from Easton to
Belvidere on the Delaware, and see its fine pools and rapids,
and then explore its bounding upper waters and tributaries, and speculate as to the vast area of spawning-ground
this river affords, and say if the states bordering on it, or
owning the tributaries, are not closing these natural salmon
nurseries against a wealth of delicate food we might enjoy.
The experiment of introducing salmon even into the Susquehanna is well worth the trial. When the question of
fishways is settled in favor of the citizens of the state, as
it must ultimately be, the many noble creeks that feed it
(they would be dignified by being called rivers in Europe)
would afford extensive spawning-beds. The summer temperature of the water of these is but little above that of

some of the fine salmon rivers of New Brunswick or of California.

If part of the expenditure of the agricultural bureau, which produces no immediate benefit to the country, was appropriated to building an efficient fishway around Niagara Falls, and salmon were introduced by artificial culture into the many fine rivers entering the chain of great lakes above, it is difficult to estimate the numbers that would make the Niagara river a highway. At throng time it would be like the waters below the falls of some of the Oregon rivers, where a spear thrown at random does not fail to impale a salmon. In France such a national enterprise would not be thought chimerical.

Within a period of ten years, the salmon fisheries of the British Provinces had declined so much as to create fears of the gradual, but sure extinction of this fish in many rivers. By legislation, strict enforcement of laws provided for their protection, and the erection of a few fishways, this decline has not only been arrested, but the numbers of salmon so much increased, as to bring back the prices at Quebec and Montreal to the point at which they stood twenty years ago. To Mr. W. F. Whitcher, the able and vigilant head of the Fisheries Branch of the Crown Land Department, much credit is due, for his efficient agency in arresting the destruction, and re-instating most of the rivers to their former fruitfulness. The St. Lawrence at this time has eighty-seven tributaries well stocked with salmon. The summer of 1865 was favorable for the salmon fisheries of Canada and New Brunswick. The rod fishing on most

of the rivers, **surpassed that** of any former year. The subjoined is from a Montreal **paper**:

" *Salmon Fishing at* **Goodbout**—*Season of* 1865.—The
following record **of** 22 days' salmon-fishing on the Goodbout, has been **transmitted us for** publication. We have to
direct the attention of the editor of the *Field*, **and the**
sporting community generally, to Mr. Gilmour's magnificent
day's sport **of 46** fish, and to ask if it has been beaten **else-**
where? We believe it is the largest on **record**:

June.		No. of Fish.	No. 1 Rod. Mr. Noble.	No. 2 Rod. Mr. Croes.	No. 3 Rod. Mr. Gilmour.	No. 4 Rod. Mr. Law.
	20	4	0	1	0	3
	21	7	0	1	0	6
	22	10	1	2	0	7
	23	7	1	0	4	2
	24	8	0	1	3	4
Sunday—no Fishing.						
	26	11	2	3	3	3
	27	20	0	5	9	6
	28	28	5	8	6	9
	29	26	5	6	6	9
	30	22	0	6	10	6
July	1	17	0	2	6	9
Sunday—no Fishing.						
	3	30	7	2	9	12
	4	31	2	16	6	7
	5	44	5	1	30	8
	6	23	1	7	6	9
	7	18	10	3	1	4
	8	26	9	12	4	10
Sunday—no Fishing.						
	10	54	1	4	46	3
	11	28	1	4	7	16
	12	20	8	2	4	5
	13	21	0	21	0	0
	14	23	0	2	5	16
		478	49	109	165	155

Total, 478.   Fish weighing gross 4665 lbs., viz. :

Noble,	588
Cross	1059
Law	1551
Gilmour	1567
	——
Total	4665

Averaging about 9¾ lbs. each fish."

On the Nipissiguit, the same season, the sport was excellent ; my best days running from nine to twelve salmon and a great many grilse. The score of each day was very uniform ; the largest fish 22½ lbs. I was quite surfeited, and left off during a good run of fish. If I had continued I would have made an extraordinary score.

The last report of the Commissioners of Fisheries for the state of Maine, is a work of one hundred and twenty-seven octavo pages, and contains so much valuable information, particularly as showing the feasibility of restocking their many once abundant salmon rivers, that it should be read by all who have the matter at heart. Anglers should by all means read it. If the enterprise which now characterizes the commissioners continues, we may, in the course of five or six years, have abundant sport in the fine rivers of Maine.

I have obtained from Theodore Lyman, Esq., the privilege of using the illustration of fishways, found on the opposite page. It is taken from the report of the Massachusetts Commissioners of Fisheries. The explanations on p. 120, are also from the same report.

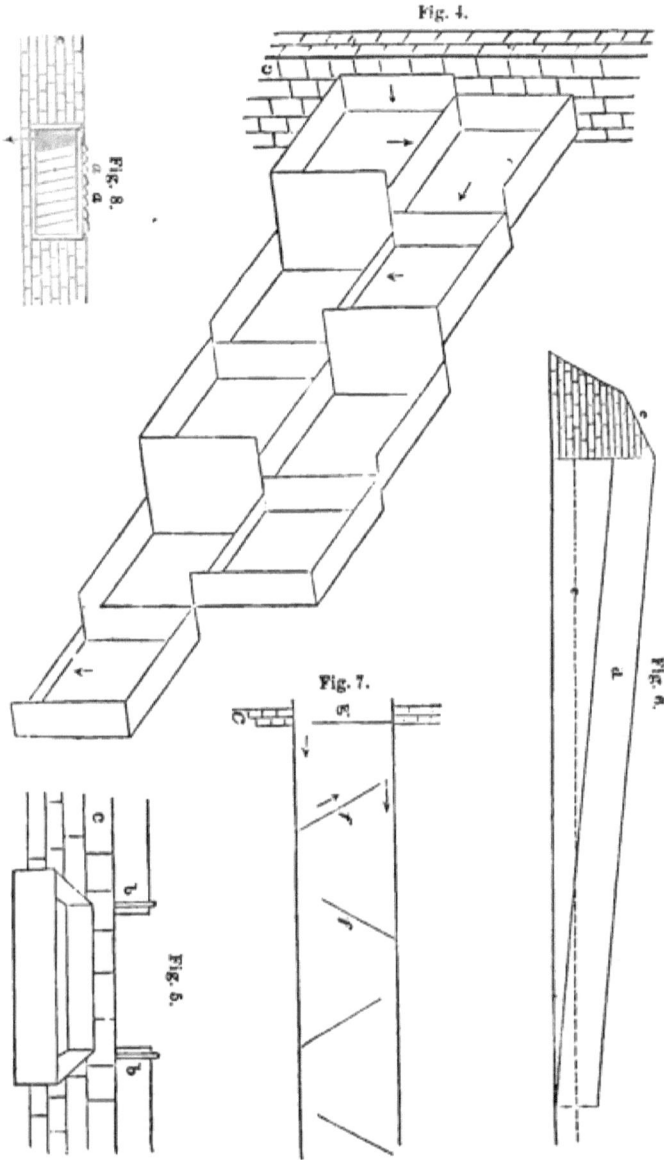

Fig. 4.

Fig. 7.

Fig. 6.

Fig. 5.

Fig. 8.

Fig. 4.—Diagram of the double Fish-stair, at Lowell, showing
the arrangement of the tanks and the course of the water. The
tanks are somewhat over twelve feet square and about two feet deep.
The fall from each tank to the next, is one foot. With 2 feet and
4 inches of water on the dam-crest, a floating body moved down
the current of this fish-stair with an average speed of less than two
miles an hour. c, the dam.

Fig. 5.—Diagram, to show how the width of the sheet flowing
into the first tank, is regulated by flashboards (b) placed on the
dam (c).

Fig. 6.—Profile of Foster's fishway, showing the trough or pass,
(d) sloping from the dam (c) to the river-bed. e, the water-line,
below the dam.

Fig. 7.—Plan of Foster's fishway, showing the up-stream slant
of the cross-bulkheads (f) and the course of the water. c, the
dam. g, the flood-gate.

Fig. 8.—Flood-gate of Foster's fishway, seen from the face of
the dam (c); a a, pieces of scantling, which may be removed to
increase the volume of water. This fishway is particularly adapted
to small streams, because it uses little water. In the absence of
any experiment, there is some doubt whether shad will freely pass
through so narrow an opening as this plan shows; but alewives and
salmon will. The cross-bulkheads are made as high as the sides
of the pass, so that the water runs deep. Figs. 6, 7, and 8, are
drawn on a scale of 20 feet to an inch.

Salmon breeding at Stormontfield.—This establishment, which has been in operation about fifteen years, is situated on the **Tay,** about five miles above Perth. The ponds occupy a piece of ground which slopes gently down to the river. The ground is bounded at the top by the Stormont- field mill-lade, **which is** led from the Tay at a point a mile higher up; the space between the lade and the river being about five hundred feet. Within these limits the whole of the operations are carried **on.** A pipe from the lade discharges at a short distance the water into a bed of gravel, **from** which **it** rises through two openings into a channel supplying the hatching-boxes. These boxes are three hundred in number, and lie in twenty-five parallel rows of twelve each, at right angles to the lade, and have a considerable slope. **Between** each row is a narrow foot- path **for the convenience of** examining the boxes, which **are six** feet long, eighteen inches wide, and twelve inches deep; the division between the boxes of each row being **cut** down half **way, so** as to allow **a free flow of water.** The boxes are filled to within two inches of the surface of the water, first with fine, then with coarser gravel, and on the top is a layer of stones about the size of road-metal Amongst these stones the impregnated ova are placed, about a thousand in each box. Running along the foot of the **rows of boxes,** is a small channel which joins a lade leading **to the** two feeding-ponds, one occupying about **a** quarter and the other a full acre, **the latter** having been added

---

* A condensation of a description found in the Fisherman's Maga- zine, London, with some additions from "Harvest of the Sea."

within a few years. A channel connects the ponds with
the river, for the passage of the smolts to sea, a **perforated**
sluice being opened at the proper time for their egress.
The smolts can be detained by a sluice near the river when
any of them are to be marked.

The time of incubation here, is from a hundred to a
hundred and thirty days. The fry remain in the hatching-
boxes **five** or six weeks, **and then** find their way to the first
pond, where they remain for **a** year, and are then turned
into the second pond, that the succeeding brood of fry may
occupy the first. From the second pond, when they become
smolts, they are turned into the river through the channel
referred to above. Marking them is done generally by
clipping or notching the adipose dorsal fin. The fry are
fed regularly on boiled liver grated fine, rising to the sur-
face in thousands when it is thrown in.

The spawning fish are taken at Almond Mouth, about
three miles distant, with the common draught net, and
manipulated there. When a rise in the river sufficient to
interfere with taking the fish is apprehended, they can be
taken some days before they **are** fully mature, and kept **in**
the mill-lade mentioned at the beginning of this article;
being **kept within bounds by two rows of iron** bars set
across the lade, one row about **a** hundred yards from the
other. Mr. Peter Marshall, the superintendent of the works,
is the operator. Holding the female firmly or having her
held, he brings his hand with a gentle pressure down **the**
belly, when the ova are ejected into a pail of **river** water;
manipulating the male in the same way, he extrudes the milt

and sets the pail aside for awhile, when the water is poured off and fresh water substituted; after renewing it a second, and it may be a third time, the eggs are ready to be placed in the hatching-boxes. It is estimated that the female salmon has about a thousand eggs to each pound of her weight, therefore the ova from fifteen fish of twenty pounds, or twenty of fifteen pounds, or thirty of ten pounds, will give three hundred thousand eggs.

When this fish factory was first established, the single pond could only be stocked alternate years, from the fact that part of the fry became smolts the second, and the remaining portion the third year. The latter of course would destroy the brood of young fish if turned into the pond from the hatching-boxes. This led to the construction of the second pond for the accommodation of the parr that remained until the third summer, so that the production of fry can be increased from three hundred thousand every alternate year, to three hundred and fifty thousand every year.

From the information I can gain as to the loss of salmon-eggs in incubation, it is about ten per cent. in Scotland and Ireland, and more than double of that at Huningue.

One of the consequences of the operations at Stormontfield, up to 1865, was an increase of ten per cent. in the number of salmon taken in the Tay, and, of course, a corresponding increase in the rental of its fisheries. It has also opened the eyes of owners and lessees of fisheries on this and other rivers, to the availability of fish culture, in restoring them to their former fecundity. Amongst those who have adopted this means, are Messrs. Martin & Gillone, lessees of the river **Dee** salmon-fisheries. Their establishment is at Tongueland, on the **Dee. In 1865** they produced from ova laid down **the previous autumn,** over 100,000 young fish. They do not expose **the ova to** the weather as at Stormontfield, but occupy a room **seventy feet** long **in a** lumber store-house, **connected with a** *biscuit bakery*. **It is in** contemplation, by some **spirited** gentlemen, **to endeavor to increase** the produce of the Severn, and **to stock some of** the other rivers of England with salmon. **Even the polluted Thames** is included in the number; side **drains** for the filth **discharged** into it by London, **having been** talked of. *The Thames Angling Preservation Society* have a hatching establishment, and **have introduced the** grayling. In the season of **1863–4 they** turned out about **40,000** young fish,[*] 12,000 of which were salmon, the remainder common trout, sea trout, Rhine salmon, **ombre** chevalier, &c.

The following account of **Mr.** Ashworth's undertaking **on the Galway, is from Mr. Francis's book on Fish Culture.**

"Several successful **undertakings in pisciculture have been carried out in Ireland.** · The first of any note, perhaps, **was at** Outerard, near **Galway, in 1852. The Galway**

---

[*] **Mr. Francis, a writer on** fish culture, in a recent letter, expresses a doubt as **to** the smolts being able to make their **exit to** sea through the impure water of the Thames opposite London, and **gives an** unfavorable report generally, **of the** results **of this** enterprise thus far. –

river is the channel through which Loughs Mask and
Corrib, two enormous lakes containing a vast area of water,
discharge themselves into the sea. The fishery of this
river belongs to Mr. Ashworth. In 1852, finding the
stock had been terribly reduced from a variety of causes,
he established a breeding-place at Outerard, in a small
tributary stream. Here twenty boxes were laid down, after
the same fashion as the plan, already explained, adopted at
Stormontfield. This plan, carried out by Mr. Ramsbottom,
was the model whence Stormontfield was taken. These
boxes were stocked with about 40,000 ova, which in due
time came to perfection. Subsequently, owing partly to
the opening of a wide Queen's-gap in the weir, Mr. Ashworth's fishery multiplied itself in value manifold, and
he cast about, adding a still larger area to the field of his
operations.

"Lough Mask, which discharges into Lough Corrib, is
separated from it by a very rugged channel, and a lofty,
impassable fall; consequently, although Lough Corrib
abounded in salmon, none had ever been seen in Lough
Mask. Moreover, the many gravelly tributaries which
salmon love to spawn in, rather discharged themselves into
the upper part of Lough Mask, which again receives the
waters of one or two smaller lakes, than into Lough Corrib;
and as the capabilities of production of a fishery are
bounded by the area of its spawning-beds, this proved a
serious check to the further increase of productiveness in
the fishery. Undaunted by difficulties, however, Mr. Ashworth set to work, ameliorated the stream, put salmon-

11 *

stairs to the impassable fall, and stocked the head waters of
Lough Mask with half a million of **salmon ova. These**
operations have **been so lately** completed, **that** we hardly
know as yet what measure of success will attend them; **but
I see no** reason for doubting their success, and, if **so, a**
capable area of about thirty square miles will be added to
Mr. **Ashworth's already˙ valuable** fishery, **and in a few**
years' time the fishery will realize a handsome fortune.
This shows what can be done **by** pisciculture, **in** its broad
sense, **and a little practical common sense combined."**

To the foregoing **I** would add, **that from information**
obtained from another source, **Mr.** Ashworth **laid down**
in the **season of** 1861–2, no less then a million and a **half**
of ova.

I would also state that Mr. Frank Buckland, a naturalist
who takes much interest **in fish culture** in England, has,
since the publication of **Mr.** Francis's book, **examined the**
ground between lakes Corrib **and Mask. His** report is
adverse **to the** efficiency of the fishway **there used.** He
says that the natural outlet from the upper to the **lower**
lake, is underground, **through broken and cavernous** rocks,
and that the channel for the fishway is in the bed of an
abandoned **canal, three and a half miles long,** through
rocky ground˙ full of fissures and sink-holes. That the
passage, even with the improvement made by laying down
a thousand **feet of** iron pipe, three feet in diameter, is
impracticable to salmon in the spring of the year, from the
force of the current; and in summer, from the scarcity **of**
water. And further, that the young fish leaving **Lough**

Mask, would most likely do so by some of the many sub-terranean passages, and be lost in the bowels of the earth. The foregoing, in substance, is from " The Field," of Nov. 19th, 1864. Mr. Ashworth, in his prize essay on the culti-vation of salmon fisheries, says, " I have lately expended £1700 in the construction of a salmon-passage and ladder, between Loughs Corrib and Mask, and through which salmon have passed in the winter of 1865, into an exten-sive district of new breeding-ground from which they had been previously excluded." This is the last we have of the passage alluded to. Whether the fish have passed it, in numbers, and if so, whether Mr. Buckland's prediction of the fry getting lost in the bowels of the earth has been realized, I am unable to state.

I am indebted also to Mr. Francis's book, for an account of Mr. Edward J. Cooper's experiments at Ballisodare, Ireland.

" This undertaking, which was really an experiment, shows how great difficulties can be overcome by persever-ance, and how a fishery can be created where none has previously existed. Mr. Cooper owns two rivers, the Owenmore and the Arrow, which unite some two and a half miles from the sea and form the Ballisodare river. On these rivers are three falls ; the lowest, which is a suc-cession of falls over high ledges of rock, is within a short distance of the sea ; the next, which is a short distance above it, is called the Upper Ballisodare Fall. This fall is impracticable to fish, though fish had been known to sur-mount the lower one occasionally, but not often. The entire height of the two falls is about seventy feet. The highest, which is on the Owenmore, near the village of Collooney, has but one fall; but this one is higher than either of the falls which comprise the lower one and the Upper Ballisodare Fall, and is entirely impracticable.

"The ladder applied to the Upper Ballisodare Fall was at first brought out into the lower water too far down the stream from the fall, so that the fish in running up missed it. It was therefore found necessary to turn it, so as to bring the embouchure of the ladder close to the foot of the falls. A few pairs of fish had always been in the habit of entering the river and running up to the lower falls, and the plan adopted to stock the river was that of catching the fish and placing them in the river above the falls, so that they might spawn in the river. After sundry failures, the ladders being completed, and several fish being put up above the falls, and some fecundated ova deposited in the river, a large quantity of salmon-fry was observed to be in the river. These, at the usual time, became smolts and disappeared. This was about April, 1857. On June 26th the first grilse was observed at the fall; by July they were plentiful, and so continued till the end of the season. The river was not fished in 1857.

"I had much more and interesting particulars from Mr. Cooper in reference to this fishery, but cannot find space for it here. The account was fully given in "The Field" in December, 1858, and from that paper I extract the follow- ing table, showing how completely the experiment succeeded. The table was kept by an agent whom Mr. Cooper appointed :—

" ' 1857. August 24. Saw several salmon in the hole under the fall of Collooney.

" ' September 24. The river between Ballisodare and Collooney is now well stocked, salmon being visible in almost every deep hole, and a number being congregated between Collooney Bridge and the hole under the fall.

" ' October 3. A flood being in the Owenmore, I shut the water off the Collooney ladder to see if there were any fish passing up, and found seven salmon and one white trout in the pond Of these seven, five were males.

" ' October 13. Examined Collooney ladder, and reported to Mr. Leech that there were salmon in it. Twenty-seven salmon were found in it, the great majority of them being females.

" ' October 15. Lowered the sluice of Collooney ladder again, but got no fish.

" ' October 28. Again examined the ladder, and got three male fish.

" ' October 30. Four male and two female fish taken out of ladder and put up.

" ' November 3. Sixteen male and eight female.

" ' November 4. There were ten fish in the ladder, which were not removed, as Mr. Leech was not present.

" ' November 5. Nine fish, not removed.

" ' November 6. Seven ditto, ditto.

" ' November 7. Eleven ditto, ditto. I went to Balliso-

I

dare on this day, and saw several large fish leaping at the upper ladder.

"'November 9. We put up from the ladder twenty-four male and fifteen female fish.

"'November 23. Lowered the sluice again; twenty-five male and twenty female fish found in the pond. A few of these were large fish, say 14 lbs. or 15 lbs. weight.

"'November 30. The fish are now beginning to spawn in great numbers in the Owenbeg river.

"'December 3. Thirty-six male and forty-five female fish found in the ladder.

"'1858. January 5. Saw a few spawning-beds in Owenmore.

"'January 9. In river Arrow and tributaries found twenty-nine salmon redds.

"'February 14. Walked the Kilmorgan river (a tributary to the Arrow), and counted twenty-one redds.'

"In the early part of this year, 1858, we seldom fished. In the month of February we took five fish; in March three; in April two; in May ten; in June thirty-nine. We did not, in fact, begin to fish regularly till the 1st July. During this month we took 868 salmon, and up to the 20th August (the close of our season) 530 more—the year's take averaging very little more than 4 lbs. each. Mr. Culbertson's notes on this year are: 'Spring-fish showing in February. One of 9 lbs. taken in the net, was a fry marked by Brown in 1856. In March got another about the same weight. Only a few fish through this month. Fry coming down in April, and more plentifully

in May : but I do not think so many in the river as last
year. On 13th May saw nearly one hundred jumps from
six to eight o'clock in the evening ; they were from 8lbs.
to 12lbs. weight. On 9th June was first grilse at lower
fall ; about the end of the month they were very plentiful.
Among the fish taken by the nets on 6th July, seven were
fry marked by me last year. and they weighed **5½ lbs. to**
6 lbs each.'

"Since the end of the close-season, many reports have
been sent me relative to the numbers running up. From
my inspector's book I take the following : ' Aug. 28. At
Ballisodare, numbers of salmon in every part of the river
between bridge and lowest fall. **Sept. 1. .** Collooney ladder
literally full of fish. They did not run in such numbers
last year until November, being over two months earlier
this **year. Sept. 6.** Plenty of fish immediately above
Collooney Bridge. Sept. 25. Collooney ladder swarming,
and plenty showing **in** every place between bridge and
fall. October 3 **to 6.** Heavy floods. Collooney ladder
resembles a steeplechase, as we see them clearing the
steps in pairs, and some very good fish. Oct. 8 and 9.
Plenty of fish still on the run. Oct. **16.** I have been
watching the salmon jumping and playing at Collooney
fall and ladder. I have visited the ladder daily this week,
and from the numbers in it, am convinced that they
could be removed from top of ladder with the hand.
Nov. 27. Great numbers of fish in Collooney ladder.'
In addition to these notes of my inspector, **one of my**
water-keepers reported having **counted 267** salmon in one

hour ascending the Collooney ladder; and Mr. Culbertson has written to me to say that he reckoned 100 in less than half an hour making up the rapids at Ballisodare. On yesterday, Dec. 2, there were so many fish in the pond at Collooney, that Mr. Leech took up no less than six at once in a common landing-net.

"EDWARD J. COOPER.

"Markree Castle, December 3.

"P.S.—Since my letter was written, the Earl of Enniskillen has visited my fishery; and I extract the following from his notes, entered in inspector's book :—

"'On the 9th (Dec.) I visited Collooney ladder and saw immense quantities of fish running up. Frequently saw four fish at the upper step jumping together. On the 10th again at Collooney. Not nearly so many fish moving this day; counted at upper step nineteen in five minutes. Turned off the water, and put up 256 fish. This day (11th) counted 102 fish jump at the upper step in five minutes. Turned off the water; the pond actually alive with fish, in general larger and fresher from the sea than those of yesterday. Put up 246 fish, and then stopped, as the fish were getting sick in the pond. I am confident that we did not take half the number out, and that we left from three to four hundred in the pond.' "

Introduction of Salmon into the Doohulla.—The following extracts and condensation of letters to Mr. Francis on the subject, show the origin and early progress of this enterprise. The subjoined is from Mr. Ffennel, inspector of fisheries.

"In relation to the Doohulla river,—I should rather say the Doohulla waters, because there is nothing which can well be dignified by the name of river connected with the concern. There are several small loughs or lakes which now discharge through two artificial cuts, one connecting the upper lakes with the lower one, and the other connecting all with the sea, and more in the character of mere ditches than of rivers. The whole catchment area (as engineers call it) of these small lakes is very inconsiderable; they always contained some white trout which ascended through a tortuous stream or brook, when heavy rains created occasionally sufficient water in its rugged bed; these favorable opportunities however were few and very far between. This place was purchased some years ago by Mr. John Knight Boswell, of Monkstown, near Dublin. He requested me to assist him in such measures as might be adopted for the improvement of the fishery.

"The main principle carried out, was that of connecting the waters of the several loughs; cuts were made to effect this—the old stream was dammed out, the water was run through an additional lake before unconnected with the others. The speculation was a complete success, though a valuable white trout fishery only was created when Mr. Boswell sold it, realizing a large profit for his outlay."

The following, which relates to the same waters after coming into possession of Mr. Cooper, is from a letter of Mr. Ramsbottom :—

"It is four years this month since the first lot of ova were deposited, viz., 18,000. These, when hatched, were kept
12

in the nursery beds and ponds for about two years and three months as smolts, and then turned into the river perfectly ready for sea. It was from the above lot of smolts we marked 700 in March, 1862, and which have during the season just passed returned as grilse, being now a little over three and a half years old.* I am also happy to inform you that I have just received a note from my son to say that he has for the first time seen grilse on the spawning-beds of the river at Doohulla.

"That your readers may more clearly understand, I append a table of the dates :—

"18,000 ova deposited in 1859.

"Ova hatched February, 1860.

"Fry kept in nursery ponds until May, 1862, being nursed for two years and three months; but I would here remark that a few of the fry, and only a few, appeared to be ready for sea when about thirteen months old.

"Turned out of nursery ponds ready for sea, May, 1862.

"Returned as grilse (after being at sea from thirteen to fifteen months) in June, July, and August, 1863.

"You will see that when the first grilse returned (in June), it must have been three years and four months old."

It will be seen from the foregoing how small a stream can be made exceedingly productive if net-fishing is pro-

---

* It will be seen by this, that it will sometimes require three years and a half from the time of hatching to produce a grilse. On the contrary, a smolt may go to sea when something over a year old, and return, a grilse, in two months; making at least, two years and four months difference in the time of maturity.

hibited for a few years at its mouth, and the salmon protected on their spawning-grounds. There are no doubt
many such along the coast of New England that could be
stocked, and salmon cultivated with as much profit as at
Doohulla.

The project of stocking the rivers of Australia with
salmon was commenced in 1864. After a long discussion
as to the manner of sending out the ova, a hundred thousand salmon and three thousand trout eggs were packed in
two hundred boxes; moss being used in packing, much as
we do with the ova of trout in this country. The two
hundred boxes were closely surrounded by thirty tons of
ice in the hold of the ship Norfolk, which sailed on the
21st of January. The ship was seventy-seven days in
making the passage, and arrived at Melbourne on the 15th
of April. The greater number of the boxes were at once
sent off to Tasmania, reaching Hobart Town on the 20th,
where suitable arrangements had been made for hatching
on the river Plenty. On opening the boxes it was found
that more than two-thirds of the ova had perished. This
occurred where they were tightly packed and the moss was
deadened and had assumed a brownish tint. In the boxes
where the moss was green and somewhat loose, they were
still alive.

The temperature of the water in which they were hatched
varied from 46° to 49°, some of the ice left from the Norfolk being used to keep it below the latter point on warm
days. Mr. Ramsbottom, son of the noted fish culturist,
had charge of the hatching; but with all his care only

three thousand fry were produced from the thirty thousand eggs that arrived in sound condition. These were healthy, but did not grow as fast as some of the young trout. While the friends of the enterprise were congratulating themselves that at any rate they had three thousand young salmon, there was a mysterious disappearance of the greater part of them. Some, it was thought, found their way into the river; only about five hundred remained in the pond, and these also after a while were allowed to escape to the river. To this "small point," as a Yankee would say, had this much-talked-of introduction of salmon into Australia been "whittled down." The enterprise, however, was commendable in those who attempted it, and we say all honor to its patrons.

There are reports of grilse having returned, whether from this small migration, or from the hatching of subsequent importations of ova, I have not been able to learn definitely. But the five hundred even, if protected, will in due time make salmon abundant. The following, copied from the Hobart Town Mercury, I have clipped from the report of the Vermont Fish Commissioners:—

"The first batch of salmon have been sent out to sea, and we shall have a second batch to let loose at the end of the year. When Mr. Ramsbottom, in charge of the salmon ponds at the Plenty, turned the first batch into the Derwent at the close of 1865, he fixed upon February, 1866, as the date of their return from the sea, and they have been true to their time. They began to return in the month of February, and now seem to be returning in considerable numbers.

"After enumerating the instances where salmon had been seen, the writer concludes by saying :—

"All doubts of the return of the first batch of salmon in greater or lesser numbers are therefore at an end. We cannot say that the Derwent swarms with them. But enough has been said to show that they have returned in considerable numbers."

The following statistical information is from the report of the Vermont Commissioners of Fisheries :—

Mr. Ashworth has communicated to the International Congress to Promote the Cultivation of Fisheries the following table of the number of salmon taken in fisheries of the Galway :—

In 1853 the number taken was 1,603
" 1854 " " " " 3,158
" 1855 " " " " 5,540
" 1856 " " " " 5,371
" 1857 " " " " 4,857
" 1858 " " " " 9,639
" 1859 " " " " 9,249
" 1860 " " " " 3,177
" 1861 " " " " 11,051
" 1862 " " " " 15,431
" 1863 " " " " 17,995
" 1864 " " " " 20,512

During the past two years the number has been increased, but we are not able to give the exact figures.

12 *

Ballisodare.—During the eleventh year from the time these fishways were built, the number of salmon taken in these waters was over ten thousand.

Stormontfield.—Mr. Ashworth also submitted tables giving the yearly rental of the fisheries on the Tay river, Scotland, from the year 1828 to 1864. "In 1828 the annual rental was £14,574 10s. In this year an act was passed which made net-fishing legal up to the 14th of September, instead of the 26th of August. The annual rental gradually dropped off from year to year, till 1852, when it was only £7973 5s. The public mind then became awakened, and the law was repealed, and all fishing ceased on the 26th of August as before. There was great opposition to the repeal of this law. The fishermen insisted that it was an unjust abridgment of their rights. They could not perceive the necessity of protecting the breeding salmon that would be likely to pass up during this interval of nineteen days. They insisted that the more they were permitted to fish the more fish they would catch. In addition to this wholesome law, an establishment was commenced at Stormontfield, for breeding salmon artificially. The annual rental steadily increased under this new system as follows :—

"In 1853 it was £8,715 17s.
" 1854 "   "   9,269 6s.
" 1855 "   "   9,977 13s.
" 1858 "   " 11,487 2s.
" 1859 "   " 12,884 14s.
" 1860 "   " 13,827 10s.

In 1861 it was £14,109 15s.
" 1862 "   "   14,080 12s.
" 1863 "   "   14,257 16s.
" 1864 "   "   15,000 00s.

"These official documents, the concurrent testimony of all whom we heard speak upon the subject, and the great abundance of salmon we saw in the market of England, convince us that good results have followed the efforts to restock the streams of Great Britain.   It may be proper to remark in this connection, that we estimated the amount of salmon for sale in the London markets to be more than double all other fresh-water fish on sale.   The price has been affected by the increase of supply.   They were selling in July last at one shilling (twenty-four cents) per pound.   Six years ago salmon were sold in London at over a dollar per pound."

From B. J. Lane, one of the special commissioners for Irish fisheries, we obtained their reports for a series of years.   In them there is evidence of steady progress.   In the report of 1865 they commence by saying:—

"We have great satisfaction in being able to report the steady and progressive improvement of the fisheries committed to our charge.   That improvement is, however, more real than apparent.   Its proofs are found in the shoals of smolts that descended to the sea last spring, in the multitudes of fry that swarmed in the rivers during the summer, and in the unprecedented number of breeding fish that have so lately thronged the spawning-beds.   Its effects appear in the increase of the number of men living

on the fisheries, and of the funds collected for the purpose
of preservation. In no previous year, as far back as living
evidence will take us, have the rivers of Ireland been so
well stocked with salmon, young and old."

That their anticipations for a continued increase were
well founded, is evident from tables submitted in the
report for last year. From them it appears that the whole
amount of salmon shipped over the seven railroads in
Ireland in 1865, was 790 tons, 14 cwt., and 3 qrs. In
1866 there were shipped over the same roads, 1092 tons,
10 cwt., and 2 qrs.

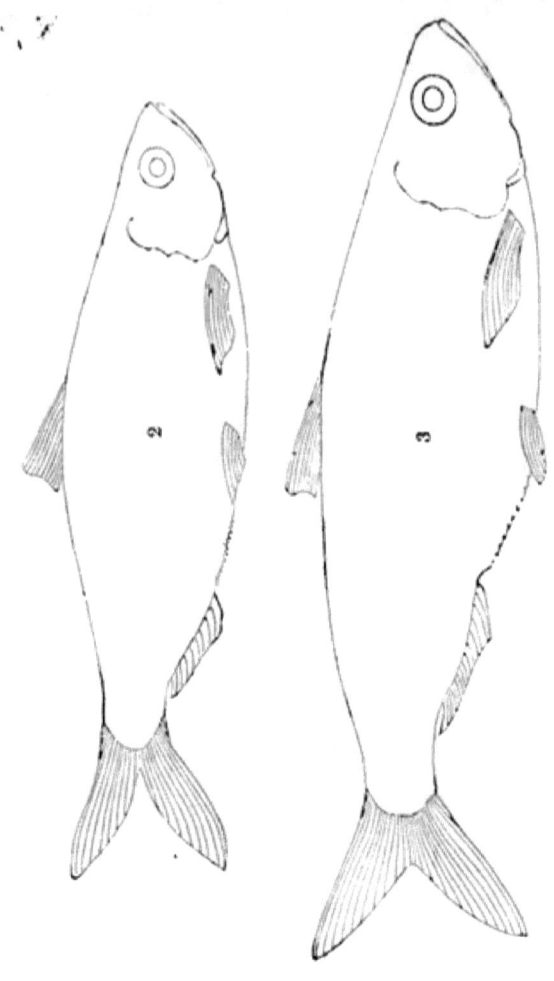

CHAPTER VI.

CULTURE OF THE SHAD.

The Shad.—Its instincts, and analogies to the salmon.—Migrations.—Former abundance.—Incubation of its ova.—Its growth.—Its introduction into rivers flowing into the Gulf of Mexico, by Dr. Daniell.—Hatching its spawn at Holyoke.—Ascent by fishways over dam of Susquehanna Canal Company.—Report of Col. James Worrall. *The Alewife.*

An account of the specific characteristics of this fish is unnecessary here, and would scarcely interest the general reader; we will, therefore, allude only to its instincts and habits, bearing on the subject-matter of this chapter.

The shad belongs to the great family of herrings (*Clupeidæ*), so useful, and it might be said, almost indispensable to man. Although there are two varieties which visit our rivers, *i. e.*, the white shad, and that with a row of spots on its sides, they are known as the same species *Alosa præstabilis*, and, doubtless, occupy the same spawning-grounds, at the same time, and breed promiscuously the one with the other. Its geographical range extends all along our Atlantic coast; and through the laudable efforts of Dr. W. C. Daniell, has been introduced into the Gulf of Mexico, by stocking the Alabama river by means of artificial propagation. This gentleman based his hopes of accomplishing this enterprise, on his knowledge of the unerring instinct of this and other anadromous fishes, returning to their native rivers to reproduce their species.

The *Clupeidæ* show many analogies to the salmon family, not possessing, however, the adipose dorsal fin. The most noble species of each—the shad and the salmon,—resemble each other in their migratory habits, and both attain that rapid growth and excellent flavor, for which they are distinguished on similar feeding-grounds, and likely, to a great extent, on the same food; although the locality of these feeding-grounds, where they do not overlap, may occupy different parallels of latitude. There can be no question that soft-shelled crustacea, the young of molluscs, small fish, and the lower orders of marine life, are consumed in large quantities by each.

It is generally believed now, that the shad, as well as the salmon, does not wander far at sea from the mouth of its native river; and in seeking it may coast along for some distance from the north or south, and thus give the impression that the great shoal may come from either point. At the north, the old theory was, and still is with many, that shad come from the south, while Dr. Daniell alludes to the supposition on the coast of Georgia (though he doubted it), that they come from the north.

Notwithstanding the analogies of the shad and salmon just mentioned, it is surprising that the former retains its fleshiness and delicate juices quite up to the time of spawning, while the latter continues to fall off from the day it enters fresh water. It has even been insisted on by many, that the longer a shad has been in fresh water before spawning, the better its condition; as many of those taken just before the season closes, and high up the rivers, are finer than the early run. This is likely erroneous, as the late run proceed at once to their spawning-grounds, not lingering as the great body do, but travelling hundreds of miles in a few days. Fresh run shad have been taken at the head of tide on the Susquehanna, with small salt-water fishes in their stomachs so perfect that their species could be identified. I mention this fact as an evidence of the rapidity with which shad sometimes travel. After they enter fresh water, it is generally believed that they do not feed, as they are invariably found with empty stomachs. It is true that a shad will rise at an artificial fly occasionally, or take a minnow, as I know from experience, but on opening them, these, as well as other anadromous fishes, are found without food. Amongst these I instance the herring, the alewife, the salmon, and Canadian sea trout. It is reasonable to suppose that shad are omnivorous, and that some of the algæ which are gelatinous and highly nutritive, contribute to their rapid growth.

Shad, at one time, entered every river on our coast which furnished the requisite spawning-beds, and ascended until some barrier opposed their course; every tributary was crowded with them. Civilization, and its attendant enterprise, prosecuted without provision for the passage of the fish to and from their spawning-grounds, have driven them entirely from some rivers, and lessened their numbers so materially in others, that shad are now considered rather a luxury, than one of the chief staples of life, in their season. In view of this alarming decrease, many of the States have appointed Commissioners of Fisheries, and are constructing fishways over impassable dams. The New England States, by concerted legislation, have a joint commission, which gives us hope of a speedy restoration of shad and salmon to rivers from which they have been expelled.

In the report of the Commissioners of Fisheries for the State of Vermont (October 11, 1866), it is said of shad, that they " select their spawning-grounds in bodies of water deeper and warmer than those occupied by salmon. The deep eddies below dams and waterfalls are generally selected by them. The eddy below Bellows Falls was formerly a favorite spawning-ground for shad. The one below Holyoke dam in Massachusetts, is now occupied for that purpose, and thousands of shad are now annually caught at that place." This was also the case below Fairmount dam long after the Schuylkill was obstructed there, and but for the city gas-works, it would still have been a spawning-ground. Even now, a few shad continue to spawn there. A few years since, when returning from the dam where I had been fishing for white perch, two or three young shad (likely pursued by rockfish) leaped into my boat. This occurred in the latter part of May, and the fry were then between three and four inches in length. The remarks just quoted, as well as my observations, are corroborated by the experiments in artificial propagation at Holyoke last summer, and prove that shad instinctively deposit their spawn where it is kept suspended by the action of the water, if such a place is accessible.

The short term of incubation (60 or 70 hours), and the fact of this fish being so prolific, are palpable arguments in favor of its artificial propagation. By such means they can be immediately introduced into upper waters and tributaries of our rivers, if fishways are **provided for** their passage up and down. In eddies where sun-fish, **perch,** chub, roach, and other small fish congregate (being led thither, **no doubt, by an** instinctive knowledge of **the food** they are to find), the suspended and moving ova of shad must offer easily attained morsels, and it is not likely **that** any large proportion escape the ravenous devourers, **or that** one out of five of the helpless fry live to migrate to sea. All Philadelphia fishermen know how tempting a bait shad roe is to any fish, from the splendid rockfish down to the grovelling catfish. That it would pay to **keep the fry for** a short time in **ponds of river water, is problematical, but** well worth the experiment.

The Massachusetts Commissioners of Fisheries, in their **last** report, comparing the statistics of Mr. T. D. Stoddart, as given in the "Harvest of the Seas," with other authorities, estimate that of the eggs of salmon which are **not** devoured, one-third become parrs, that two-thirds **of the** parrs become smolts, that one-twentieth of **the smolts be-** come grilse, and that one-tenth of the grilse become salmon. Thus showing that only one out of fifteen hundred **eggs** produces a full-grown salmon if deposited naturally, and the ova, fry, and grilse subjected to the usual chances. Or, that the produce of twenty thousand ova at the end of the third year is only seventy grilse, seven full-grown salmon, fifty thousand new parrs, and two hundred thousand eggs. The twenty thousand eggs thus producing

13   K

only seventy-seven fish fit for the table in three years. To show the advantages to be derived from the artificial propagation of shad, the report alluded to continues :—

" By the shad, thanks to the admirable experiments of Green, we may illustrate the results of natural and artificial propagation side by side. We assume that the male is fecund at one year, that the female carries spawn at two years, and lays from 10,000 to 12,000 eggs to each pound of her weight, and that males and females are in equal numbers. Considering what is known of the hatching of the eggs, by the natural process, and assuming that the young are destroyed in the same proportion as those of the salmon, the following fractions may be deduced :—

$\frac{1}{3}$	$\frac{1}{3}$ of all eggs laid, get impregnated and escape being eaten by other fishes.	
$\frac{1}{80}$	$\frac{1}{30}$ of these hatch.	
$\frac{1}{4000}$	$\frac{1}{50}$ of those hatched grow to one year.	
$\frac{1}{20000}$	$\frac{1}{5}$ of the yearlings grow to two years.	
$\frac{1}{40000}$	$\frac{1}{2}$ of the two-year-olds grow to three years.	

" It would hence appear, that of 40,000 eggs of shad laid in the natural way, only one arrives at the age of three years. Now suppose two pairs of adult shad should come to a river each year, for three successive years, and there breed; what would they and their descendants amount to at the end of that time? The following table, calculated from the data foregoing, will answer this question. ·

Natural Breeding.

Beginning of First Year.	Beginning of Second Year.	Beginning of Third Year.	End of Third Year.
4 Shad. 1750 Young.	{ 4 Shad. { 1750 Young. 35 Yearlings.	{ 4 Shad. { 1750 Young. 35 Yearlings. { 7 two year-olds. { 1750 Young.	4 Shad. 35 Yearlings. 7 two-year-olds. 3 three year-olds. 35 Yearlings.

Total... 84

"Even at this rate, and allowing that all shad die at three years old, the number of three-year-old fish in a river, derived from a single pair, would double in about eight years, although, for several years, there would be, of course, no three-year-olds at all in the river, the original pair having died. But, since the number of the largest fish is always small, compared with those of less size, and as these large ones are most liable to get caught, it may well be understood that the river fishermen think that both shad and salmon have 'decreased in size,' and that they are obliged to make their net-meshes smaller. The gain by artificial propagation of shad, lies at the very outset, and consists in the increased percentage of spawn that may thus be hatched; the ratio of the artificial to the natural being at the most moderate estimate, as seventy-two to one. Starting with this difference, and taking the other proportions just as in the above table, we should have the following results from the artificially hatched spawn of two pairs of large shad, taken three years in succession, *added to* the spawn of their mature progeny within that period :—

Artificial Breeding.

Beginning of First Year.	Beginning of Second Year.	Beginning of Third Year.	End of Third Year.
*126,000 Young.	*126,000 Young. 2520 Yearlings.	*126,000 Young. 2520 Yearlings. 504 two-year-olds. †3,969,000 Young.	2520 Yearlings. 504 two-year-olds. 252 three-year-olds. 158,760 Yearlings.

| Total.. | 162,036. |

" Compared with the former table, the results in favor of artificial propagation are as 162,036 to 84, or, as 2000 to 1, nearly. This is nothing unbelievable. * * But it is a difference that ought to call the attention of all thoughtful persons to this subject. It would be very little labor or expense to set free 100,000,000 young shad in the Connecticut, and these might reasonably be supposed to return us nearly a half million of two-year-old fish. Fifteen hundred large females would yield the required amount of spawn, and this is not more than a half of one per cent. of the females now yearly taken in the river."

The supposition that shad remain at sea two years is yet to be proven. I know, from personal observation, that their growth is rapid, for I have taken scores of them in August, when fishing in a deep tideway for white perch; the size averaging six or seven inches in length, which at least equals that of the generality of smolts. If the

---

* From the eggs of two females :—$\frac{9}{10}$ of 140,000.

† From the eggs of the two-year-olds.

smolt returns the following summer a grilse of from three
to five pounds, why may not a shad attain a weight of two
and a half or three pounds in the same time?

In a report of the Fish Commissioners of one of the
New England States it is said that a few male shad nine
or ten inches in length are sometimes taken in the Connecticut river; and it is assumed that these have spent one
winter at sea. On this, which is a mere supposition, the
theory has been started that the females and most of the
males remain at sea two years. May not these males have
remained in the river all winter, the milt developing in the
mean time as it does in the male parr of the salmon? We
know how much shorter time is occupied in the hatching
of the spawn, and the more rapid growth of the fry of the
shad. In three or four months a young shad will grow to
a size which a smolt only attains in fifteen or it may be in
twenty-seven months. With this wonderful precocity of
egg and fry, I cannot see why its growth at sea should not
be as much as two or three pounds by the next spring or
summer. If a few thousand shad fry could be confined to a
limited space by leading off a side stream from one of our
rivers, and marked, after they had grown to five or six
inches, by cutting off the hinder part of the dorsal fin, and
then turned loose, it is quite likely that some of them might
be taken in the river near the place of their nativity the
following summer, and the problem be solved.

The following, from the proceedings of the Academy of
Natural Sciences, Philadelphia, communicated through the
Smithsonian Institute, shows how the pioneer movement in

13 *

introducing shad into the rivers flowing into the Gulf of Mexico was made :—

" *On the Introduction of the American Shad into* **the** *Alabama River. By W. C. Daniell, M. D. of Savannah, Ga.*—My success in establishing the white shad in the Alabama river being now complete, I propose to give you a detailed statement of the matter.

" Having long doubted the generally-received theory of the annual migration south from the northern seas, of the white shad, and of the consequent annual migration thither of the young fry hatched from the eggs deposited by their parents in our fresh-water streams, I made inquiry of our fishermen, and learned that minute but distinctive differ- ences were readily detected between the white shad taken in the Savannah river and those taken in the Ogeechee river, eighteen miles south of the Savannah river. Fully satis- fied of this fact, I readily concluded that the young shad that descend to the sea never go so far from the mouth of the river descended as to lose their connection with it, and that they ascend in the spring the same river which they had descended as young fish the previous summer. Then the feeding-ground, so **to speak,** of the shad is in or near **the** mouth of the river. If the young shad does attain its growth at the mouth of the Savannah and of the Ogeechee rivers, may there not be equally good feeding-grounds at **the** mouths of the Alabama and other rivers flowing into the Gulf of Mexico? To solve this question, I, with the **aid** of my friend, Mark A. Cooper, Esq., whose residence **on** the Etowah river, in Barton county, supplied an eligible locality for the experiment, in the early summer of 1848 had placed in a small tributary of the Etowah river the fecundated eggs of the white shad, which I had myself carefully prepared at my plantation on the Savannah river, ten miles above this city, from living parents. These eggs, so deposited by Major Cooper, were daily visited by him until they had all hatched. I sent another supply of fecundated eggs to Daniel Pratt, Esq., at Prattsville, near Montgomery, Ala., in 1853 or 1854, as he writes me, which he deposited in a small creek. Inasmuch as he left home soon after, and was absent 'some weeks,' he can only report that during that absence heavy rains raised the waters in the creek, and washed away the 'pen' in which he had placed the white-shad eggs supplied ·by me. Nothing can therefore be safely affirmed of the success of this second deposit, nor is it important, as in 1851 or 1852, the white shad had already been taken in the fish-traps at the foot of the Falls of the Alabama, at Wetumpka, and of the Black Warrior, near Tuscaloosa, though unknown to me at the time of supplying Mr. Pratt with the fecundated eggs.

"Through the kindness of a friend at Montgomery, Ala., a shad taken from the Alabama river was sent to Professor Holbrook, of Charleston, S. C., and he wrote me that he 'felt certain' that the fish received and examined by him was identical with the white shad of our Atlantic rivers. I have a letter from Charles T. Pollard, Esq., of Montgomery, Ala., of 6th inst., in which, speaking of the white shad in the Alabama river, he says: 'They have gradually increased in quantity since they first appeared, and have year by year increased in size, until, to use the words of a native of South Carolina, who lived many years near Sistera Ferry, on the Savannah river, they are now equal to the best Savannah river shad.'

"The white shad have chiefly been taken in the fish-traps at the foot of the fall at Wetumpka and near Tuscaloosa. One, I am informed, has been taken from a trap at the head of the Coosa river, near Rome, in this state, and only some sixty miles below the locality in which the eggs were deposited by Major Cooper, in a tributary of the Etowah river. I also learn that some few have been taken with a dip-net near Selma.

"I think that we may safely conclude that the white shad may be as successfully established in the Mississippi river as it has been in the Alabama. Since feeding-grounds for that delicious fish exist at the mouth of one river flowing into the Gulf of Mexico, may they not exist at the mouths of other or all the rivers discharging into that sea? Time must answer that question.

"Savannah, April 19th, 1866."

It is to be regretted that some memoranda concerning the incubation were not given in this communication. It would have been a matter of much interest to compare observations of this kind with those of Mr. Lyman, of the Massachusetts Fish Commission, who says, "Green was not able to hatch more than 2 per cent. of the ova deposited on the natural river-bed."

The following account of the hatching of shad-spawn at Holyoke is from the admirable report of the commission just named. All the facts connected with the incubation are so interesting, and at the same time so new, that I quote Mr. Lyman's observations almost entire :—

"*Artificial Breeding of Shad.*—Early in last summer, Seth Green offered to come, at his own expense, and try to hatch the eggs of the shad at Holyoke, provided the New England Commissioners would furnish the necessary apparatus.

"Green began his experiments the first week in July. He put up some hatching-troughs, like those used for trout, in a brook which emptied into the river. Having taken the ripe fish with a sweep-seine, he removed and impregnated the ova in the way already described for trout. These, to the number of some millions, he spread in boxes; but, to his great mortification, every one of them spoiled. Nothing daunted, he examined the temperature of the brook, and found, not only that it was 13° below that of the river (62° to 75°), but that it varied 12° from night to day. This gave the clue to success. Taking a rough box, he knocked the bottom and part of the ends out, and replaced them by a wire gauze. In this box the eggs were laid, and it was anchored near shore, exposed to a gentle current that passed freely through the gauze, while eels or fish were kept off. To his great joy, the minute embryos were hatched at the end of sixty hours, and swam about the box, like the larvæ of mosquitoes in a cask of stagnant water. Still, though the condition of success was found, the contrivance was still imperfect; for the eggs were drifted by the current into the lower end of the box,

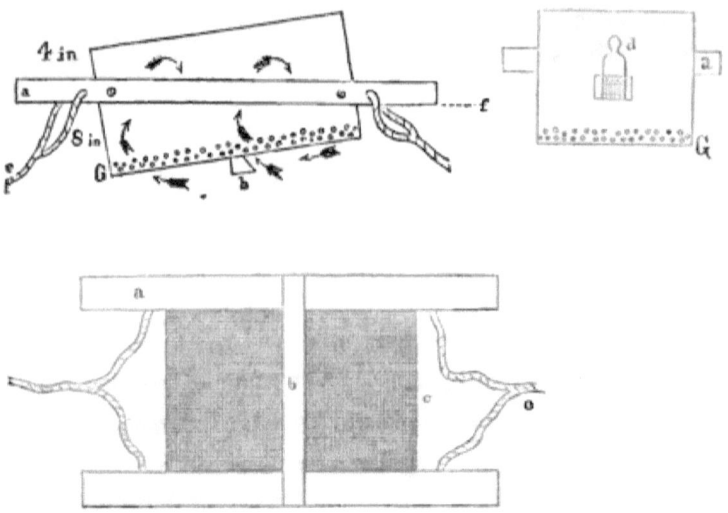

FIGS. 1, 2, 7.—Green's patent hatching box seen from the side, end and bottom. Scale, 1-20th. *a*, side floats 3.4" long; 2" by 3" square, set with screws. *b*, bottom cross bar, bevelled, to throw the current upward. *c*, wire-net bottom 14 wires to an inch. *d*, trap in hind end for escape of young fish, covered by wire-net, 8 to an inch, and with a covering slide. *e*, anchoring cord. *f*, water-line. G, spawn.

and heaped up, whereby many were spoiled for lack of fresh water and motion. The best that this box would do, was 90 per cent., while often it would hatch only 70 or 80 per cent.

"The spawn-box he at last hit on is as simple as ingenious. It is merely a box with a wire-gauze bottom, and steadied in the water by two float-bars, screwed to its sides. These float-bars are attached, not *parallel* to the top line of the box, but at *an angle* to it, which makes the box float with one end tilted up, and the current striking the gauze bottom at an angle, is deflected upwards, and makes such a boiling within as keeps the light shad eggs constantly free and buoyed up. The result was a triumph. Out of 10,000 ova placed in this contrivance, all but seven hatched. In spite of these delays, and of the imperfect means at hand for taking the fish, Green succeeded in hatching and setting free in the river many millions of these tiny fry.

"As no way is now known of keeping shad in ponds or pools, they must be watched at their breeding-grounds, and when the spawn begins to flow freely from them, operations may commence. The fishing must take place by night, because (near Hadley Falls, at any rate) no ripe females are captured by day; those taken are all spent, or not yet ready to lay. This may be because they are in the deep holes, spawning, or because they are above, in the quick water. The seine must not be hauled quite ashore, but the bight of it must remain in the shallow water, that the fish may be kept alive. Thence they are taken out, and the spawn impregnated in a tub, or a large pan of water. Many scales will fall in the water, and must be carefully picked out, before the ova are distributed in the floating boxes, wherein they may lie about one-fourth of an inch deep. The boxes must be lashed end to end, in lines of convenient length, and it is well to surround them with a log boom, to keep off rubbish brought down by the stream. They should be placed conveniently near the shore, in a gentle current, but not so near as to risk being left dry by a fall of the river. They will now appear as if they had nothing in them, for the eggs are almost as transparent as the water itself; but if they turn milky, and look like half-boiled sago, they are spoiled.

"The contents are not, however, to be thrown away, without taking up some in the hand, when it will likely appear that but a small part are addled, while the rest remain transparent. With further progress the embryo may, with a weak glass, be easily seen moving in the egg, which then is not so clear, and at the end of sixty hours (with sunshine and water at 75°), the box will be found alive with tiny fry, almost transparent, except the eyes, swimming freely, with their heads up stream. In confinement they cannot be kept, because the yolk-sac does not suffice for their support for more than one or two days. But care must be taken to liberate them in a *safe place.* Green observed that, on setting them free among the shallows near shore, the dace (*Argyreus*) and other little fishes rushed to the spot, and commenced jumping at them. In the stomach of a dace, he found fourteen shad fry. Then, by a series of most ingenious experiments, he discovered that the fry, so far from frequenting the shallows, like many minnows, *made directly for the main current, in mid-river.* How different this from the young trouts that lie almost helpless for forty-five days, and then are fain to hide behind stones and roots! Whereas, these minute, transparent, gelatinous things push boldly for the deep, swift current, where they are too insignificant to be attacked by the great fishes. Will the physicists tell us what 'correlation and conservation of force' produces this, or will the Darwinians set forth how, some millions of years gone, a particular shad fry, finding by accident that he did not get eaten in deep water, transmitted a deep-water instinct to his children, who thereby flourished, while the shoal-water fry got in due time exterminated?

"So the fry must be let go in the proper way by towing **the boxes into mid stream,** or by liberating them during **the** night, when their enemies do not feed. In either case, **the** trap-slide must be raised, when they will be carried gradually through the coarse netting by the current. This operation must be performed as soon as all the ova are hatched out. There ends the nursery care; for we know no method of keeping the young till they have gained size and strength. What we may hope to avoid is, the **enormous** loss which the eggs themselves suffer, when deposited by the natural method.*

"**The ovaries of a** full-grown shad weigh at the spawn**ing** season about thirteen ounces, without the membranes. With a common lens, three sizes of ova are at once distinguished. The first have a diameter of $\frac{8}{100}$ to $\frac{9}{100}$ of an inch. **These are** transparent and ready to **be laid**; the second, $\frac{4}{100}$ to $\frac{5}{100}$ of an inch; the third, $\frac{2}{100}$ of an inch. **These two smaller sizes** are opaque; they are still found after **the** fish has spawned, and **are** the crops ready to mature the next year and the year after. This state of the

---

* With the utmost care to secure every favorable surrounding, Green was never able to hatch more than *two per cent.* on the natural river-bed. Only those eggs hatched that chanced to catch in an **angle** of the gravel, where they had the current all about them. This does not take into the account those that are not impregnated, or are devoured, or **covered by mud, &c., &c.**

14

ovary has its parallel in the turtle, and possibly in all of the vertebrata.

"It is scarcely necessary to add that the microscope shows other and smaller ovarian eggs. An ovary of the size above mentioned contains about 70,000 ova, ready to be laid. Their diameter increases, as soon as they are put in water and impregnated, from $\frac{9}{100}$ to $\frac{13}{100}$ of an inch. This is by the endosmosis of water between the yolk and the shell membrane.* Of the embryonic development, we have, as yet, only an imperfect outline to present. Forty-one hours after impregnation, the condition of the embryo is, on the whole, in advance of that of *coregonus* on the thirty-third day. The under surface, from the nose to the beginning of the ventral, is in close contact with the yolk, which is composed of a great number of rounded divisions, such as are seen in the complete segmentation of that body, while its surface is flecked with pigment stars, of which a less number may be distinguished on the forward part of the trunk. That part of the embryo which swings free makes a spiral half turn, so that the dorsal fin is turned toward, instead of from, the yolk-sac. The head, which is pointed in front, and flattened, bears no resemblance to that of the grown animal, and it would be, perhaps, fanciful to compare it even to such forms as *Petromyzon* (Lamprey eel.) A large portion of it is occupied by the

---

* The same takes place in a less degree in the egg of *Coregonus* (white fish.) (Carl Vogt, loc. cit. p. 27, Pl. I. fig. 9.) Accustomed only to eggs of trout, Green was much astonished to behold the mass of ova swell to near twice its first bulk.

eye, which fills proportionately at least four times more space than in the adult. **The** choroid coat, not yet closed below, partly encircles the crystalline lens, above which **may be** distinguished a **clear space**, which **is a** portion of the vitreous humor. The form of the brain may already be distinguished, especially when fore-shortened from the **front.** It is probable that the pectoral fin already exists, but, from the extreme transparency of the tissues, its outline could not be caught. From the well-marked nuchal bow, the flattened body tapers gradually to a fine point, and is bordered, above and below, by an embryonic dorsal and ventral which spread into a spatula-like caudal fin, and it should be observed, **that** neither **in this stage nor in the** newly-hatched, does there exist any unevenness of the margins of these fins, that should indicate their approaching separation; whereas, the newly-hatched salmon already shows very distinct dorsal, adipose, caudal, anal, and ventral fins; and the little *Coregonus*, though less advanced in this respect, shows plainly the boundaries of these organs. Near the base of the caudal is now to be seen the end of the alimentary canal, passing at an angle across the breadth of the fin. The heart may be observed beating, and the embryo itself moves itself round and round within its prison, by a series of convulsive jerks. This motion is **called by the breeders,** 'life in the egg.' *

---

* In this **stage Green succeeded** in keeping eggs alive in damp moss for six days, in a low temperature. But **they are very hard** to transport long distances, and cannot be hatched in cold water.

"The specific gravity of the eggs at all stages is very small—barely enough to sink them in still water—a great contrast to those of the trout, which go down almost like shot.

"The newly-hatched young is $\frac{37}{100}$ of an inch long. It swims actively by a continuous and rapid vibration of the body, and keeps its head to the current, perhaps to get the food that is carried past.* The yolk-sac, whose longer diameter, already in the egg, was parallel with the body, now appears still more ovoid in form. The pectoral fin is easily seen, and the finger-like canals in it indicate that its rays are forming. The embryonic, dorsal, caudal, and ventral fins are continuous one with another, and extend round the whole body, back of the yolk-sac. In the caudal a few faint, radiating fibres indicate the formation of rays. The choroid has completed its circle, and the eye has nearly the outward look of that in the adult. Along the course of the alimentary canal, quite to the anal opening, and over the yolk-sac, the pigment stars are more numerous and defined. A little indentation indicates the mouth, which lies under the eye, and opens as a curved slit. The general mass of the brain is easily made out. Along the centre of the body, a more translucent stripe indicates the dorsal cord, above which the range of muscular bundles begins to be distinct.

---

* The current carries the fry gradually seaward. Hence it is, that since the erection of the Holyoke dam, young shad are no more seen there; because, by the time they are large enough to be noticed, they have all drifted lower down the river.

"Within eighty-two hours after hatching, great development has taken place. The tail, though not forked, has taken on its triangular **form**, and is made up of fine, radiating fibres. **The embryonic dorsal** and ventral are reduced in breadth, whereby the anal opening **is** brought close to **the body, the** base muscles of the true dorsal may also be seen as it begins to form. Along the body the transverse muscles show themselves distinctly both above and below the lateral line. The pectoral fins have now their fibres complete, and resemble two little flat brushes. **The** mouth is pushing forward towards its normal place. **It** seems to have, in the under **lip, a notch,** perhaps **the** point of future union of the maxillaries. **The** yolk-sac no longer plays an important part, and is reduced to very small dimensions. But the most striking change is the development of gills, four on a side, and each in its gill-pouch. The gills themselves can be distinguished, like little bows, along which run their veins and arteries. These, together with the size and position of the eyes, give the under **surface** of the head rather the look of that of a skate embryo than of a shad.

"Such is a hasty sketch of three periods of embryonic life in this *Alosa*. Of the young, at three months, outlines have already been given.* It should be added, that **their** jaws are, at this age, armed **with fine, sharp,** slightly curved teeth, nearly continuous along the upper maxillary and intermaxillary **pieces,** with a few at the point of the

---

* See plate at the commencement of this chapter.

L

lower maxillaries. None, apparently, on the vomer. These are necessary for the capture of the water beetles that then constitute a part of their food. The jaws of the adult are, as is well known, smooth.

"Of the further growth of the shad, we cannot as yet speak with certainty, although there are pretty good grounds for an opinion. Mr. Frederic Russell, late Commissioner from Connecticut, first called attention to some small *Alosæ*, about nine inches long, called by the fishermen, 'chicken shad,' or 'Connecticut river alewives.' He was led to consider them partly grown fishes, from the fact that they all were *males*. Of many hundreds examined, only one female could be found, and there the ova were not developed. The fish taken for artificial breeding at Holyoke were then compared, and it was found that they were of three, if not of four distinct sets or sizes. The smallest were the 'chicken shad,' and were all males; the next were but half the size of the largest, and were males and females; so also were the largest of all. Hence we may at least guess, that the young of the autumn go down, as minnows of four inches, to the sea. The next spring the males are fecund (so too in the salmon parr), and seek the fresh water, urged by the sexual instinct, and are the chicken shad or yearlings. Not so the females, which, not yet sexually developed, remain in the salt water, or in the estuaries. When two years old both sexes are fecund and seek the river together. These are the half-grown or two-year-olds. The third season they are large fish, and may be termed three-year-olds. But these three-year-olds have, in the ovary, at least two crops of eggs ready, though undeveloped, for the next two seasons. Nature does not prepare her seed only to die! Old fish become barren. These two crops of eggs are to be laid, and for that the fish must live at least two years more. The impression that **prevails among** fishermen, both here and in Europe, that shad die after spawning, the first year, comes only from the familiar fact that fishes are in meagre condition after spawning, and that some of the weaker probably do die, and are seen floating. There was a similar idea about lamprey eels, which was to the effect that they made fast by their sucker and then slowly decayed "*

---

* Concerning the indisposition of some persons **to believe in** the utility of fishways, **Mr.** Lyman, one of the Massachusetts Fish Commissioners, gives the following :—

" When the fishway at Lowell was building, some of the factory superintendents (very intelligent men about *factories*), said, **that the fish must have a** schoolmaster to teach **them to go up those steps!** The **next** year shad and salmon *did* go up, and without any schoolmaster. **The nearer we get** to the truth, the more it stands **out, that artificial propagation and** free passage over dams, **are the two great conditions of restocking rivers.**"

The same writer takes the subjoined " fling" **at certain slow,** cautious **people :—**

" **This feeling** gets strength **from the** loose impression that game, **like the Indian, is** doomed, **and** that the last shad or trout is soon **to be caught,—a sort of Dr. Fear-the-worst theory,—**

> ' The former did maintain
> The man would take all medicine in vain.'

" This kind of sentiment is shown by the uncomprehensive way

The subjoined reports for the years 1866 and 1867, made by Col. James Worrall, the Commissioner appointed by the Governor of Pennsylvania, under the Act of March 30th 1866, contain information of much interest to the citizens of the state. His description of the fishway at the Colum-' bia dam, will show the reader how such means of passage for the shad are constructed, and how the fish find their way up. He also explains the reason of the delay in build-ing fishways at other dams on the Susquehanna, as pro-vided for under the above Act. For these reasons I have deemed it advisable to give both of his reports in full :—

I.

"HARRISBURG, PA., December 3d 1866.

"DEAR SIR :—In fulfilling the duties devolved upon me under the act of 30th March 1866, ' relating to the pass-age of fish along the Susquehanna and certain of its tribu-taries,' I have the honor to report as follows :—

---

in which legislative committees often receive applications from peo-ple who petition for the control of particular streams, or creeks, or ponds, for the purpose of raising fish or oysters in a systematic and economical way. At once the members begin to ask whether this control would not abrogate some grant of the Pequot Indians to Fear-the-Lord Crowell, in the year 1639; or some ancient right of the inhabitants of Harwich Centre to dig one peck of quahogs per man on that particular ground.

"These same committee-men would not treat a petition for a railroad or a cotton-mill in this way, and simply because they *believe* in the success of a railroad or of a mill, but they do not believe in and do not know about the success of fish or oysters."

"Immediately after my appointment, by your Excellency, I consulted all the authorities on the subject within my reach, and finally devised a plan which was in the form of steps commencing at the comb of the dam, and falling or stepping down, one after another, at the rate of six inches per step; each of these steps being also a trough ten feet wide, to contain a constant supply of water two feet deep for the fish to rest in during their ascent.

"The width of the flight of steps was to be from two hundred feet on the main stem of the Susquehanna to a proportional width for its smaller tributaries, and the whole was to be constructed of good substantial crib work, such as is employed and approved in the construction of dams in Pennsylvania.

"I had this plan carefully draughted and specified, and before the 1st of June I sent it in, plan and specification, to the following corporations owning dams on the streams mentioned, namely: The Susquehanna Canal Company; The Pennsylvania Railroad Company; The West Branch Canal Company; The Wyoming Valley Canal Company, and The North Branch Canal Company. As these corporations owned all the lower dams on the river, and which, if not altered for the passage of fish, there would be no use in altering dams located above them, and as I knew that they all, except the Susquehanna Canal Company, held their property by purchase from the state, without encumbrance, as alleged, and deemed themselves, therefore, exempt from the operation of the law, I did not notify individuals or corporations owning dams above them;

for even should such accept notice, comply with the law and alter their dams, fish would be debarred from reaching them by the neglected dams below, and there would be expense and trouble for nothing.

"In pursuing this course I have not obeyed the letter of the law, but I trust to be forgiven when the circumstances are considered.

"My surmises in respect to these companies proved to be correct. None, except the Pennsylvania Railroad Company, regularly acknowledged even to have received my notification, nor have I heard from any of them since.

"The Susquehanna Canal Company, owning the dam at Columbia, however, have complied with the law in every respect, as far as I was able to direct them how to do so.

"On or about the 1st of June I met Mr. B. Andrews Knight, their president, at Columbia, and conferred with him on the subject, and he expressed his willingness to carry out the plan, but suggested some modifications, which I did not like to accept, until I could sustain myself by other authorities on the subject, and our meeting was adjourned until in July, that I might be enabled in the mean time to do so.

"I proceeded immediately to the New England States; conferred with the chairman of the Fish Committee of the Legislature of Connecticut, the Hon. Mr. Avery, and presenting credentials from your Excellency to the Governor of Massachusetts, Governor Bullock, was introduced by the Hon. Oliver Warner, Secretary of the Commonwealth of

Massachusetts, to Theodore Lyman, Esq., who has charge of the subject in that state.

"In Connecticut I was informed by Mr. Avery that they did not consider the river (the Connecticut) obstructed by any works of theirs which existed in it, and that they so intended to answer the state of New Hampshire, that state having officially requested to know if any such obstructions existed.

"In Massachusetts I found that they had not advanced in these improvements further than we had, they being just then engaged in devising plans for the Merrimac, and perhaps other of their streams.

"They, however, had given intelligent consideration to the subject.

"Mr. Lyman is well known as a naturalist, and he had availed himself of consultations with Prof. Agassiz, whose reputation, I need not say, is, in the same pursuit, world wide. I could not learn that in the other states of New England I would be able to add to the information obtainable from these high sources in Massachusetts, so I proceeded no further than Boston.

"In July I met Mr. President Knight again on the dam at Columbia, and there, in consultation with himself and Mr. Daniel Shure, the able superintendent of the Susquehanna Canal, a plan was devised, chiefly by Mr. Shure, with some modifications suggested by my New England experience, which plan has been since carried out, at a cost of some $5000 to that company, and I have reason to hope that it will prove to be a ' success.'

"If my hope should prove well-founded, some small number of shad will make their way as far up the river next spring as Duncan's island, a distance of nearly fifty miles higher up than they have been able to reach for many years, and this number will increase from year to year, if not too much thinned out by fishing, until we may hope for an adequte supply of this spring delicacy, being brought back to localities so long unjustly deprived of it.

"I say small number, for I have recently received a letter from Mr. Lyman, of Massachusetts, the gentleman before alluded to, to whom I had communicated the progress of our operations, warning me that I 'must not be disappointed if my shad do not go up so fast or so far as I hope. It is not the tendency usually of fish to make much exertion to *pass beyond* the beds where they were spawned,' and he particularly wishes me to 'cause reliable observations to be made on this very point, and if the fish do go over the dam and pass far above it in really large numbers, that I would tell him of it, as it would be a point of interest in natural history'—(See last number (October or November) of the proceedings of the Philadelphia Academy of Natural Science, on the planting of shad in the Alabama river), and he adds, 'if they do not go freely over, being satisfied that they could if they chose, you must transport some from below into the basin of the dam above, and then let your legislature forbid fishing above the dam for five years. That is the term allowed in Maine to restore barren rivers.'

"I think we need hardly take the trouble to transplant

fish from the lower to the upper levels, for once or twice that the Columbia dam has been broken, they have made their way above it, and have been caught in small numbers at Duncan's island.

"But what Mr. Lyman says is nevertheless true; that the fish will make almost irrepressible exertions to return to the beds where they were spawned, while to pass beyond there, they will take but little trouble.

"The spawn (fry) of the few, however, that make their way up, will return by resistless instinct in the following season, and it may be well to consider his other recommendation, that the fishing above the dam should be somewhat restricted by legislative enactment for a limited period, until our great Susquehanna shall be cured of ' barrenness.'

"It remains for me to describe to you the device which has been inserted in the Columbia dam.

"The dam itself is about six feet high, and about a mile and a third long, and is located on a rough, rocky bed. The channel below is rapid and much interrupted by large rocks, worn by the water. The fish channels in these rapids are tortuous and much spread over the whole bed of the stream.

"A point was selected within about a quarter of a mile of the York county shore, where the fish 'most do congregate' from all the lower channels every spring, and where many of them have been annually taken; and at this place a section, forty feet long, was cut clean out of the

15

dam, a coffer dam having been first erected above to keep off the water.

" In this opening, a new subdam was erected, so that its comb or highest elevation would about equal the level of the water below the principal dam when the fish are running (a little over three feet say). The lower slope of this subdam was placed at an inclination of one in fifteen, and the sides of the aperture in the main dam were dentated or framed in a series of offsets, so as to promote the formation of eddies in the current passing over the subdam.

" When the fish are running then, in the spring, the water in the aperture will be under the influence of gravity in opposite directions. The lower water will try to attain its level, the top of the subdam and the upper water rushing through the aperture will meet and certainly drive it back, but with a force considerably impeded by the cushion, so to speak, of lower water.

" The fish will be nosing along the foot of the main dam, as is their wont, and finding its passage open, agitated though it be by these contending currents, they will endeavor to pass up, and let us hope they will succeed. But should they fail in the first few trials, there are the recesses at the sides where the eddies are sure to be formed, and where they may gather strength for a renewal of the trial. I am informed, by persons in the neighborhood of Columbia, who have seen this aperture of ours with the water running through it, that there are many passages in the Conewago rapids below. which are much more difficult of ascent than this is; and which, of course, the fish must easily pass, or they would not be caught, as they now are, at the base of the Columbia **dam, their next** obstacle.

"Such is the result of our labors at the Columbia dam, and we have but to wait now until spring to see what action the **fish, our** long absent friends, will take upon the subject.

"If **our** inducements are not sufficient, we may, in the future, be able to improve upon them, and **Mr. President** Knight has expressed his willingness to render all reasonable aid in making such improvements as, after experiment, may seem to be required.

"The next two **dams in** streams, contemplated **by the** act, are first : the **Middletown Feeder dam, crossing** the **Swatara a short distance from its mouth, and the Duncan's** **Island dam, crossing** the Susquehanna at or near Clark's **Ferry. These** both belong **to the** Pennsylvania Railroad Company, whom I notified, according **to law, and who** acknowledged the receipt of the notification. On November the 1st, nothing had been done **to either of these dams,** and immediately after that **day I had placed in the hands** of the district attorney of **Dauphin county, J. W. Simon-** ton, Esq., a written account of **my proceedings. If the** case be **carried to the** courts, and **a decision should be had** against the constitutionality **of the act, there will be no** use in prosecuting the companies **higher up the stream** If the **act should hold, and the** Pennsylvania Railroad Company be **compelled to alter its dams, the point will be** settled for the **upper companies, and there will be no more** trouble. So I did not initiate legal proceedings **in respect**

to those companies, deeming it better to await the decision
of the courts, in reference to the case of the next dams
above Columbia."

II.

"SIR:—Having been re-appointed by your Excellency
to the position of Commissioner, under the Act of March
30th 1866, relating to the passage of fish in the Susquehanna and its tributaries, I have the honor to submit the
following report:—

"The passage for fish constructed in the Columbia dam,
and described in my last report, I have every reason to
believe is a success.

"It is notorious that shad have been caught of the very
finest quality and in respectable numbers as high above the
Columbia dam as Newport, on the Juniata.

"The numbers actually taken, during the past season,
between Columbia and the Juniata, are variously estimated
at from ten to fifteen or eighteen thousand, by men in whom
full reliance can be placed.

"In my last year's report to Governor Curtin, I stated
that the various companies owning the lower dams on the
Susquehanna and its tributaries were duly notified, according to law, of what was required of them, under the act,
and that no company had responded except the Susquehanna Canal Company, who had complied with the act to
my satisfaction, by the construction of the designated weir.

"I laid information, strictly in accordance with the act,
against the Pennsylvania Railroad Company, who, at that

time, owned the next structures which barred the access of the shad to the upper river.

"This information was duly reported to the District Attorney of Dauphin county, but was not acted upon last year, and thus one season has been lost in the progress of our 'reconstruction.'

"This year, however, true bills have been found, both against the Pennsylvania Railroad Company, the company owning the dams last year, and the Pennsylvania Canal Company, the party owning them at this time; and there is every reason to believe that the question of the constitutionality of the law will very soon be settled in the courts.

"Should this question be put at rest so that this corporation shall be compelled under the law to erect the weirs, I have not any doubt but what shad will make their appearance once more above Duncan's Island, in the Susquehanna; and if this first company constructs, the others who were duly notified, as stated in my last year's report, namely, the North and West Branch Canal Companies and the Wyoming Valley Canal Company, must also comply or otherwise stand a lawsuit, which it is not supposed that they will do with the record against them.

"The whole matter then depends upon the result of this suit. If the law now in existence be inadequate to produce the desired result, it will be for the legislature to consider the matter further.

"The people on the Susquehanna, between Columbia and Duncan's Island, and up the Juniata, as far as New-

15 *

port, have had a taste of fish ; and those living above those points being informed that with an expenditure of a few thousand dollars at each dam, this delicious luxury can be brought again to their doors, it will not be at all surprising if they should feel exceedingly anxious that a law should be passed benefitting them in the same way.

" Large numbers of the spawned fry of the shad have been observed at various points making their way down the river during the fall, and the bodies of the old fish— those that had fulfilled their mission in spawning—were also seen at various points, in large numbers, late in the season, floating down with the current.

" I should not be surprised, therefore, if the catch in the coming season would double or treble the number taken during the season last past, for it is a well-known instinct of this branch of the finny tribe that they return unerringly to the localities in which they were spawned, unless prevented by some insurmountable obstacle interposed during their absence.

" The erection of fish dams (weirs) in the river, however, will tend very materially to diminish this desirable result, and public opinion in Dauphin, Cumberland, and Perry counties is so strong against these devices, that I believe but a single one was erected along the borders of those counties this year, and that one was promptly suppressed by law.

" Having heard, however, that some of those nuisances were about to be, or had been erected, along the river nearer to Columbia, I caused the citizens to be requested to lodge information against them.

"No such information has been lodged, and I have not been able to ascertain to what extent the downward passage of the spawn has been interrupted in the localities spoken of. The main dams in the river are scarcely a greater obstruction to the passage of shad than these fish-traps—they catch the spawn (fry) in their meshes, and there the little creatures die by the thousand.

"It is in the hands of the people to remedy this crying evil. The laws against the erection of such structures are sufficiently stringent to put a stop to them altogether; but unless those interested will lodge information, the system will continue, and although the most efficient weirs (fish-ways) shall be made in the large dams for the passage of fish up the stream, unless the way for the spawn (fry) to get down be left open, no increase in the catch from year to year can be expected.

"There is no state, county, or township officer whose business it is specially to watch this infraction of the law, and I would suggest that it be made the duty of some such official in the counties bordering upon the river to have an eye upon it—notifying all persons against putting up such structures, and that if they should still persist in doing so they will be proceeded against in the most summary manner.

"A little active interest taken by the public in this regard is all that is necessary, and it cannot be many years until the shad shall be fully reinstated in the Susquehanna and its tributaries for hundreds of miles."

THE ALEWIFE.

THIS species (*tyranus*), of the same genus as the fine fish just treated of, is the gaspereau of the Canadians, the alewife of the New England states, and the herring of the Middle and Southern States. The means to be used for its restoration to the streams from which it has been driven are so identical with those now being resorted to for the purpose of bringing back shad and salmon, that I have not thought it necessary to make more than this brief allusion to it.

One habit of this species, here and further south, is somewhat different from the habit which prevails with it at the north. I allude to its entering very small streams to spawn. In the Delaware it does not ascend the upper waters as far as the shad, not being abundant above the terminus of the tide. The same may be said of it to the southward. Here, as in the Eastern states, there are several runs differing in size, the earlier being larger fish. South they have been, and continue to be, so abundant that no thought of their becoming scarce has ever been entertained. As an evidence of their abundance, I quote as follows from the "American Anglers' Book :"—

"In Maryland and Virginia they have even been used as manure, as the small species known as 'manhaden' and 'mossbunkers' have been farther north. In Virginia and North Carolina, the custom of visiting the 'fishing-shores' annually for a supply of herrings to salt down, still exists as an 'institution,' and the inhabitants for many miles back from the rivers that furnish these fish, come every spring and take away immense numbers of them.

"One of the greatest hauls with a seine that I ever heard of, was made by a fisherman on the Potomac near Dumfries, Va. With one sweep of his long net he encompassed a school which supplied all applicants. He sold them as long as they would bring a price, and then, after furnishing them to the people of the immediate neighborhood without charge, lifted his net and allowed the remainder of the imprisoned fish to escape.

"The herring will occasionally take a bait, and on a sunshiny day in May, when the wind is from the south, will jump at a piece of red flannel tied to a hook. An old Scotch merchant of New York—a superannuated trout-fisher—some years back was in the habit of fishing for them with a fly, from the decks of vessels in the East River."

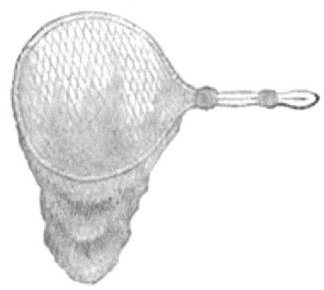

M

CHAPTER VII.

NATURALIZATION OF FISHES.

General remarks. SALMONIDÆ.—*The Brook Trout.*—Instances of its naturalization. *The Lake Trout.*—Mr. Robinson's letter on its propagation. *The Schoodic and Sebago Salmon.*—Extract concerning its habits and propagation, from Maine Fish Commissioners' Report. *The Sea Trout of Canada.*—Advantages of naturalizing it. *The Grayling.*—New species found in Michigan. *The White Fish.* —Its excellence, habits, and manner of propagating. *The Otsego Bass.*—Not a bass. *The Smelt.*—General remarks. PERCIDÆ.— *The Rock Fish.—The Crappie.—The Black Bass of the Lakes.*—Its adaptability to naturalization. *The Black Bass of the West and South.*—Its introduction into the Potomac.—Mr. Wright's score of fish taken with the rod.—**Their** naturalization in mill-ponds. SILURIDÆ.—*Small Species.*—Their excellence as food.—Manner of cooking them.—Their proposed **introduction** into England. CYPRINIDÆ.—General remarks on. ESOCIDÆ.—Injurious results from introducing them.

I USE the term naturalization as the most appropriate in reference to fishes which are to be introduced into a new habitat.

Not only in France and England is this branch of fish culture claiming the consideration of thinking and enterprising persons, but in this country its great advantages are beginning to be appreciated. The French government and people have become aware of the value which lies in hitherto waste and uncultivated waters, and, as I

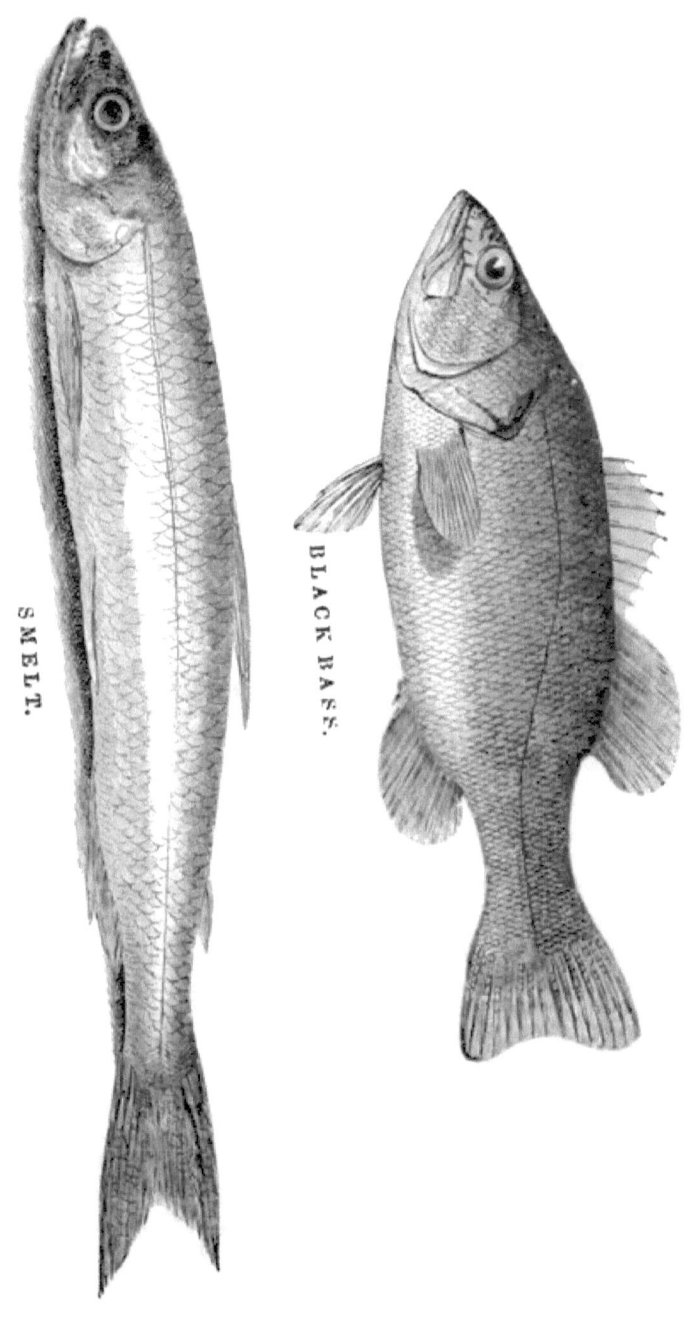

SMELT.

BLACK BASS.

have remarked on a preceding page, have made considerable progress in turning them to profit.

The fact that certain fishes are not found in certain waters is no indication that such waters are not suitable to them. I know of several instances on fine brisk streams where trout were unknown above high falls, until a few were passed over, and thus introduced above. Here they are prolific, and grow as large as their progenitors in the waters below. Lakelets and new streams have also been successfully stocked with these fish. I also know of natural and artificial ponds, as well as mill-ponds and rivers, where the two species of black bass have been introduced, and where they have multiplied and grow to the size they do in the waters they were taken from.

Waters have no doubt been accidentally, or it may be said, providentially, stocked with percoids, cyprinoids, and pike, by the ova of these fish (which are surrounded by a glutinous substance) adhering to the legs of wading birds, which have transported them in their flight from one river or lake to another. Some even suppose that the eggs of fish have been swallowed by birds in one stream, and passing undigested through them, have been deposited in other water. The latter theory is scarcely tenable; with the ova of trout or salmon either would be impossible. Referring to the stocking and replenishing of certain waters of the Mississippi Valley with percoids, I hope I shall be excused for again quoting from the " American Anglers' Book :"—

"I have alluded on another page, to the replenishing of the lakelets, found so abundantly scattered along the margin of the Mississippi, through its alluvial bottom lands, by the occasional overflow of that river. This phenomenon is strongly presented to the notice of observing anglers in the neighborhood of St. Louis, and one is apt to wonder where the great numbers and varieties of the perch family come from, to stock those sluggish waters. In thinking over the matter, I have fallen back on my favorite theory, the *instinctive migration of surplus production*, as applicable to fresh-water fishes, as well as to salt water or pelagian genera.

"If the reader will take the trouble to look at a good map, he will see that the states north and west of the confluence of the Mississippi and Ohio, are threaded for thousands of miles by rivers of gentle flow, and dotted with innumerable lakelets, which, to a great extent, are the feeders and sources of the Mississippi. These are the breeding-places of bass, crappie, and other percoids; most of them spawn early in the spring, soon after the ice has left the lakelets; and as most fresh-water species instinctively run down stream after spawning, it is easily conjectured how large schools of these fish are hurried along by freshets, and deposited in the ponds that are fed by the overflow of the great river.

"After a rise in the Mississippi, the lakes and ponds that skirt its course, above the mouth of the Ohio, and down through the regions of cotton and sugar, are filled with fish of this family.

"In the ponds which have been replenished in this way in the neighborhood of St. Louis, their numbers decrease

very little the first summer; the second season they spawn
and breed, as in their native waters, but if the ponds are
not refreshed by an overflow of the river every two or
three years, the waters lose the chemical condition necessary to the reproduction of fish, from a continued infusion
of decayed vegetable matter, and the lakes become barren,
until another overflow of the mighty river comes rushing
through, clearing them of foul, and filling them with fresh
water; and restocking them at the same time with fish, and
most numerously with percoids.

"Below its junction with the Ohio, the Mississippi has
made, in the course of time, many a "*cut off*," forcing its
way in times of flood, across the neck of a peninsula or a
bend, in seeking a more direct course, and leaving considerable bodies of water, of a horse-shoe shape, as the old
channel closes. These are fed by the annual or occasional
overflow of the river, and their waters refreshed and restocked with fish, as just described. Bruin Lake, opposite
Grand Gulf, Mississippi, is a water of this kind, and is said
to contain bass (or as they are there called trout) of immense size. I have been told by an angler, that he has
taken there, in a day's fishing, thirty of these fish, whose
aggregate length was sixty feet."

In naturalization, care is required that predatory fishes
are not introduced into waters with more valuable species;
black bass, for instance, should not inhabit waters where
the young of salmon and shad are reared. We occasionally find through the country, pig-headed individuals who
have introduced pike into ponds which were well stocked

16

with trout, because the former were larger fish. The consequence of course is, that the valuable and more beautiful trout are exterminated by these fresh-water sharks in a few years.

The quality of the water should also be considered, cold or warm, clear or muddy, swift or sluggish; and such fish introduced as are natural to the stream or pond.

As it is inferred that naturalized fish will propagate naturally, it is necessary that suitable spawning-beds should be accessible to them in their new home. A cool, well-shaded lakelet, which it is intended to stock with trout, should have spring brooks or rapid streams entering; these should be provided with an abundance of gravel in gentle and shallow currents. For fish of the carp and perch families, aquatic weeds and grass or brush should be furnished, on which these fishes deposit their spawn; which is agglutinated together, and adhere to aquatic plants or stones by means of the viscid matter which surrounds the eggs. Bundles of faggots tied irregularly may even be placed in parts of a pond where they are likely to spawn for their accommodation. The impregnated ova could be collected, if desired, as it is in China, and transported adhering to the twigs, in water, or stripped off, if done gently, and sent away in small vessels.

The naturalization of species belonging to the perch family is, or should be, a matter of importance to the people of the Western States. Many an insignificant stream which now affords a home only for small worthless species might be dammed and stocked with bass obtained from

larger waters. A supply of fish food which is now pre-
carious and only obtained by a long trip to rivers and
lakes, might be thus made certain and brought to one's
own premises or immediate neighborhood.

Concerning the hybridizing of fish, I would here remark that many erroneous notions prevail, and some very
impracticable suggestions have been made by those who
should know better, about crossing different genera or
species. When fish culture was in its incipiency, some of
the learned men of France, amongst whom (if I remember
correctly), certain renowned biologists were included, suggested crossing the pike with the salmon. I have no
knowledge of any results from experiments of this kind
which are reported to have been made at Huningue, but I
doubt whether the ova of one genus (to say nothing of that
of a different family), can be impregnated with the milt
of another. If species of the same genus were even
crossed, it is reasonable to suppose that the progeny would
not be endowed with reproductive powers. They would,
doubtless, be mules. There is a limit to the violation or
interference with certain laws of nature, and hybrids when
produced, are inferior animals. We see it in the produce
of the horse and ass, where the reproductive power is lost;
and in the mulatto, where the physical condition of the
Caucasian or the negro, in most cases, deteriorates. Experiments in hybridizing, therefore, may develope certain
truths that might be interesting to biologists; but that
new species or mules of larger growth or greater excellence
can be thus produced, it is unreasonable to hope for.

It is my purpose to treat separately, and under its appropriate head, of the species of each family which I have thought may be advantageously naturalized.

SALMONIDÆ.

Having already treated at length of the cultivation of the true salmon (*S. salar*), I will proceed with other species of the same genus.

THE BROOK TROUT (*S. fontinalis*).—This, as well as its nobler cogener, has already occupied so much space that further notice of it might be deemed superfluous. Still its cultivation is a matter of so much importance that I shall offer some remarks on its naturalization.

No sooner is a line of travel opened to within a reasonable distance of any part of the country where trout are abundant, than the backwoodsman, in league with the city fish dealer, commences a war of extermination. Urged on by the high price they bring in market, all manner of means, fair and foul, are used to take them, and they are sent to the cities in season and out of season. Sometimes trout of unusual size are offered for sale even in the streets of New York just after they have spawned, and inconsiderate people buy them, when they are no more to compare to the same fish in June than a handful of dried apples are to a Newton pippin. We also see them garnished and displayed in the windows of restaurants in October and November, and those who are ignorant of the flavor of a trout in good condition, eat them because trout are considered a delicacy. I forget how many tons of trout are estimated to have been sent from the Umbagog region to Boston last fall. Another cause for the decline of trout streams is **the relentless manner in** which these **fish** are pursued with **hook and line.** **Fish of all sizes, from the length of one's** finger upwards, **are** strung **or basketed by country** bait-fisher or city angler with his flies. **The poor ambition** possessing each, that he may boast of the *numbers* **of trout** he has exterminated, without **regard to size; for with such** the fingerling counts one, as does the fish that **runs one's line** off the reel. **With this** state **of** semi-barbarism **existing—and it appears** almost impossible to **ameliorate it—it is evident that** naturalization and arti-ficial propagation **must be resorted to in** more thickly set-tled **parts of the country, if we wish to** prevent these **beautiful** fish **from becoming almost as rare in** our streams **as salmon now are.**

I **have alluded in** the introduction to this article, **to the stocking of the upper parts of streams with this fish, and** could **cite instances** in **which they have been quietly intro-duced into others,** where, after **a few years, those who** transplanted **them were** rewarded with good fishing, **until the** knowledge **of such** fact **caused the brook to be over-**fished.

The Cuttyhunk **Club,** an association of anglers who **have established** themselves **on the** island bearing that name, **are about** introducing **brook trout into a fine fresh** water **pond on their grounds. In a** letter, bearing date April 25th, **a member of the club says:** "We have not **got** along far **enough at Cuttyhunk to** give any decided

16 *

result. We have had 21,000 spawn from Seth Green, of which we think we have hatched and have in good lively condition all except about 2000. These fish we have in boxes, fed by a cool spring, and arranged under Green's personal inspection, and attended by Capt. Simons, an enthusiastic and very careful person. We have plenty of water to keep these little fellows confined until this fall, when we shall turn them into a pond of ten acres and about twenty feet deep, cool, fed by springs. No outlet except what leeches through the sand into the sea. In very heavy weather the sea sometimes dashes a little salt water into this pond, which lies about four feet above high tide, and this we think a good feature. We have now about 300 fish of a quarter of a pound each in this pond with lots of feed."

Having occupied so much space with the cultivation of the trout, I shall conclude by giving the following from the Maine Fish Commissioners' report concerning its naturalization :—

" Maj. S. Dill, of Phillips, writes to the Maine Farmer: ' In the fall of 1850 I put into the Sandy river ponds ten or twelve trout; for seven or eight years no indications of them were to be seen, notwithstanding thousands of people crossed those ponds every year. Since 1857 it is judged that not less than 2000 pounds have been taken out annually. So far as I have been able to inform myself, never a fish had been seen in either of those ponds prior to my *colonization.'* "

THE LAKE TROUT.—Of these we have many species, from the gigantic *S. Namaycush* to the lesser trout of our smaller lakes. They are known in Canada as "Lunge," in some of the Eastern States as "Togue," the average of the species in the smaller lakes not exceeding three or four pounds. Experiments were made last winter by Mr. Robinson, of Meredith, N. H., in hatching the ova of the lake trout found in his vicinity. In a letter to Mr. Ainsworth he says : "In regard to our lake trout, I am making the experiment of hatching them, under the patronage of the New Hampshire Commissioners. I am well satisfied with the result thus far, considering my want of knowledge in the business. I think that, with a little more light on the subject, I can make a *perfect* success. I lost a great many spawn by bringing them home in buckets, sitting in the bottom of a wagon, and others by being jarred in a boat beating to windward in a heavy sea. All I transported without jar are hatching well. There is no real trouble in obtaining the spawn. The fish come on the shoals to spawn, and can be taken in mesh-nets without at all injuring the fish. I captured some 250 fish of both sexes, and after manipulating, returned them to the lake and killed but few. Those I took were of the proportion of five or six males to one female. The amount of spawn I should judge would be about the same as salmon, say about 2000 for a two-pound fish and upwards, to 10,000 for a ten-pounder."

There is but little doubt that any of the species referred to can be naturalized in lakelets that are suitable to the black bass of the northern lakes. They do not appear to be prolific, as they are not found in great numbers in the lakes they now inhabit; nor is the flesh of any of them comparable to that of the true salmon, the land-locked salmon, or the brook trout. The last report of the Maine Fish Commissioners contains the following remarks on their habits :—

"Late in October they resort to shoal water, and spawn on rocks and ledges. They come suddenly, finish the operation in a few nights, and immediately retire to deep water. It has been noticed that the females come to the spawning-grounds first. The first night of their appearance nearly all will be females, and at the last nearly all males. They are accompanied and followed by a motley throng, composed of nearly all kinds of fishes in the lake, eels and hornpouts predominating. Probably few of the eggs escape them."

THE SCHOODIC TROUT, or more properly salmon (*S. gloveri*), and the Sebago salmon (*S. Sebago*), I am inclined to believe are identical. Both are doubtless land-locked salmon, having lost the instinct of migration to sea many, many generations back. It is likely that at some remote period natural obstructions prevented their migrations to the ocean, and the habit of reproducing in fresh waters without going to sea to recuperate was forced upon them and became an instinct. These modified salmon (if I may so call them) are now permanent in Sebago and Schoodic lakes, although there appears to be no obstruction to the marine migrations of the latter. These fish could probably be naturalized in the smaller lakes of New England and New York. In the Umbagog region they would, without doubt, do well. Chautauque Lake, near the dividing line between Pennsylvania and New York, could likely be stocked with them; at all events such an enterprise is worth the experiment.

The following interesting account of the Sebago salmon is taken from the Maine Fish Commissioners' Report:—

"This species was once quite abundant in the waters connected with Sebago Lake; but torch and spear, and exclusion from the spawning-grounds, have made great inroads on their numbers. Probably not more than a thousand of them are now taken annually. Nathan Cummings, Esq., of Portland, has given us much information about these fish. He says that when the Cumberland and Oxford Canal was building, during the first winter the workmen sent away fifty barrels of them. Mr. Cummings used to fish for them very successfully at the outlet of Sebago Lake, but for some years he has tried them there to no purpose. They are still brought in limited numbers into Portland each spring and fall, mostly from the lower part of Crooked and Songo rivers.

"The principal breeding-grounds of this salmon at the present time are on Crooked river, below Edes Falls, in the town of Naples, and in Bear brook, at the head of Long Pond, near Harrison village. They make their first appearance in the direction of their spawning-beds about the 1st of September; in Crooked river a little earlier than in Bear brook. In the latter stream the males come first alone, and run back and forth in the mouth of the brook until the last of the month, when they are joined by a few

females, but these are still very few until the 15th of October. Soon after this date they begin **to ascend** the rapids
to spawn. It is not often, however, that any of them are mature and commence spawning until the 20th. They come
then in considerable numbers, and soon finish spawning.
Very few are found in the brook as late as November 14th,
although probably they sometimes spawn later. Crooked
river **is a larger stream, and** they report different habits in
some respects. **The very first** that come into the stream
are males, but after that **the females seem to head** the advance, and the males follow them; taking the whole of
September, the males are not more numerous than **the**
other sex. In the whole season there are more males.
They sometimes continue to spawn very late. The state
of the water has a great influence on their motions at this
time. A rise is followed by a plentiful run of fish.

"Their beds are made in the gravel where the current
is rapid, but just on the verge of a ripple in the water;
rarely seen **on** the lower side of a ripple. They make
large excavations, the sand and gravel from which are
carried out **by the current,** and form **a** mound below.
These excavations are sometimes three feet in diameter,
and **are made by more than** one pair. A large number of
both sexes are sometimes seen together in one hole. No
fighting is observed amongst the males. It is more common, however, to see a single pair working together, lying
side by side in the nest. They make the excavations by
fanning **with the tail,** no digging with the head being observed. **On favorite** grounds the nests **encroach** on each other

on all sides, frequently lying one above another, like a row of potato hills; but whether one pair makes more than one nest has not been ascertained. The **work** of spawning is carried **on at night, and by** day the fish are rarely to be seen on **the beds.** Their ascent of the stream **also occurs by night. The** old fish eat nothing during this season; **but small** males are taken with their stomachs full of eggs. The adult males are very different in appearance from the other sex, being much deeper and thinner, with larger and more pointed heads.* The lower jaw is furnished at the spawning season with a singular recurved process, some-**times near** an inch in length, **which shuts into the roof of** the mouth; **it is conical in** form, either truncated or with the apex bent backward. On an adult male of one pound weight this was present, but not so fully developed as in the larger specimens. In younger individuals it was want-ing. Both jaws in this sex are so curved as to prevent the closing of **the** mouth. A male of six inches length had a forked tail, eight or **nine** black bars across the side, twelve large vermilion spots on the side. One that **measured** eight and one-half inches in length, has the same forked **tail, and the** bars on **the** side, **but** they **are** very faint, and the vermilion spots have changed to maroon; **the hook** on the jaw not yet visible.

"The spawning-grounds of this species are very limited. Those **of Long Pond** are confined **to Bear brook. Those** of Sebago **are mostly limited to two or three miles of**

---

* This difference **in** the forms of the male and female **is** peculiar **to** all the species of the genus *Salmo* at the spawning season.

Crooked river. In former times they ranged at the spawning season the whole length of Crooked river, as far, at least, as North Waterford, and great numbers of them were taken at many points; but they were never known to ascend the river at any other season than fall, farther than the first gentle rapids near its mouth. This is rather singular; for the sea salmon (*S. salar*) ascends rivers of smaller size than this in June, and passes the summer in them. The grand fishing-place in May was from the junction of Crooked and Songo rivers several miles down. The fish took bait eagerly, and were then in superior condition. They left this ground as early as the last of May, but at the outlet they were taken much later. In the lake itself they were only caught in the track of the rafts that came down across the lake into Presumpscot river, and the arrival of the rafts at the outlet was always the signal for good fishing there. In Long Pond they are never caught —only when entering the brook, and in the spring only a few small ones are taken there.

"The size attained by the Sebago salmon is very considerable. The average of those taken in the fall is, for the males, 5 pounds; for the females, a little more than 3. A female 25 inches long weighs 5 pounds; a male of the same length weighs 7 pounds. Of two males 29 inches long, one weighed 9 pounds 14 ounces, the other 11 pounds 4 ounces. Some extreme weights may be given. One was taken the past season at Edes Falls that dressed 14½ pounds. The largest on record was caught by Mr. Sawyer, of Raymond. Its weight was 17½ pounds, and is vouched for by

Franklin Sawyer, Esq., of Portland. These old fish are seldom caught with the hook; and of those taken in the spring and summer, when they are in season, the average weight would be less than indicated by the above.

"These fish are said to be about as plenty as they were ten years ago. But it is strange that they can maintain their numbers against such persecution as follows them. The spear is very fatal. In Bear brook nearly all the breeding males are destroyed before the females are ready to spawn. In 1858 a law was passed for their protection, which would enable them to recruit their numbers were it enforced.

"We consider this variety worthy of being propagated and disseminated through the state."*

THE SEA TROUT (*Salmo Canadensis* of Hamilton Smith).—From all my researches the only scientific account given of this fish is by the present writer.† Hamilton Smith, though he named it, scarcely refers to its specific characteristics. It is decidedly distinct from the varieties of *S. fontinalis* which migrate to and from

---

* Mr. Nathan Cummings, of Portland, Maine, has communicated to the Massachusetts Fish Commissioners the following concerning the agility of the young of this fish:—

"The young are very agile. Some of them, bred artificially by Mr. Robinson, at Meredith, N. H., were put, when quite small, in a tank, into which, from a height of nine inches, fell a stream of water flowing through a one and a half inch hole; whereupon the lively parrs leaped up the stream, and into the upper tank, like harlequin going through a clock-face."

† See American Anglers' Book, page 238.

17   N

salt water, and which acquire a larger size and darker
tinted flesh by feeding upon crustacea found there. Nor
has it but slight affinity to the sea trout (*Salmo trutta*)
of Scotland and Ireland.

These fish come in large schools into the Canadian and
New Brunswick streams. On their arrival they are beautifully bright and of surpassingly delicate flavor, but like
the salmon, which they precede a month or so, they lose
their brilliancy and flesh up to the time of spawning, which
is in October. As far as I have examined them their
stomachs are empty after entering fresh water, while an
occasional brook trout taken in the same pool has a well-
filled paunch. They are, therefore, purely anadromous, and
like the salmon attain all of their growth and flavor at sea.
On this account they are desirable subjects for naturalization, and should be introduced with the salmon, and be
made to participate in the facilities which are now being
created to enable them to ascend our rivers. Four pounds
is not an unusual size; they are sometimes taken as high as
six and seven pounds.

In the summer of 1865 I stopped with a friend at
Harris's, on the Tabasintac, an inconsiderable stream half
way between Chatham and Bathurst, New Brunswick, to
enjoy the sea-trout fishing. My friend captured a goodly
number of them under a pound weight, near the house
after taking our tea. The next morning we travelled seven
miles down the creek in a large "dug-out," drawn by a
pair of stout horses, rumbling along over cobble-stones
down to the junction of the Escadillach. Here, in less than

four hours, at midday and under a bright sun, we captured four and a half bushels of these handsome fish and left off from pure satiety. A hundred of these fish were over two pounds in weight, and many of them four pounds, although our attendant lamented that there were no *large ones* in the pool. In fishing with two flies on ordinary trout gut, the fish, having a dead pull against each other, would break loose. After losing many flies in this way, we each fished with a single salmon fly, generally a worn-out one, left from my former summer's tackle; and as long as there was dubbing or feather on the hook they would seize it freely. Their sharp teeth, which are much more formidable than those of our brook trout, made a frequent renewal necessary. We would have ceased this havoc sooner, but young Harris, who drove our aquatic vehicle, said he hauled the pool with a seine two or three times during the summer for a stock of trout to salt down; we accordingly kept on until we had taken the quantity above given, to save him the trouble of making the pool a visit with his seine.

These fish frequent and spawn in the Miramichi, on which river (I have been informed by Rev. Livingston Stone, of New Hampshire), a salmon-hatching establishment will be started the coming autumn. Of course it is to be supposed that those who have charge of it, will not neglect so favorable an opportunity of procuring the eggs of the sea trout and giving them the opportunity of making sufficient progress in incubation to insure their safe transportation to the states.

At the time of writing the foregoing chapter on the

cultivation of the salmon, I was not aware that so spirited and praiseworthy an undertaking as the one alluded to was contemplated, and gladly make this digression to commend it. The necessity of manipulating salmon on the stream and transporting the spawn immediately after impregnation, when the ova are so apt to lose their vitality by being agitated, and not allowing sufficient time in hatching-troughs for the early development of the young fish in the eggs, has been almost the only bar to the success of those who had the task of introducing salmon into the rivers of New England. It is a matter of gratulation that this difficulty is about to be obviated. Not having Mr. Stone's letter at hand at the time of writing this, I am unable to say whether it is an enterprise of his own, or of the New England Fish Commissioners, but shall throw some light upon the question in an appendix.

Thymallus.—To this genus belongs the English grayling. Dr. Richardson, in his " Fauna Boreali-Americana," gives an account of two species. Another has lately been discovered in some of the affluents of Green Bay. It is described as a fish of rare beauty and excellence. While on a trout-fishing excursion lately in the north-western part of Pennsylvania, I met with a very intelligent, though not scientific person, who informed me that he, last summer, while exploring some timber lands on the Oconto and Au Sable (though I can find no such stream as the latter on the map), met with a new kind of trout, which he had never seen before. From his description it was, doubtless, this new species of *Thymallus.* He informed me that it took readily a bait of the flesh of one of its fellows, a worm having been used to capture the first fish, and that it was very beautiful and of delicious flavor. Cannot some of the spirited commissioners of fisheries of the New England States **introduce** this new fish into their waters?

WHITE-FISH.—Lake herrings, Otsego bass, and species known by other local names are included in the genus *Coregonus*. It is likely that we have no less than ten distinct species, from the fat-beladened *C. albus* or *sapidissimus* and *C. quadrilateralis* of the Arctic regions, to the little lake herring found in the Saranac lakes. They are all peaceable dwellers in the depths; approaching the **shores,** or the rapids of some affluent in autumn to spawn, at which time most of those found in our markets are taken.

It is said that no food has ever been detected in the stomachs of these fish. In this respect they show a marked analogy to the shad and herring. It is said of them also, that on rare occasions they have been known to take a bait and even to rise to a fly; their food, though, is a matter of mystery. They are not predatory, as will be seen from the mouth and jaws. Although their food may consist of minute crustacea, they are, perhaps, to a certain extent, herbiverous, as cyprinoids are,* and may find certain fresh-water algæ in the deeps where they feed.

---

* Fishes that are considered purely predatory in their habits, are, **in some degree,** omnivorous. A striped **bass** will take a bait of shad roe; I found once **in** the throat of one, several roots and stalks of some succulent aquatic grass. A trout or a salmon will also take a bait of the roe of one of its own species.

17 *

The Large-White Fish (*C. albus*), is a fish of rare delicacy. Its flesh and skin contain a large proportion of gelatine. In autumn, at spawning time, it is difficult to broil it because of the fat; which dripping on the coals ignites and frequently envelopes gridiron and fish in a blaze. Its fatness even disfigures it. With head sunk in its shoulders, it presents the appearance of the body of a shad with the head of a herring. This, with its congener (*C. quadrilateralis*), furnishes a large amount of food to the northern Indians. Twenty-five years since a goodly portion of the Chippeways, who were permanently encamped at Sault St. Marie, subsisted chiefly on them, taking them in large numbers in the rapids with dip-nets. In the regions around the lakes of northern British America and Hudson's Bay, it also furnishes a large proportion of food. Its flesh cloys less than that of any other fish, and it can be eaten for months without getting tired of it.

The average size of this fish in the upper of the large lakes of the great range, is somewhat over three pounds; they have been taken in Lake Superior weighing as much as ten and twelve pounds. The usual size of those brought to our city markets is about two pounds. They should be naturalized in every lake that will afford them a suitable habitat.

The following from the last Maine report throws much light on their manner of propagation :—

" Mr. Clark is engaged in the fishery in Detroit river He estimated the total catch of white-fish in that river alone, this year, to be half a million or more in number, weighing a million and a half of pounds, or seven hundred and fifty tons. At the retail price in Boston these would be worth $250,000. Mr. Clark has a pound with an area of an acre and a half, six feet deep, made by enclosing with stakes a portion of Detroit river, in which he keeps white-fish from November until the last of the winter, when they are caught out and marketed. They are first taken with a seine before they have spawned, and most of them spawn here in the pound. The operation is in the following manner: the opposite sexes approach each other, turning partially on the side, and the male appearing to attach himself by his soft flexible mouth to the female near her gills; then both fish dart off through the water together, and as they go the female ejects the eggs and the male the milt, in such a way that they mingle together and fall to the bottom. They move ten or twenty feet at a time, and each time eject several hundred eggs. Mr. Clark placed sieves on the bottom at night, and in the morning found many thousand impregnated eggs on them. Mr. Clark has taken the pains to procure, pack, and send to us two separate lots of these eggs, to assist us in ascertaining the best mode of packing and transportation. Of the first lot, packed in cotton batting, in sand and in river grass, a few survived the journey, out of fifty thousand; but of the other lot, packed in river mud and partially frozen, not one survived.* Further experiment would, no

---

* The only mode of obviating this destruction of ova in transportation, is to have them partially incubated before sending them away.

doubt, bring to light a method by which they could be successfully brought."

THE OTSEGO BASS (*C. otsego*).—This fish bears the very inappropriate name of "Bass" in Lake Otsego, while it does not bear the most remote affinity to any of the numerous genera of bass. Thus far it is unknown in any other water than that which gives it its specific name. It is said even to surpass the larger white-fish in excellence. Its average size is not much more than half that of *C. albus*. It could likely be naturalized in small lakes of a more southern latitude than the large white-fish, and is well worthy of the attention of those who take an interest in diffusing the best species.

The smaller species of this genus are not unworthy of the notice of those who would like to see a variety introduced in the many lakelets which dot our Northern and Middle States. The fera, of which millions are hatched at Huningue and sent to all parts of France, are similar to those we call lake herrings.

THE SMELT (*Osmerus*).—Of this genus we have two species. Those usually found in our markets (*O. viridescens*) are taken in great numbers on tidal rivers north of Boston, and along the coast of the British Provinces. The annual value of those sent from Boston exceeds a hundred thousand dollars. They are retailed in our markets at from fifteen to thirty-three cents a pound, and make a most palatable dish for breakfast or supper. The roe is particularly delicate. They are so abundant at the head of tide, where they come to spawn, on some of the rivers emptying into the Bay of Chaleurs, as to be used for manure; a barrel of them in abundant seasons selling for sixty cents. The average length is not over seven inches, although they have been taken as long as twelve inches.

Both here and in England the smelt has been naturalized in fresh-water ponds and lakes; although an interference with their partially anadromous habits, produces generations of smaller and, perhaps, less palatable fish. The reports of the New England Fish Commissioners give several instances of their naturalization in fresh waters. The Maine report for 1867 has the following:—

"Smelts are scattered all over the state. It seems probable that we have more than one species. Whether either of them is identical with the salt-water smelt we cannot say, but the resemblance is very close. In several localities they attain a large size. Those of Harrison are said to exceed half a pound in weight, and those of Belgrade to measure fourteen inches in length. In spring they approach the shores, and are sometimes thrown upon the land by a heavy wind, and perish in great numbers, the shores being lined with the dead. About the 1st of May they ascend the streams. In Monmouth they run into some very small rills that lead into Cochnewagn Pond, and are dipped out in considerable quantities. In May 1867, after it was supposed they were all gone, a fresh run occurred, that yielded thirty barrels. In quality the fresh-water smelts are fully equal to those from the tide-waters. Those from Monmouth have been placed side by side with smelts from Damariscotta, and received the preference."

The smaller species, *O. sergeantti*, found in the Passaic and Raritan, and discovered lately in the Schuylkill and tributaries of the Delaware, is preferred by many, to those brought from the north. ·The peculiar odor of a freshly taken smelt, resembling that of a newly pulled cucumber, is observed readily in the more southern species, and epicures accord to it a great superiority over the northern fish. They are found with us only in winter and early spring, when they spawn and then disappear. They never ascend above the head of tide, neither do the northern species, from all I have learned of them in New Brunswick and Canada. From the success that has attended efforts to introduce the northern species into fresh water, it is evident that these are not without claims to naturalization.

In this notice of these beautiful and delicate little fish I may appropriately allude to their food. An examination of their dentition, and I may say of their stomachs also, evinces an extremely predatory nature. During the last winter I took from the pouch of one of the northern species, three undigested shrimp, two of the small fry of some marine species, and a half a dozen ova, as large as the eggs of our brook trout. Some years ago I made a similar examination of a number of smelt and found that all of them had been feeding bountifully on shrimp. I was not aware until then that these lively little crustaceans could be found in winter. The fact of their being found along our north-eastern coast at this season of the year is suggestive of the vast amount of marine food accessible to pelagian and anadromous fishes at all times. Small crustacea, both in winter and summer, and the larger, when they shed their hard coats, must contribute largely to the sustenance of fishes that inhabit salt and brackish water.

PERCIDÆ.

We have many fishes included in this family that can be readily naturalized. They are found both in salt and fresh waters. Our fresh rivers, lakes, ponds, lagoons, and bayous are rich in genera and species. They are all hardy fish, firm of flesh, and excellent eating.

THE ROCK FISH, or Striped Bass (*Labrax lineatus*), is

> " A fish of wonderful beauty and force,
> That bites like a steel trap, and pulls like a horse."

Some ineffectual attempts have been made to naturalize it in fresh-water ponds by those who have not taken into consideration that it is to a great extent an anadromin, and that to continue its generations in size and perfection, it must necessarily make yearly migrations to salt water. I have no doubt it would deteriorate in purely fresh water as much as the salmon or shad, if this law of its nature was set aside. Still if it grew to half its accustomed size, when prevented from going down to salt or brackish waters, it might be profitably naturalized in fresh ponds and lakes. From all I have learned of its habits, it reproduces in tidal creeks and coves where fresh streams enter, and not above tide, as the salmon. A friend, whose statement I consider reliable, informs me that in some of the shallow waters along our southern coast, he has dipped

up a hand-net full of the fry. **They are** seldom found—
at least not in large numbers—above the head of tide until
they have attained some size ; and their pushing, predatory
instinct must induce them to ascend so far only for feed.
This species is **rare in** the waters of the Gulf of Mexico
or the rivers and bays connecting with it.

THE WHITE PERCH (*Labrax pallidus*).—This is a beautiful fish ; silvery bright in tidal rivers, and on open rocky
or sandy bottoms ; of greenish or golden hue where it lives
amongst **grass and aquatic** weeds ; **and of** darker tint
when it inhabits discolored waters, and muddy **or** peaty
bottoms. Southward, in tidal streams, it **may be enume-
rated** with anadromous fishes. In the Middle and Eastern
States it is **not** unfrequently found in fresh-water lakelets
or ponds having no communication with salt water. At the
south its average size is larger than at the north ; and it is
with surprise that we find northern ichthyologists underrat-
ing it in this particular, and fish commissioners alluding to
it as a fish unworthy of their consideration for culture.

A white perch of twelve inches will weigh nearly a
pound. I have taken them of this size in numbers in the
Chesapeake and **Delaware** Canal, which in its course occu-
pies a considerable **length** of an old mill-pond and St.
George's creek. These fish breed here in the coves, and
the canal no doubt receives fresh accessions from the Delaware through the locks* at Delaware City. South of

---

* **A** singular fact, I am credibly informed, is noticed here
every spring. **The** alewives, or herrings, as we term them, collect

Philadelphia as far as Savannah, white perch occupy an important place amongst "pan fish." They are hardy and prolific, and much better eating than the yellow or barred perch. **If they could be made to take** the place **of the latter in ponds or lakes where these** now abound, it would **be a great desideratum.**

THE CRAPPIE, so called by the habitans of French extraction in Missouri, and "Sac a lai" by the creoles of Louisiana, is the *Pomoxis hexacanthus* of Cuvier. This is one of the most beautiful percoids known. **It is found in** sluggish waters from the Carolinas southward on **the At-** lantic, **and in the** bayous and lakelets of the **Mississippi** Valley, from the **Gulf to** Minnesota. **An excellent en-** graving **and a full description of** it can be found in the "American Anglers' Book," p. 111. It exceeds some- what the white perch in **size. It** bites freely at a baited **hook, is** a good pan fish, and well **worthy, if** only for its beauty, of naturalization in the eastern states.

The BLACK BASS of **the Lakes (***Grystes nigricans***) has** been naturalized in many of the lakelets **of New** England and **New York,** and might be introduced in such waters further **south. These** fish, some years back, made their

---

in large numbers, apparently with the effort **of passing** through the **locks into the** canal. **It is said that a herring** fishery **might be** established here that would be worth some thousands **of dollars,** but for its interfering with the passage of the boats. **It may be** that some **of them pass through the** locks **and spawn in the canal,** and the fry pass **out,** thus keeping up this yearly crowd of appli- cants for admission.

18

way through the Erie Canal into the Hudson. They
appear to prefer the mouths of streams entering this river,
and are but seldom found in the tideway. Professor
Agnel, of West Point, about nine years since, procured a
stock of them from Saratoga Lake, and introduced them
into Wood Lake, a beautiful sheet of water some six miles
west of the Hudson. Here they thrive wonderfully, and
have been taken four or five pounds in weight. The Professor, who pitches his tent every summer by his pretty
lake, uses the artificial fly and his trout-rod exclusively in
taking them.—May his shadow never grow less, or the
bass refuse to rise to his red hackle !

On a preceding page I have given an extract, which
shows the progress the Cuttyhunk Club* had made towards

---

* The Cuttyhunk Club takes its name from the island where it has
been established ; the most westerly of the Elizabeth Islands, off
the coast of Massachusetts. It is about four or five miles long and
half as wide. This association was established here in 1864, its
originators being induced hither by the fine striped bass-fishing to
be found along the shores. Besides the trout and the black bass
pond, the club controls by lease of land and otherwise, the shoot-
ing on the island also. Originally there were twenty-five members,
the number has since been increased to sixty, and the capital of the
club to $25,000 ; each member contributing twenty dollars annually.

The commodious and comfortable hotel of the club, with ice house,
fine spring water, and other accessories, is near the beach, and
opposite some of the best stands for striped bass-fishing. A tariff
of hotel prices is fixed every season, and each member is allowed
to invite a friend who is *not a member*, to accompany him and partake of the sport. The club also, at their meeting in the month of

stocking their trout pond. The following is from the same letter:

"Our bass-pond of sixty acres, and twenty feet deep in some places, adjoins that intended to be occupied by the trout, and is separated from it, by a small embankment extending across a narrow neck of land, which, in low water, is sometimes dry. Early in the spring of 1866, we put into it twenty-nine large black bass, and as many more during the summer, to make the number exceed one hundred. We think those we put in early spawned the same season, as a numerous progeny (about one and a half inches long) were observed by the men who had charge of the pond. The young bass are readily distinguished from the perch, which had already occupied it. I can not say how large the bass have grown by this time. We shall restrict the fishing to the fly. As regards the perch, we have no apprehension of the injury they may do the bass, but have fears that those in the smaller pond will be destructive to the young trout. We shall therefore try to seine out the perch from the latter, during the coming summer. As we do not contemplate feeding the young trout after we put them in the pond, we will rear them in troughs until autumn, by which time, we hope they will be large enough to take care of themselves, and escape any perch that may be left after dragging the pond with the seine."

It will be seen by the foregoing, to what an extent the

May each year, occasionally extend special invitations to brethren of the angle. Wholesome regulations prevail, and good order characterizes the assemblage of the members.

artificial propagation of trout, and the naturalizing of bass
may be made to contribute to the sport of the angler.   In
a few years, a pond of sixty acres will afford abundant bass-
fishing, and one of nine acres a fair amount of trout-fishing.   As the angling in both will be subjected to wholesome restrictions, the ponds will not be depleted as those
have been, which are open to all fishers.   The example of
this club is worthy of the imitation of other associations of
the kind.

These fish have also been introduced into small artificial
ponds with much success.   A few days since (June 15th,
1868) I visited a friend in the neighborhood of Newburg,
N. Y., and found his pond, about three-eighths of an acre
in extent, well stocked with bass, which were a little over
a year old.   Although they did not rise well to the fly so
early in the season, we caught enough for a mess, and
found them in excellent condition.   These fish had grown
to the size of a half pound in about thirteen months.   The
margin of the pond was dotted with numerous broods of
this spring's fry.

The lake bass will grow to the extreme size of seven or
eight pounds, though four pounds is thought to be a large
fish; one and a half or two pounds may be considered a
good average.   They rise at an artificial fly in July and
August.   They generally come with a rush, and are taken
also by trolling with a gang of flies or with spinning spoon.
Crickets and minnows are used in fishing at the bottom,
which is generally done after the 1st of September.   When
hooked they leap high from the water, shaking their heads

to free themselves, and are plucky and die hard. The last
Massachusetts Fish Commissioners' Report says :—

"In 1850, Mr. Samuel T. Tisdale, of East Wareham,
succeeded, after much care, in bringing twenty-seven from
Saratoga Lake, alive, to his place, where he put them in
Flax Pond, close to his house. In 1851, and again in
1852, others were brought, and several of the neighboring ponds were stocked. The matter was kept secret, and
a 'jubilee' of five years given to the fish; at the end of
which time, they were found to have peopled these ponds,
and to have grown finely. So soon as this fact was known,
all the neighborhood at once gave its assiduous attention to
poaching, indignant that any one should be so aristocratic
as to try to furnish cheap food to the community. Their
efforts were so far successful as much to reduce the number of the fish.

"During May they come by pairs, and make a spawning-
bed on a sandy bottom in from four to six feet of water.
This they sweep with their tails after the manner of trout,
and the male remains on guard over the spawn, and drives
away the many intruders which hang about, greedy for
this savory food. In June, the young—recognisable by a
black band across the tail—are first observed, and these,
by autumn, have grown to a length of three to four inches.
At one year old, they weigh from $\frac{1}{4}$ to $\frac{1}{2}$ pound, and increase about $\frac{1}{2}$ pound yearly, till they arrive at 6 pounds,
according to food and water. They are in prime condition
in August and September, but in winter are black and lean.
The objection in certain cases to this species, is its great

18*   o

voraciousness. It destroys almost everything before it, except the perch, and even kills out pickerel by devouring the young. But in ponds already infested with pickerel and abounding in 'shiners,' it may be introduced with much profit, because it replaces bad fish by good. It should be carefully excluded, however, from all waters that contain trout, white fish or other valuable species, and from ponds *communicating* with such waters, for it is a most restless and pushing robber, eagerly searching and following the inlets and outlets of its pond. Of this propensity the Brookline reservoir gives the most curious instance. Nine black bass of 2½ to 3 pounds were put there in July, 1862. Since then, in the examination of the water-pipes leading from this reservoir to Long Pond, these fishes have been found in considerable numbers and of large size; and, moreover, either by their young or their eggs, they have penetrated the screen at the mouth of the pipe itself!* So these black bass, apparently impelled by no other feeling than that of restlessness, performed an underground journey of fifteen miles, in a brick aqueduct whose greatest diameter was six feet!" †

How easy it would be to introduce these bass into ponds where pike have exterminated the more valuable trout, or

---

* Communication from Mr. John H. Thorndike, President of the Water Board.

† Arrangements have been made with Mr. Tisdale to stock several other ponds, and the work is already begun. The best time to move the live fish is in the cool weather of late autumn or of early spring.

where only yellow perch, bull pouts, and worthless species are found. The latter would afford food for the new comers.

The BLACK BASS, of the West and South (*Grystes sal moides*). There are several varieties of this fish in the waters of the Atlantic states, from the Dismal Swamp and James river to Cape Florida. They abound also in the rivers and bayous communicating with the Gulf of Mexico on both sides of the Mississippi, and are found in all of the waters of the west, thence up to Minnesota with its numerous lakes. In the northern part of that state, lakes in close proximity are inhabited, one it may be with bass, and the other with white fish; the former discharging into the head-waters of the Mississippi, and the latter into streams flowing north towards Hudson's Bay. Occasionally, though, the white fish are found on the southern watershed.

This species is a more shapely fish than the bass of our northern lakes, resembling it, however, in its habits and its game qualities. The first figure on the engraving at the head of this chapter is a correct picture of this fish. The following account of its introduction into the Potomac was sent to me by my esteemed friend, Dr. Charles D. Meigs, of this city, two or three years ago :—

"About thirteen years since, a son of Mr. Stabler, at that time a conductor on the Baltimore and Ohio Railroad, having caught fifteen or twenty pounds of black bass in Wheeling creek, secured them in a bag-net, and, putting them into a locomotive tender's tank, carried them safely to Cumberland, and turned them into the Potomac, all of whose tributaries, down to the Great Falls, are now well stocked with them. They have multiplied exceedingly, and are said to grow to from six to eight pounds. M. desires me to tell you this. By this act of young Mr. Stabler, a region some 180 miles in length has been abundantly stocked with a large fish, good for food and sport."

Mr. Charles H. Wight, of Baltimore, who wrote me about three years ago in reference to stocking the Monocacy and Gunpowder rivers, in Maryland, with this fish, gave me the following score of catches on the Potomac in the summer of 1865 :—

2 rods. 8 hours' fishing, 125lbs. Largest fish 4¾lbs.
3 " 9 " " 326lbs. " " 5lbs. 10oz.

I infer, from Mr. Wight's letter, that they were taken with artificial flies in the neighborhood of Williamsport, above Harper's Ferry. It is said that this fish does not go below the Great Falls of the Potomac, which are about twenty-five miles above Washington. On the Gulf coast it is sometimes taken on the same feeding-grounds at the mouths of rivers, in company with the sheep's-head, attracted doubtless by the abundant supply of crustacea found there.

The different levels made by damming the Schuylkill from Reading down to Fairmount could be stocked with this valuable fish as easily, and in the same manner, as the Potomac was by Mr. Stabler. The Schuylkill is now destitute of any valuable species, except cat-fish; and our city authorities could have them transported from Pittsburgh or the Monongahela to the river bordering on Fairmount

Park, in the same way that they were taken from the Ohio to Cumberland. A prohibition to catching them for a few years would make them abundant, and afford angling where there is none at present.

The southern habitat of this bass makes it more susceptible of naturalization in this and states south of us, than the northern species would likely prove. They have been taken from the James river and naturalized in mill-ponds in the neighborhood of Fredericksburg and Warrenton, Va. In open, unshaded mill-ponds, they assume a brighter vesture than their ancestors had at the time of transplanting them. I have seen fish of four pounds taken that were quite silvery on their sides.

The small yellow-bellied bass, and the sun-fish (*Pomotis vulgaris*), should be introduced into ponds inhabited by the larger fresh-water bass, as they furnish an infinite source of amusement to juvenile anglers, and are well worthy of the frying-pan after the month of June. No species of bass, or of the perch family, however, should be put into waters where the more valuable species, as trout, white-fish, and salmon, are intended to be cultivated. The smaller perches are as destructive of the ova and fry of trout as the larger bass would doubtless prove to the young of white-fish and salmon.

SILURIDÆ.

This family includes the different catfishes, or bullpouts, as they are termed in the Eastern States. The larger species found in the western rivers grow to the size of a

hundred and fifty pounds. I have seen them cut trans-
versely into steaks and I have heard the music of the frying-pan, and have smelt them as they were fried, but never
had the curiosity to taste of them; they are coarse grained
and, it is said, are not palatable.

There is a species, the yellow catfish, found in ponds and
streams not communicating with tidal waters, as well as the
ditches and creeks which do. These are inferior to the
white or blue forked-tail catfish, whose more natural
habitat is tide and brackish water. The latter, however,
if prevented from their run to tidal rivers, become permanent above them, as they have in the Schuylkill above the
Fairmount dam. If these smaller species were not so common they would be more generally esteemed. These are
far better fish for the pan; their flesh is firm and sweet,
and resembles that of the trout or the breast of a young
chicken, more than the flesh of any other fish. "Catfish
and coffee," at the Falls of Schuylkill, was formerly, and,
to some extent, is still an "institution;" and a catfish
supper with et ceteras there, was a thing "not to be
sneezed at."

In Philadelphia they are a favorite dish. The shrill cry
of "buy any catfish," sometimes awakens the slumberer at
early morn; or the wife, or man of the house, or servant
returns from market with bunches of catfish, denuded and
beheaded. The "catties" are dipped in raw egg, rolled in
corn-meal or grated cracker, a few turns are given in the
fizzing, spitting lard of the well-heated frying-pan, and in a

trice they are served on hot plates with the accompaniment of coffee, and one's breakfast is complete.

Much of the gluten and fat which makes fish palatable, is between the skin and the flesh, and in the skin itself; thus any fish suffers in edibility by stripping it. There is a way of cooking catfish, which I think had its origin with the negroes in lower Virginia and Maryland; it is vastly superior to a chowder or a "cubrion." The fish are merely scraped as one would a trout, and not divested of heads or skins, and are stewed (not too much) with just enough water to cover them. Flitch of bacon with onions or pot-herbs are put in for seasoning, and unskimmed milk or cream is added when the dish is half cooked. Large white catfish, which sometimes grow to the size of two or three pounds, thus treated, are very fine.

Persons who have small ponds, or large either, if the water is too warm for trout, should by all means cultivate catfish. A pond of half an acre, or even of less size, if well stocked, will supply two or three messes a week for a good-sized family. These fish, though mostly herbivorous, will eat almost anything. A muddy or grassy pond is particularly adapted to them. Although they will take a small fish if presented as a bait, they are harmless to other species, and without detriment to either, can be put into ponds with bass.

In transporting catfish they should not be crowded, as they are apt to injure each other with their sharp spines. A better way, if the distance is not over a day's travel, is to saturate an old carpet, and lay it in the bottom of a

spring-wagon, then place on the carpet as many fish as it
will accommodate without finning each other. They should
then be covered with another carpet or blankets dripping
wet, on which is placed another layer of fish, and so on
until five hundred or even a thousand are so packed. For
the information of those who live near Philadelphia, I
would say, that an old man known as "Toney," and his
partner, young Krumbar, who live in the small street
nearest the Schuylkill between Race and Vine, and at the
corner of a court running towards the river, will supply
live catfish to those who want them. These men keep
them in live boxes and supply them at the moderate price
of a dollar and fifty cents per hundred.

The Acclimatization Society of England have gone to a
large expenditure of time, labor, and money to introduce
into their waters a large species (I believe the only one of
this family in Europe), *silurus glanis*, or Sheat fish, bringing it over land from the Argisch, a tributary of the
Danube, the distance of eighteen hundred miles. It is
said that this fish has attained the size of fifty-four pounds
in four years, and in extreme cases has weighed as much as
two hundred pounds. A drawing of this fish shows a wide
dissimilarity to our Siluroids; its fins having no sharp spines,
the dorsal, anal, and caudal being continuous and joining,
as is the case with the eel. Mr. Francis Francis, the
piscicultural director of the English Acclimatization Society, says : "One of the greatest wants felt in this country (England) has been a good pond or lake fish that
might be turned to actual account, in order that the huge

wastes of water with which our islands abound might be turned to actual account. This want the silurus seems likely to meet." The fish in question is described as savagely predatory; in view of which fact, and considering our smaller species of catfish the opposite, as well as excellent eating, and easily naturalized, I have suggested to Mr. Francis the benefit to be derived from its acclimation in such waters as the society he represents wishes to bring into use.

Mr. Francis was so taken with the idea that he communicated it to the " Field," which published the letter suggesting the introduction of the catfish. The matter has created some interest with those who are interested in the acclimatization of new species, and may lead to favorable results.

CYPRINIDÆ.

Of this family we have many native species, from the bulky Buffalo fish to the little roach and redfin of our small brooks; all of them are coarse or insipid, and in this country are eaten only when other fish cannot be had. In China, however, they are cultivated as they are in Germany. The English Carp; it is said, unless taken from lively rivers is not a good fish. What the carp of the Romans (who grew them to a prodigious size), was as to edibility, it is hard to infer. They doubtless considered them a luxury. After a long abstinence from piscine food, I have on some occasions partaken of broiled suckers with some relish when taken from cold streams.

19

ESOCIDÆ.

The various species of the pike family are not herbivorous, insectivorous, or omnivorous, but simply piscivorous,
subsisting entirely on fish with, perhaps, the exception of
an occasional frog.   If one wishes to exterminate the trout
of some pretty mountain lake or a pond let him introduce
any kind of pike.   " *Verbum sat.*"

CHAPTER VIII.

CULTURE OF EELS.

Probability of eels being of sufficient importance to be cultivated.—General remarks on eels.—Eel culture at Comacchio.

OWING to the rapid diminution and enhanced price of
the better kinds of fish, it is not improbable that eels may
at some future day be of sufficient importance to be cultivated. At present the prejudice existing against them on
account of their serpent-like form, and the, as yet, fair
supply of scale-fish in our markets, cause them to be under-
rated. In Europe they are thought worthy of cultivation,
as is attested by the extensive eel fisheries at Comacchio,
in Italy. In most Roman Catholic countries they form a
large portion of fish-food, which is necessarily consumed
on account of the many fast days. To those who can di-
vest themselves of prejudice, there are few more palatable
or more nutritious fishes than the eel.

As we have no occasion to refer to the family of lam-
preys (*Petromyzontidæ*), or the electric eels (*Gymnotidæ*),
we will take a cursory view of those which are generally
eaten (*Murænidæ*). These are so abundant in autumn, when
they are taken in all of our streams as they return to hy-
bernate in salt water, as not to be appreciated.

The eel at one time was considered hermaphrodite, because it is never found with spawn. After the fact was

established in natural history that no vertebrate animal could be hermaphrodite, it was thought, from the absence of spawn, to be viviparous; and a doubt still exists whether it is, or oviparous, as most fishes are. As it reproduces after its autumnal descent to salt water, it is not probable that the question will soon be decided. The ova, if it exists during its stay in fresh water, is so small that it has never been observed. There may be species of *Anguilla* inhabiting salt water exclusively, and others ascending fresh rivers in spring and returning in autumn. Or a large portion of one species may be migratory, and another portion live entirely in salt water.

The eel fry ascend the rivers of this latitude in April and May, and by fall have acquired a weight varying from a quarter to a half pound. Some remain permanently in fresh water, growing to a very large size, weighing even as much as ten pounds, and in some cases beyond that weight. These, it is reasonable to suppose, do not reproduce.

The following account of the eel fisheries at Comacchio, taken from the "Harvest of the Sea," is given for the novelty that such an enterprise would be in this country. It is suggestive of what might be done on suitable parts of our coast at some future day :—

"Long before the organization of the Dutch fisheries there existed a quaint colony of Italian fisher people on the borders of a more poetic water than the Zuyder Zee. I allude to the eel-breeders of Comacchio, on the Adriatic. This particular fishing industry is of very considerable antiquity, as we have well-authenticated statistics of its produce, extending back over three centuries. The lagoons of Comacchio afford a curious example of what may be done by design and labor. This place was at one time a great unproductive swamp, about one hundred and forty miles in circumference, accessible to the waves of the sea, where eels, leeches, and the other inhabitants of such watery regions, sported about unmolested by the hand of man; and its inhabitants—the descendants of those who first populated its various islands—isolated from the surrounding civilization, and devoid of ambition, have long been contented with their obscure lot, and have even remained to this day without establishing any direct communication with surrounding countries.

"The precise date at which the great lagoon of Comacchio was formed into a fish-pond is not known, but so early as the year 1229, the inhabitants of the place—a community of fishers as quaint, superstitious, and peculiar as those of Buckie, on the Moray Firth, or any other ancient Scottish fishing port—proclaimed Prince Azzo d'Este Lord of Comacchio; and from the time of this appointment the place grew in prosperity, and the fisheries from that date began to assume an organization and design which had not before that time been their characteristic. The waters of the lagoon were dyked out from those of the Adriatic, and a series of canals and pools were formed suitable for the requirements of the peculiar fishery carried on at the place, all of which operations were greatly facilitated by the Reno and Volano mouths of the Po, forming the side boundaries of the great swamp; and, as a chief feature of the place,

19 *

the marvellous fish labyrinth celebrated by Tasso still
exists. Without being technical, we may state that the
principal entrances to the various divisions of the great
pond—and it is divided into a great many stations—are
from the two rivers. A number of these entrances have
been constructed in the natural embankments which dyke
out the waters of the lagoon. Bridges have also been
built over all these trenches by the munificence of
various popes, and very strong flood-gates, worked by a
crank and screw, are attached to each, so as to regulate
the migration of the fish and the entrance and exit of the
waters. A very minute account of all the varied hydraulic
apparatus of Comacchio would only weary the reader; but
I may state generally, and I speak on the authority of M.
Coste, that these flood-gates place at the service of the fish-
cultivators about twenty currents, which allow the salt
waters of the lagoon to mingle with the fresh waters of the
river. Then, again, the waters of the Adriatic are admitted to the lagoon by means of the Grand Palotta Canal,
which extends from the port of Magnavacca right through
the great body of the waters, with branches stretching to
the chief fishing-stations which dot the surface of this
inland sea, so that there are about a hundred mouths
always ready to vomit into the lagoon the salt water of
the Adriatic.

"The entire industry of this unique place is founded on
a knowledge of the natural history of the particular fish
which is so largely cultivated there—viz., the eel. Being
a migratory fish, the eel is admirably adapted for cultiva-

tion, and being also very prolific and of tolerably rapid growth, it can be speedily turned into a source of great profit. About the end of the sixteenth century we know that the annual income derived from eel-breeding in the lagoons was close upon £12,000—a very large sum of money at that period. No recent statistics have been made public as to the money derived from the eels of Comacchio, but I have reason to know that the sum has not in any sense diminished during late years.

"The inhabitants of Comacchio seem to have a very correct idea of the natural history of this rather mysterious fish. They know exactly the time when the animal breeds, which, as well as the question how it breeds, has in Britain been long a source of controversy, as I have already shown; and these shrewd people know very well when the fry may be expected to leave the sea and perform their *montee*. They can measure the numbers, or rather estimate the quantity, of young fish as they ascend into the lagoon, and consequently are in a position to know what the produce will eventually be, as also the amount of food necessary to be provided, for the fish-farmers of Comacchio do not expect to fatten their animals out of nothing. However, they go about this in a very economic way, for the same water that grows the fish also grows the food on which they are fed. This is chiefly the aquadelle, a tiny little fish which is contained in the lakes in great numbers, and which, in its turn, finds food in the insect and vegetable world of the lagoons. Other fish are bred as well as the eel—viz., mullet, plaice, &c. On the 2d day of February the year

of Comacchio may be said to begin, for at that time the
montee commences, when may be seen ascending up the
Reno and Volano mouths of the Po from the Adriatic a
great series of wisps, apparently composed of threads, but
in reality young eels; and as soon as one lot enters, the rest,
with a sheeplike instinct, follow their leader, and hundreds
of thousands pass annually from the sea to the waters of the
lagoon, which can be so regulated as in places to be either
salt or fresh, as required. Various operations connected
with the working of the fisheries keep the people in employment from the time the entrance-sluices are closed, at
the end of April, till the commencement of the great harvest of eel-culture, which lasts from the beginning of
August till December."

CHAPTER IX.

CULTURE OF OYSTERS.

The Oyster.—An hermaphrodite.—Its fecundity.—*Its spawn* or "spat," and its manner of incubation.—Emission of the spat, and its destruction by marine animals —Importance of its finding something to fasten to.—Places favorable to its growth.—Transportation of seed oysters to the north.—Growth of the young oyster.—Chief object in the culture of oysters. *Oyster Culture* at Fusaro.—Its antiquity.—Its progress in France at the Bay of St. Brieuc and the Island of Rec.—English and French oysters.—Decrease of oysters in Eastern States.—Governor Wise's estimate of the area and value of oyster-beds in Virginia.

THE oyster being hermaphrodite, reproduces of itself. There are different opinions concerning its fecundity. Some writers state the number of young produced by a single oyster at half a million, others at three millions. As the produce of a large oyster is more numerous than a small one, either may approximate the truth.

On the coast of England the embryonic oysters, in mass, are termed "spat." The formation commences in the spring and through all "the months without an R," the spat is maturing or being ejected. This, like other bivalves, incubates its ova or seed within the folds of its mantle and leaflets of its lungs. The seed are contained in the mucous substance which we observe when they are in what is called the "milky state." This mass of spawn loses its

P

fluidity to a great extent as the time of its emission approaches, and is ejected for a considerable time during the summer. The spat comes forth like mist, and is dissipated at once; each little oyster, although a microscopic mite, perfect in itself. It rises to the surface at first, the same apparatus by which it attaches itself to anything at a later period now acting as a little float. After some hours, its specific gravity increasing, it gradually sinks, being carried in the mean time by wind and tide until an opportunity is afforded for attaching itself to something. In this interim it is devoured by fish and crustacea, and as it settles to the bottom by its own species and other molluscs.

Quiet creeks and bays, therefore, without strong tides, and protected from high winds by highlands or forests, are favorable to the preservation and permanent location of young oysters. To such places in the Chesapeake and other southern bays our northern oyster-growers resort for seed oysters, which they plant in favorable locations convenient to large cities where they are sold. I have seen a good-sized sloop or schooner, which had anchored at high tide on a bank of seed oysters in the Curratoma creek, on the Chesapeake, loaded in a day or two when she was left high and dry, by shovelling them in.

European writers say that the oyster commences to reproduce when it is three years old, it may earlier in our waters. The young on the coast of England when two weeks old are about the size of mustard seed; at three months old as large as peas; at five months the size of one's little finger nail; at eight months rather larger than the thumb nail; and at twelve months old the size of a silver half dollar.

In oyster culture, to arrest the drifting spat is the chief object; therefore, walls of stone or turf, hurdles of brush, faggots, and lines or enclosures of posts, are used for the purpose. When the natural drift does not bring the young oysters in contact with such appliances, mature oysters are laid so that their spat may lodge against or on them.

Fifteen years ago there was scarcely an oyster-bed of native growth in France, all having been so over-dredged as to exhaust them, when M. Coste, by direction of the government, set about restoring them and promoting their culture. In his investigations he visited Lake Fusaro. The oyster-beds here are of ancient celebrity. In past centuries the luxurious Italians built their villas by this lake to enjoy the salt-water bathing and partake of its bivalves. The Lucrine Lake, in its vicinity, is where Sergius Orata inaugurated oyster culture. At Fusaro the same mode of culture has prevailed since the time of that princely oysterman. The oysters are laid down on mounds of stone and the surrounding enclosures of posts arrest the spat. Faggots also are suspended for the same purpose from chains or strong ropes, which stretch from post to post in the lake.

Following this mode in France, the old oyster-beds in the Bay of St. Brieuc were renewed by laying down about three millions of mature oysters, and sinking faggots and constructing parallel banks. In less than six months the old shells on the beds and the faggots and banks were covered with minute oysters.

On the Island of Ree this improved mode of culture was commenced a year before Mr. Coste's experiments were under way in the Bay of St. Brieuc, and in 1864, according to Galignani's Messenger, seventy-two millions of oysters were produced, four thousand parks and claires being used in growing them. Seven thousand of the inhabitants, many of them coming from the interior of the island, were soon engaged in the occupation. The whole thing on the Island of Ree was initiated by a shrewd stone-mason, bearing the singular name of Beef. Enclosing a small portion of the shore with a rough dyke eighteen inches in height, and strewing some large stones over the area, he planted a few bushels of oysters. While attending to his proper avocation his little oyster farm was progressing, and he was able to sell thirty dollars worth of the young from his stock the first year. By doubling the size of his enclosure he doubled his sales the following season, and in four years his income from this source amounted to two hundred dollars. Of course his neighbors were not slow in profiting by his example. The consequence has been that the shore, productive in oysters many years ago, but which had become almost worthless from an accumulation of mud, was made to produce many fold beyond the yield it had given in its palmy days of old.

On the Island of Jersey and in many places along the English coast, where oysters had been grown for many years for the London and other large markets, they are now resorting to the same mode of securing the spat which the French have adopted. I have the disposition to pursue this subject, and would but for the limited space afforded. It will, however, be seen from this short notice of oyster culture that any person having command of a small portion of shore on salt water can not only grow oysters, but stock his beds and keep up a succession of crops without being under the necessity of procuring seed from a distance.

A young friend, with whom I was conversing a few evenings since, gave me an account of his visit to Lake Fusaro, where he had partaken of its oysters. To procure them a stake was pulled up by his attendant, and as many as he wanted taken off and the stake replaced. This lake is on classic ground, it is the Avernus of Virgil. It occupies the bed of an extinct volcano, and is a mile or so in extent. The youthful traveller alluded to, says that the French and English oysters are very small and insipid compared with ours, the size generally not larger than a Spanish dollar. That the larger ones are generally coppery in taste. That the average size is small is evident from their computing fifteen hundred to a bushel; or, as Mr. Francis Francis lately remarked in a letter, "six to the mouthful."

Most persons have observed the aptness of the young oyster to cling to anything with which they come in contact. The wharves of some of the cities of our southern seaboard, or walls standing in the water, are frequently covered. So also are logs and brush, and even the pendant

20

boughs of trees. These, however, are generally worthless. The oyster must be furnished on its beds with the food required to secure flavor and fatness. Many of the dwellers on the brackish waters of the south have their family oyster-beds; a place where fresh water enters is preferred.

Our cultivation of oysters has extended no further than planting them in favorable locations, some of which are known for the rapid growth they give, others for the fine flavor they impart to the oyster. Many of our fine oyster-beds in Long Island Sound and to the eastward have been exhausted, but as yet there is not much apprehension of the supply being short of the demand. Henry A. Wise, Esq., when governor of Virginia, in one of his messages, estimated the area of oyster-beds in that state at 1,680,000 acres, containing about 784,000,000 of bushels. In proposing a tax of three cents on each bushel taken, he estimated the revenue from that source at $480,000. If the waters of the state of Virginia contain 784,000,000 of bushels, what must be the total produce of all of our states bordering on the Atlantic and Gulf of Mexico?

TROUTDALE SPRING.

APPENDIX.

I.

NATURAL FOOD OF TROUT.

THE following, by Mr. Francis Francis, on the natural food of trout in ponds, lakes, and streams, offers some valuable suggestions to those who have preserved waters:—

"There is not an insect or small reptile that inhabits the soil beneath us, the air above us, or the waters around us, that is not food for fishes in a greater or less degree. Worms of all kinds, flies of all kinds, grubs and larvæ of all kinds, cockchafers, crickets, leeches, snails, humble-bees, young birds, mice, rats, frogs, beetles, all serve the turn of one fish or another, and so in turn help to produce food for man. Black beetles, for example, often looked on as a nuisance in houses, are caviare to the trout; and I have seen two or three trout devour a panful of them with the greatest avidity. Nay, I have seen a wary old six-pound stream trout, that had been tempted with every conceivable variety of bait, succumb to the temptation of a black beetle. Small frogs, just emerged from tadpoleism, they rejoice in exceedingly; and I have even seen them take young toads, though some do repudiate the taste on the trout's part. Nothing living comes amiss, but doubtless some kinds of food agree with them far better than others. But we know very little on this branch of the

subject.   It is dreamland to us, with a very little ascertained waking reality.   What do we know even of the
various breeds of the same species of fish, save the bare
fact of their existence?   What do we know of the food
and conditions most favorable to them?   Consider the
trout.   Can any fish display greater diversity or variety
of size and value than trout?   And how do we account
for it?

"Trout in one stream will be much larger, firmer, redder, and better shaped than in others.   This may, in a
measure, be owing to *the greater abundance* of food; but I
have every reason to believe that it proceeds quite as much
from the kind of food that they are enabled to obtain.   In
some rivers and lakes we find the trout large, handsome,
red, and vigorous fish; in others, we find them small and
meagre; nay, even in the same lake the fish will be influenced in a strange way by locality, so much so that the
very breed even appears to be different.   It would seem
difficult to account for this peculiarity upon any other
hypothesis than that of food and the nature of the water
and soil around them, and yet the fish appear to be a
totally different breed; and it certainly appears possible
that the character of the fish may have changed by degrees, through successive generations, and owing to being
bred and fed in a different manner from the other fish.   I
have placed trout from one stream into another, and after
years could very easily distinguish them from their com-
peers of the stream.   But it is doubtful if their progeny
would show and retain their special characteristics, though
if they interbreed with the fish of the stream, as they
would be pretty sure to, the breed might possibly be improved by the infusion of fresh blood.

"Few experiments of any note have been tried in the
feeding of fish, this being as yet almost untrodden ground;

but I once heard of an experiment being tried in the following manner: Equal numbers of trout were confined for a certain time by gratings to three several portions of the same stream. The fish in one of the divisions were fed entirely upon flies; in another, upon minnows; and in the third, upon worms. At the end of a certain period, those which had been fed on flies were the heaviest and in the best condition; those fed on minnows occupied the second place; while those fed on worms were in much the worst order of the three. The probability is, that had another pen been set off, and the fish fed with a mixture of all three species of food, the fish in it would have far exceeded any of the others in weight and condition.

"Some rivers notoriously produce larger trout than others, although the character of the soil they flow through may to all appearance be very similar. I will instance two, both of which are tributaries of the Thames—the Chess, a branch of the Buckinghamshire Colne; and the Wick, a little stream running through High Wycombe. I select these two streams, because they are only some ten or twelve miles from each other, and because they are as nearly as possible of a size. Now, it is generally supposed that the very best and most fattening food provided by Nature for the trout is the may-fly, or green-drake. This fly abounds in profusion on the Chess; it is rarely if ever seen on the Wick—in fact, it may be said not to exist there. The minnow, likewise supposed to be most excellent and nourishing food for the trout, is also a stranger to the Wick; or if it exists there, is not found in any considerable number. Sticklebacks and miller's thumbs are found in places, though they do not abound in all parts of the stream. The caddis, or case grub of the smaller flies, however, is very abundant; and in some of the hatch-holes there are a considerable quantity of leeches.

20 *

"On the Chess a trout of two pounds would be a very fine one, the fish averaging from half a pound to a pound and a quarter. On the Wick it would be an ordinary fish; indeed, they are not considered fair takeable fish under a pound and a half. They are often caught of four and five pounds, and I have known them to run up to seven or eight or even ten pounds; and this in a small stream, little more than a good-sized brook, is a most astonishing size; for not only do these fish acquire this unusual weight, but they arrive at it very rapidly indeed. I have had many opportunities of knowing how they will increase under favorable circumstances, as one of the fisheries on the stream belonging to a friend of mine was on one or two occasions almost destroyed by bleach and tar water—some forty or fifty brace of fish being all that were saved : none of them were over two pounds, and yet, in two years, many of them had grown to six and seven pounds' weight.*

"Taking the Wycombe fish as a breed, I may say that they are the heaviest and thickest fish, for their length, it has ever been my lot to see; while the color of the flesh of a good fish, instead of the ordinary pale pink of a really well-conditioned trout, is often of a deep red, much redder, indeed, than that of salmon. On the other hand, the Chess fish are not particularly handsome, shapely, or well colored. Here is a point well worthy the consideration of those who wish to take up the science of pisciculture. What particular species of food can it be which not only makes up for the total absence of the may-fly and minnow, but so feeds the fish in this admirable little stream, that there is no river, large or small, which I have ever seen in all Eng-

---

* Since this was written, I regret to say that again have the whole of his fish been destroyed by filth sent down from above.—F. F., 1864.

land, can for its size equal it in production? What, then, can be the particular food that fattens them so rapidly?

"My own impression is, that the fresh-water gammari, or pulex, to which I have previously referred, have not a little to do with it, for these insects abound in this stream even to profusion—to a greater extent, indeed, than I have ever found them in any other brook. The trout feed upon them voraciously; and it is a very common thing to find in the trout a mass of these insects, half digested, and as large as a filbert. I have seen the trout picking them off the walls, which pen the stream in some places, as rapidly as a child would pick blackberries from a hedge; and I am induced to think that this insect has, as I have said, much to do with the fineness of the fish; and the more so, because, wherever I have found it to exist in any quantity, I have invariably observed that the trout are of fine size, and in unusually good condition.*

---

* "These insects of course thrive better in sluggish than in rapid water, though they do well enough in either when there are weeds. They are peculiarly well adapted for lakes; and were I owner of a lake, I would leave no stone unturned to introduce them in large numbers. They feed upon almost anything, and are the scavengers of the water. They are very fond of the large fresh-water mussel, and destroy and eat them in large numbers. These, which are easily introduced, should be as food for the trout food. Where the streams are too rapid for the plentiful production of the gammari, it would be by no means a bad plan to make here and there (where the situation of the soil and the banks suited such a plan) small shallow ponds, supplied with water by means of a small pipe, and having an exit to the stream. In these the requisite kind of weeds might be planted, a stock of these little insects turned in, and some kind of offal or other food occasionally being cast to them, and the insects left to thrive and increase. They would of their own accord make their way into the stream, where they would afford excellent food for the trout. Other kinds of insects might be also placed in such food-breeding ponds, where they might propagate and multiply

"In lakes, also, it is a very common thing to find the trout in one lake large, bright, and well fed, and in another, very similar in appearance, and perhaps only a bare half-mile distant from the other, they will be long, black, and lean, with heads out of all proportion to the thickness of the body. In another, probably but a similar distance from the first two, the trout will be abundant, but very small, though bright and well colored. These varieties, I have every reason to believe, are caused partly by a difference of water, produced by the absence or presence of certain plants, these of course giving a difference of food. To exemplify this : I remember some years since, while fishing in a wild part of Donegal, near the little village of Ardara, coming upon a cluster of small lakes. The trout in some of these lakes were small, bright, and very plentiful; in others, they were of a good size, but not handsome. But in one of the lakes, a small one—a mere pool, of perhaps a couple or three acres in extent—my attendant informed me that the trout, though of a dark color, owing to the peat color and depth of the water, were large and well-shaped, and of good flavor, often running up to five and six, and even seven or eight pounds' weight. But the lake was what is termed among anglers 'a sulky lake,' that is, the fish very rarely rose well at the fly, and probably it might be fished a dozen times without producing a single fish, though there were times and days, if the angler chanced to hit upon them, when very good fishing might be had, and when the lake appeared alive with fish. I fished the pool, however, and had the good fortune, by sinking the fly, to take one

---

in safety. By such a method as this almost any amount of the food best suited to the trout might no doubt easily be produced. *For if we increase the stock of fish, we must, of course, if their size and weight is to be kept up, grow food for them somehow*, and this seems not to be a very difficult plan."

of the trout, a strong, well-shaped fish, though somewhat
dark in color, and of two pounds' weight. We also caught
specimens of the fish in the other lakes, and the difference
between the fish I have already mentioned. While fishing
the small lake I accidentally allowed my fly to sink to the
bottom, and on pulling it up again with some difficulty I
brought up a large piece of a thick moss-like green weed,
with which the bottom of the pool appeared to abound.
On examining this weed more closely, I found it swarming
with a variety of insects, chiefly water-snails, the small
crustacea that inhabit fresh water, and large quantities
of the caddis of some considerable fly. The abundance of
food thus found at the bottom of the lake fully accounted
not only for the large size and good condition of the fish,
but also for its being a sulky lake, or for the trout not paying much attention to the flies upon the surface of the
water. For they had no difficulty in procuring any quantity of food they needed at the bottom, without swimming
hither and thither to seek it, or giving themselves the
trouble to come to the top. Colonel Whyte also mentioned
a fact somewhat of this nature, some time since, in the
' Field.' He related, that wishing to improve the size and
condition of his fish in a small lake, he cast into it a bushel
of the small crustacea, which are often found on water-
weeds. These increased rapidily, and as they did so his
trout increased in size and improved in condition wonderfully; but it is also fair to say, that they became much
shyer of rising to the fly. Probably the reason why the
fish sometimes rise well to flies, and not at others, in lakes
like those of Donegal (which are by no means few), is
owing to the fact that the abundance of caddis at the bottom may be undergoing some transformation, into flies perhaps, which ascend rapidly to the top of the water, and the
trout are thus led in pursuit of them to the top of the water,

where the insects rest, and are easily captured. If anglers, being aware of this fact, made some little study of entomology, so far as to know about the time when these insects undergo their transformations, they might not be induced to seek such lakes so often in vain. In the instance I have noted the lake is deep, and the water dark; and the fish at the bottom, engaged with ground food, do not see the flies at the top.

"In the great Irish lakes, as Lough Erne, Lough Arrow, the Westmeath lakes, and others, the large trout which inhabit these lakes never come to the surface in any number, save at the rise of the may-fly. In a good fly season they rise with great freedom, and wonderful takes are made; at other times they can only, save at rare intervals, be picked up by spinning. Of course I am not referring to the small things that get on the shallows, but to the sly old fellows who scorn a midge-fly. On the Thames, also, the large Thames trout are always more upon the rise and on the lookout for flies when the big stone-fly (which is a perfect monster on the Thames), puts in an appearance in April, or when the few green drakes that are found in it show themselves. It is not to be supposed that these large fish will take notice of anything but large flies, because it would take myriads of the smaller ones to make a meal for them; and therefore it should be the aim of the pisciculturist to increase, by every means in his power, by the importation of larvæ, &c., the larger flies, if he desires to improve the fly-fishing in any lake or river.

"Again, I will instance the fish in Loch Leven, which grow to a fine size, and are almost always in superb condition. The bottom of the lake, in places, is grown over with a peculiar weed; in this is found a great variety of insects, chiefly crustacea, as small snails of various sorts: the lake also abounds in the more minute entomostraceæ.

Large quantities of both are often found in the stomachs of the trout when taken. Here sport with the fly is generally good, because the **lake is** shallow and clear, and the fish see the **fly well. In other** lakes again, where these **species of weeds, which form the** harbor and subsistence **of these insects, are wanting, it will usually be** found that **the trout** are small, or, if large, **ill-fed and meagre. I know also** a **small lake in** Wales, where the fish never take **a fly** until after dark, when fish from two to three pounds' weight (an unusual size for Wales) may be taken. This lake abounds in leeches, and the trout are very fine in it. A quarter of a mile off is a similar lake, in which trout do not thrive **at** all, and, indeed, are seldom found; while about a mile **from it are one or two small** lakes, in which the trout **do not average three ounces. And yet the char-**acter **of the lakes, and the soil in and about all of** them, **are apparently** precisely similar.

"Yet one more instance I must select, to show the changeable **and contrary habits** of fish. In a large mill-pool, belonging to a friend at Alton, are some wonderfully fine trout, the trout running from two to twelve pounds. To take trout of five and six pounds with the fly, and to **hook them** of even larger size, **is not at all uncommon.** Last season (the summer of '64) I took four fish in two evenings, which together weighed close upon seventeen pounds, and magnificent fish they were. Yet the fish in the stream that feeds the pool seldom get beyond two pounds, or thereabouts, in weight; of course there is a great deal of food in the pool, mainly consisting of water-snails and sticklebacks. **Some** years the fish run very freely at the minnow, and do not notice the fly much, but **in other years the minnow is at a** discount, and the fly at a premium. I have never seen any very large flies in the pool, yet the flies the fish take are usually large palmers—

like nothing, I should think, which they can be in the habit of seeing. This case differs entirely from any I have remarked elsewhere, and it is to me as yet, I confess, a piscatorial puzzle. A close analysis of the contents of the pond, as concerns insects and weeds, would no doubt throw some light on this interesting fact, which I hope some day to be able to make, as it appears to combine the best sport and the largest fish—which is precisely the point we desire to arrive at.

"It cannot be doubted that the condition and size of trout, as well as other fish, depend almost wholly upon the supply of food, and I think I have shown that the particular kinds of food are also a great desideratum. Now, it being known that particular kinds of weed are favorable to the production of certain species of insects, what can be easier—when the soil is favorable to such a measure—than to transplant a sufficient quantity of these weeds, and the larvæ of the insects which will almost always be found to abound in them, from one lake and from one stream to another? For example, with respect to the gammari so often noted, what could be easier than to transplant weed? This would serve as food for the large fresh-water mussel found in almost all waters, and it would serve as food for the gammari, which in turn would serve as food for the fishes. It may be said, with regard to some lakes and streams, that they are so gravelly and rocky, that the weeds would hardly thrive in them; but it is seldom indeed that some nooks and corners do not exist, in or about the banks of lakes and streams, where there may be found sufficient soil, which, with a slight admixture of the natural soil, and a judicious planting of these weeds, may not be made to grow them to some small extent; and the weeds, once introduced, will gradually increase year by year, forming their own soil, and naturally producing those requsites which are the most

favorable to their production. Of course judgment must
be exercised in carrying out such experiments, quite as
much as would be exercised in the introduction or cultivation of a new food-producing plant in agriculture. We
acclimatize every species of agricultural plant, and examine
its qualities and capabilities, for cattle, or for ourselves;
we study the soil and manure suited to it, &c., &c.; we
have shows and prizes for the best specimens of agricultural productions, and thousands of persons assemble to note
and study them; but who ever thinks of acclimatizing an
apparently worthless water-weed?"

II.

MESSRS. MARTIN AND GILLONE'S SYSTEM OF HATCHING AND REARING YOUNG SALMON.*

In addition to the group of salmon-breeding ponds at
Stormontfield, a very successful suite of breeding-boxes has
been laid down on the river Dee, in the Stewartry of Kirk-
cudbright, by Messrs. Martin and Gillone, the lessees of
the river Dee salmon-fisheries. Mr. Gillone, who is an
adept in the art of fish culture, was one of the earliest to
experiment on the salmon, and so long ago as 1830 had
arrived at the conclusion that parr were young salmon, and
that that tiny animal changed at a given period into a
smolt, and in time became a valuable table-fish. These
early experiments of Mr. Gillone's were not in any sense
commercial; they were conducted solely with a view to
solve what was then a curious problem in salmon-growth.
In later years Mr. Gillone and his partner have entered
upon salmon breeding as an adjunct of their fisheries on
the river Dee, for which, as tacksmen, they pay a rental of

---

* From the "Harvest of the Sea."

21   Q

upwards of £1200 per annum. The breeding-boxes of Messrs. Martin and Gillone have been fitted up on a very picturesque part of the river at Tongueland, and the number of eggs last brought to maturity is considerably over 100,000. The présent series of hatchings for commercial purposes was begun in 1862–3 with 25,000 eggs, followed in the succeeding year by a laying down of nearly double that number. The hatchings of these seasons were very unsuccessful, the loss from many causes being very great, for the manipulation of fish eggs during the time of their artificial extraction and impregnation requires great care— a little maladroitness being sufficient to spoil thousands.

The last hatching (spring 1865) has been most successfully dealt with. Messrs. Martin and Gillone's breeding-boxes are all under cover, being placed in a large lumber store connected with a biscuit manufactory. This chamber is seventy feet long, and there is a double row of boxes extending the whole length of the place. These receptacles for the eggs are made of wood; they are three feet long, one foot wide, and four inches deep, and into the whole series a range of frames has been fitted containing glass troughs on which to lay the eggs. The edges of the glass are ground off, and they are fitted angularly *across the current* in the shape of a V. The eggs are laid down on, or rather sown into, these troughs, from a store bottle, on to which is fitted a tapering funnel. The flow of water, which is derived from the river, and is filtered to prevent the admission of any impurity, is very gentle, being at the rate of about fifteen feet per minute, and is kept perfectly regular. The boxes are all fitted with lids, in order to prevent the eggs from being devoured, as is often done, by rats and other vermin, and also to assimilate the conditions of artificial hatching as much as possible to those of the natural breeding-beds—where, of course, the eggs are

covered up with gravel and are hatched in comparative
darkness.

It may be of some use, particularly to those who are
interested in pisciculture, to note a few details connected
with the capturing of the gravid fish and the plan of
exuding the ova practised at Tongueland. The river Dee
is tolerably well stocked with fish, as may be surmised from
the rent I have named as being paid for the right of fishing. Mr. Gillone adopts the plan, now also in use at Stormontfield, of capturing his fish in good time—in fact, as a
general rule, before the eggs are ripe—and of confining
them in his mill-race till they are thoroughly ready for
manipulation. Last season—*i. e.*, in November and December 1864, and January 1865—as many as thirty-six
female fish were taken for their roe, the number of milters
being twenty-five, the total weight of the lot being 454 lbs.,
or, on the average, six and a half pounds each fish. According to rule, the weight of the female fish taken having
been 283 lbs., these ought to have yielded 283,000 eggs,
but as several of the fish were about ripe at the time they
were caught, they spawned naturally in the mill-race,
where the eggs in due time came to life. The plan of
spawning pursued at Tongueland is as follows:—Whenever
the fish are supposed to be ripe for that process, the water
is shut out of the dam, and the animal is first placed in a
box filled with water in order to its examination; if ready
to be operated upon, it is then transferred to a trough filled
with water about three feet and a half long, seven inches
in breadth, and of corresponding depth, and the roe or
milt is pressed out of the fish just in the position in which
it swims. As soon as the eggs are secured, a portion of
the water is poured out of the wooden vessel, and the male
fish is then similarly treated. The milt and roe are mixed

by hand stirring, and the eggs then being washed are distributed into the boxes.

Mr. Gillone carries on all his operations with the
greatest possible precision. He has a large clear glass
bottle marked off in divisions, each of which contains 800
eggs, and he numbers the divisions allotted to each particular fish, which are sown into a similarly numbered
division in his box, so that by referring to his index-book
he can trace out any peculiarity in the eggs, etc.

III.

CULTURE OF CARP.*

In ancient times there used to be immense ponds filled
with carp in Prussia, Saxony, Bohemia, Mecklenburg, and
Holstein, and the fish was bred and brought to market with
as much regularity as if it had been a fruit or a vegetable.
The carp yields its spawn in great quantities, no fewer than
700,000 eggs having been found in a fish of moderate
weight (ten pounds); and, being a hardy fish, it is easily
cultivated, so that it would be profitable to breed in ponds
for the fishmarkets of populous places, and the fish-sales-
men assure us that there would be a large demand for good
fresh carp. It is necessary, according to the best authorities, to have the ponds in suites of three—viz., a spawn-
ing-pond, a nursery, and a receptacle for the large fish—
and to regulate the numbers of breeding fish according to
the surface of water. It is not my intention to go minutely
into the construction of carp-ponds; but I may be allowed
to say that it is always best to select such a spot for their
site as will give the engineer as little trouble as possible.

---

* From the "Harvest of the Sea."

Twelve acres of water divided into three parts would allow a splendid series of ponds—the first to be three acres in extent, the second an acre more, and the third to be five acres; and here it may be again observed that, with water as with land, a given space can only yield a given amount of produce, therefore the ponds must not be overstocked with brood. Two hundred carp, twenty tench, and twenty jack per acre is an ample stock to begin breeding with. A very profitable annual return would be obtained from these twelve acres of water; and, as many country gentlemen have even larger sheets than twelve acres, I recommend this plan of stocking them with carp to their attention. There is only the expense of construction to look to, as an under-keeper or gardener could do all that was necessary in looking after the fish. A gentleman having a large estate in Saxony, on which were situated no less than twenty ponds, some of them as large as twenty-seven acres, found that his stock of fish added greatly to his income. Some of the carp weighed fifty pounds each, and upon the occasion of draining one of his ponds, a supply of fish weighing five thousand pounds was taken out; and for good carp it would be no exaggeration to say that six pence per pound weight could easily be obtained, which, for a quantity like that of this Saxon gentleman, would amount to the sum of £125 sterling.

IV.

DISCOVERY OF ARTIFICIAL FECUNDATION BY JACOBI.[*]

In 1763, Jacobi, a lieutenant in the small principality of Lippe-Detmoldt, first announced, in the pages of the "Hannover Magazin," a periodical published in the town

---

[*] From Agricultural Report, 1866. By Theodore Gill, M. D.

21 *

indicated by its title, the results of experiments, conducted for about thirty years, on the artificial fecundation of the salmon and trout, and this memoir, in its entirety or in abstracts, was published in Berlin and Paris, and the discovery directly communicated to several of the prominent naturalists of the day, especially Buffon. Jacobi even received from the English government a pension, in appreciation of the importance of his discovery. Artificial fecundation, soon afterwards practised on a larger scale at Noterlem, also in the kingdom of Hanover, yielded favorable results. Jacobi having recognised the nature of the sexual relations of the fishes, and that the female, when spawning, was followed by the male, who dropped his milt over the ova of his companion, and thus fertilized them, inferred that nature may be imitated and assisted by man. He therefore took a clean wooden bucket or shallow tub, and emptied into it a pint of clear water. Taking then a female salmon whose ova were mature, he expressed them by a gentle pressure of the hand down the abdomen, and treated a male fish in the same manner, discharging his milt over the ova.

The ova, thus fertilized, were then placed in a box made for the purpose, and which is thus described by Jacobi, as translated by Fry :—

"The box may be constructed of any suitable size : for example, eleven feet long, a foot and a half wide, and six inches high. At one extremity should be left an opening six inches square, covered by a grating of iron or brass wire, the wires not being more than four lines apart. At the other extremity, on the side of the box, should be made a similar opening, six inches wide by four inches high, similarly grated. This one will serve for the escape of the water, the other for its entrance, and the grating will prevent water-rats or any destructive insects from reaching the eggs. The top of the box should be closely shut for the same reason; but a grated opening, similar to the rest, six inches square, may be left to give light to the young fish. This, however, is not absolutely necessary.

"A suitable place should then be chosen for the box near a rivulet, or what is still better, near a pond supplied with running water, from which may be drawn, by a little canal, a stream, say an inch thick, which should be made to pass continually through the gratings and through the box.

"Lastly, the bottom of the box, to the thickness of an inch, should be covered with sand or gravel, and over this should be spread a bed of stones of the size of nuts or acorns; thus will be made a little artificial brook running over a gravelly bottom."

The fecundated eggs are spread " in one of the boxes so placed, and the water of the little rivulet passes over them, care being taken that it does not run with such rapidity as to displace and carry away with it the eggs, for it is necessary they should remain undisturbed between the pebbles."

"Care must be taken to remove, from time to time, the dirt which is carried by the water and deposited on these eggs; this can be done by stirring about the water with a quill feather."

Using such precautions, and profiting by the experience gained in the course of his experiments, Jacobi perfectly succeeded in his attempts, and to him belongs, unquestionably, the merit of first artificially fecundating the eggs of fishes, or at least, the first publication of the principles of the art and of the results which would logically flow from it.

V.

ARTIFICIAL SPAWNING-BEDS.*

While artificial fecundation apparently fulfils the chief requisites for the propagation of some fishes, such as the salmonids, there are others for which it cannot be employed with equal advantage. Nature has, in such cases, been assisted by the preparation of places suitable for the deposit of the ova and milt of the fishes which it is desired to propagate, and by the preparation for such of beds which will be instinctively resorted to by them. This practice has been especially employed in France, and has been very recently advocated by the celebrated academician, M. E. Blanchard, professor at the museum of natural history, &c., in an excellent work on the fresh-water fishes of France. The obvious advantages resulting from the exposition of an author's own words, induce the writer to submit a translation from M. Blanchard's work :—

"In view of the present condition of the rivers and canals of France, the idea of artificial spawning-beds would appear to be a most happy one. M. Millet, before the Society of Acclimatization, has insisted, with great earnestness, on the preference to be given, in many cases, to artificial spawning-beds over artificial fecundation. M. Coste has justly remarked that artificial fecundation is not all-sufficient, and yet a contrary opinion is generally prevalent. No one has forgotten the marvellous results which we were to obtain by means of artificial fecundation ; fishes, left to themselves, could not thrive and have a numerous progeny. Their duties should be assumed by us, and the advantages would be incalculable. More than fifteen years have elapsed since

---

* From Agricultural Report, 1866.

these seductive announcements were made, without having yet furnished brillant results.

" Among fishes, some, as the salmon, deposit their ova in slight excavations, in gravel, or in the interstices between stones; others, as the perches, and cyprinids (carp, bream, roach, &c.), attach their ova, agglutinated together by means of a viscid matter, to aquatic plants, stones, or any bodies to which their eggs can be fixed. It is especially for the last that artificial spawning-beds might sometimes be advantageously prepared.

" The construction of an artificial spawning-bed is a very simple matter. A framework of sticks or laths should be made, and to such framework, boughs, furze, and aquatic plants should be fastened by cords, in such a way as to form irregular structures. It is also easy to give to structures of this kind a circular form, by taking hoops for frameworks. The form, and especially the size to be given to these spawning-beds, would necessarily vary, according to the character or the size of the body of water in which they are to be immersed. They should be held to the bottom of the water by stones, and fastened to a stake or post on the bank. When kept in place in this way they can be easily drawn out of the water, if it becomes necessary to do so.

" It will be readily understood that these artificial spawning-beds will be especially serviceable in those streams and canals which are so clear as to be devoid of any natural spawning-beds.

" For the salmonids, which spawn on a gravelly bottom, and whose ova remain free, artificial spawning-places are very simple and readily prepared. It is only requisite to cover in certain places the beds of rather shallow and rapid streams, near the bank or the bottom of rivulets, with a thick layer of gravel or pebbles, and to prepare slight excavations or furrows, like those made by the salmon or trout, to deposit their eggs in.   M. Millet also recommends that small heaps of pebbles should be raised at the edges of these furrows.   By means of these contrivances, trout, especially, would often be attracted, and be content to stop and spawn in places which they would not otherwise frequent, and where it would be convenient to keep them.'

VI.

THE GOURAMI.—ITS HABITAT, OR NATIVE COUNTRY.*

Among foreign fishes, none has excited so much interest, in an economical point of view, or has been the subject of so many attempts at acclimatization among the French, as the celebrated gourami—the *Osphromenus gourami* of naturalists.†   A somewhat extended notice of its peculiarities and relations to other fishes, its habits, and of the attempts made to acclimatize it in France and her colonies will, therefore, doubtless be acceptable.

The native home of the gourami is the fresh waters of the Malaccan islands—Java, Madura, Sumatra, and Borneo; and from the inhabitants of those islands we derive the name as well as the fish itself.‡   It has been attributed as a native to China, but erroneously.   It has been introduced into China, however, as well as into Pinang, Malacca, Mauritius, Reunion or Bourbon, Martinique, and Cayenne.   The gourami attains a very large size, and, reaches, *it is said*, five or even six feet in length, and a

---

* From Agricultural Report, 1866. By Theodore Gill, M. D.

† This species is also known as the *Osphromenus olfax*, but the prior name is that here adopted.

‡ The proper pronunciation would be best indicated by *gurahmee*.

P

weight of more than 110 pounds. It may be readily understood, however, that it attains these large dimensions only under very favorable circumstances, and fish of 20 pounds' weight are not very common.

The gourami belongs to a family of fishes which has always provoked interest by the singular adaptations for holding supplies of water in peculiar reservoirs or organs developed from the first of the gill arches, and which has obtained for the family the name of fishes with labyrinthiform "pharyngeals," or *Labyrinthici*. Like other bony fishes, the gourami and its kindred have four cartilaginous arches, and each of these bears on the external or convex edge a gill which is double, or composed of two leaflets; behind these arches are two somewhat flattened bones, contiguous at their internal edges, and bearing minute teeth, called the lower pharyngeal bones, and above, connected with the ends of the posterior gill arches, are other flat teeth-bearing bones, known as the upper pharyngeals—these, too, are shared with most fishes; but, in addition to these, a peculiar superbranchial organ is developed from the third or terminal portion, or articulation of the first branchial or gill arch; this organ is composed of thin, more or less expanded laminæ, or leaflets, which form more or less complicated chambers or cavities. These chambers receive and contain a supply of water which furnishes sufficient to moisten the gills and enable them to perform their functions of aerating the blood long after the fish has been isolated from the water; this structure is also associated with contracted branchial apertures or gill-holes, while the gill-covers are closely appressed to the shoulders, and the fish is thus enabled still better to eke out its supply of water. As a consequence of this beneficent provision, we find that the fishes of this family are enabled, in an extraordinary degree, to sustain deprivation of water, and that some at least can leave the waters, or the places now dried up which they have inhabited, and travel on land for some distance, to seek more favorable resorts. It is to this family that the celebrated climbing fish of the East Indies (*Anabas scandens*) belongs; and to this same family equally belongs the *Pla Kat* of Siam (*Betta pugnax*), which is raised by the Siamese for game purposes, individuals of the species being pitted against each other, and fighting with as much vim and animosity as their warm-blooded rivals, the game-cocks. Still another species (the *Macropodus viridi auratus*) is said to be reared for ornamental purposes by the Chinese, like the goldfish, and its beauty is sufficient to entitle it to such a distinction.

In form these fishes somewhat resemble the Centrachids, or sunfishes, of our streams and ponds. They differ extremely among themselves in the development of the fins; this is especially the case with respect to the dorsal or back fin, for in some it occupies the whole length of the back, while in others, as the *Pla Kat*, it is confined to a short space near the middle; the anal and ventral fins are little less variable, but it would lead us too far to detail such modifications.

Characteristics.—The gourami may be said, in general terms, to somewhat resemble a rock-bass or sunfish, but having a smaller head and a still smaller mouth comparatively, a very long anal fin reaching from the breast nearly to the base of the caudal fin, and the ventral fins inserted nearly on a line with the pectoral, the first soft ray being very long, lash-like, and almost or quite equalling the whole length of the fish. There are from eleven to thirteen spines, and an equal number of soft, jointed rays in the dorsal fin, while the anal has from nine to twelve spines, and from nineteen to twenty-one soft rays; the ventral fin has a spine and five rays, the first of which is the elongated one already referred to; the others are short and small. The color of the old is a nearly uniform dark olive green or brown, **but** the young is ornamented by seven **to** nine slightly **oblique blackish bands** crossing the body; at the **base of the pectoral fin** there is a distinct black spot, **and another roundish** spot exists on the side of the caudal **peduncle in front of** the fin and above the **lateral line.** The **jaws are** armed with a band of fine teeth; **the roof of the** mouth is smooth.

The gourami, in its native country, has always been esteemed for the delicacy of its flesh, and Commerson, the traveller, to whom we are indebted for our first precise description of the fish, has in rapture exclaimed that he never tasted, among **either salt or fresh water** fishes, **one more ex-**quisite in **flavor than the gourami**—"*nihil inter pisces tum marinos tum fluviatiles exquisitius unquam degustavi.*" In such esteem is it held, that the Dutch colonists at Batavia **are said to** keep them in very large earthen jars, removing **the water** daily, and feeding it with aquatic plants **or** herbs, **and** especially the one called *Pistia natans,* a species belonging to the *Araceæ* or Arum family.

In a state of **freedom, the gourami** lives, **by preference, in warm, still, or** stagnant and somewhat muddy waters. It **it very sensitive** to changes of temperature, and **even in** the island of Bourbon **retreats in the winter toward the** bottom of the ponds where the water is warmest, and bury-**ing itself in the mud, if** present, seems to remain in a torpid state while the cold **lasts.** The greatest heat appar-**ently** does not incommode **it, and in** summer it ascends to **the surface of the water, basking** in the sun, and, often **protruding its mouth above the water,** swallows the atmo-spheric **air.**

While the gourami **is** essentially a vegetarian, and its diet is indicated, by the extremely elongated intestinal

22

canal, which is many times folded on itself, it does not confine itself to any special plants, nor, indeed, to the vegetable kingdom, for its supply of food, and on account of its miscellaneous feeding has obtained from the French the epithet of *water pig*, or *Porc des rivières*. Besides the leaves of the *Pistia*, already mentioned, and all other species of araceæ which it seeks with avidity, it will eat cabbage, radish, carrot, turnip and beet leaves, lettuce, and most of the wild plants which grow in the water, nor does it refuse earth-worms, frogs, or even cooked meats.

In its movements, the gourami is usually slow, swimming leisurely and majestically along, and takes its time in making its meal; it is, however, capable of rapid movements, and when frightened or disturbed, will dart away with great swiftness; when first confined in narrow quarters, it will also attempt to escape by leaping out of the water. It will take the hook baited with worms.

In its sexual relations, and the care which it takes of its eggs, it somewhat resembles the sunfishes of temperate North America and the Cichlids of the warmer portions of the continent and of Africa. In spawning-time, the males and females pair, and each pair select a suitable place and construct a rude nest. "Like all intelligent animals, it will only propagate when it is insured a suitable temperature for its eggs and young—a fit retreat wherein to build its nest, with vegetation and mud to make it, and the aquatic plants suitable for the food of the young. The bottom must be muddy, and the depth variable; in one place at least a yard, or metre, and convenient to it, several metres deep. It prefers to make its nest in tufts of the grass called *Panicum jumentorum*, which grow on the surface of the water, and whose floating roots, which rise and fall with the tide, form natural galleries, under which the fish may conceal itself." In one of the corners of the ponds, among the plants which grow there, the gourami attaches a spherical nest, composed of plants and mud, and resembling in form those of certain birds.

Each nest is about fourteen centimetres, or between five and six inches in length; the male and female labor assidously in its construction, and continue their toils till it is completed. In five or six days, or a week at furthest, it is finished. This aptitude of the gourami to make a nest is facilitated, when the pairing-season has arrived, by placing in the water, almost at the surface, a large branch of bamboo (*Bambusa arundinacea*, Wild.), to which are attached bundles of fine dog's-tooth grass. The gourami takes this grass and forms with it its nest in the branches of the submerged bamboo, in the same way that the silk-worm avails itself of the branch which is presented for it to make its nest on. Toward the end of the months of September and of March, in the island of Bourbon, propagation takes place. The nest made, the female deposits its eggs, of which there from about 800 to 1000. After the eggs have been deposited, and while they are becoming matured, the parents remain near the nest, prepared to drive away intruders.

The eggs are soon hatched, and the young then find in their nest "a refuge where they are free from a thousand dangers which would threaten them for the first days of their life. Besides, they find in the macerated vegetable matter, which partly composes their nest, their earliest food, and which is most suitable for their delicate condition. Soon afterwards they make short excursions from the nest under the guidance of the mother fish, who is prepared to give them aid in case of need. They do not disperse, but keep together in bands. The young still retain the yelk-bags, which trail behind like two long appendages from below the anterior portion of the belly, and seem to assist them in maintaining their equilibrium."

The rate of growth is not rapid, and at the age of three years, the fish is only about nine inches, or twenty-two centimetres, long; but at that age it is said to be able to propagate its race. Those kept in vases or small ponds are still slower in their growth, which is even arrested at a comparatively small size. The small fishes are most esteemed as food. Their flesh, it may be added, is firm, and of a pale straw or yellowish color.

Attempts to acclimatize the gourami.—In such esteem has this fish been held that none, save the goldfish, has been the subject of more exertions to acclimatize in different countries, and if we literally accept the word *exertion*, even the goldfish cannot be excepted, for, although it is true that that species has been more generally introduced into foreign waters, little or no exertion seems to have been necessary to effect that object. The history of the attempts and success in the acclimatization of the gourami may not only be useful with reference to eventual efforts to introduce it into the United States, but the experience gained may be of advantage in the treatment of others. A somewhat extended narrative, compiled from the writings of Cuvier, Rufz de Lavison, Auguste Vinson, and others, is therefore submitted.

As already remarked, the gourami is now found in southern China, but has been probably introduced into that country, although the date and circumstances of its acclimatization are unknown to us. It has likewise been introduced into some of the islands of the same archipelago and near those of which it is a native. But the history of its introduction into the dominions of the French in different quarters of the world is better known and of greater interest.

The first effort on the part of the French of which we have knowledge was made in 1761, when several naval officers—chief of whom were **Captains De** Surville, Joannis, and De Magny—took **some fishes to the Isle** of France or Mauritius, **but, it is said, rather for the gratification of the** sight and **for** exhibition in vases than with reference **to its eventual naturalization in the island.** M. **De Céré, who has** been accredited with the introduction of the goldfish **into** France, and who was at the time mentioned commander of the French troops in the island, also interested himself in the introduction of the species. Individual fish placed in ponds propagated; some escaped into the contiguous streams, and **the species had become already domiciliated** in the **island when Commerson, the naturalist traveller, visited it in 1770.**

The gourami was next introduced into the neighboring island of Bourbon or Reunion in 1795, at first through the efforts of M. Desmaniéres, a resident of the island, and who imported specimens from Mauritius; but his example was soon followed by others. His experience has been given by Mr. Vinson, and, on account of its important bearing on the subject of its acclimatization in other **lands, is repeated** in his own words. M. Desmaniéres had, "**on his estate of** Bellevue, situated **on the upland of the quarter** Sainte-Suzanne, a magnificent natural body of water with two islets abounding in aquatic plants. Everything appeared to be propitious for the raising of the gourami, **but** the low temperature of this part of the island had not **been taken into** consideration. The fishes **lived, but did not propagate.** M. Desmaniéres **at first thought that the large size** of the pond **might be the cause of this, and he had** made **two vivaria, which may** yet be seen, and which were supplied by the large pond. **In these vivaria** the gouramis were **placed, but the** result was no more **fortunate.** He

22 *   R

received from the **Isle of** France additional fishes, but still had no success. Finally, having **transferred his** fishes into **a** vivarium near the seashore, he succeeded in inducing propagation. This experiment had, however, taken thirty **years, and during this** time, success in propagating the **species in** the island **had become** despaired of. As has been **seen,** acclimatization often depends on causes **very** simple in appearance, but which are **only discovered after** a long time. **Since the period named, the fish has** been **widely spread** through the island," and is now abundant.

The next earnest attempt **to introduce the species into a** distant country was made at **the instance of M.** Moreau de Jonnes, who, in 1818, induced the "minister of marine" of France to order the transportation of specimens to the French possessions **in the** West Indies. Accordingly, in April, 1819, a hundred small fishes were intrusted to the care of M. De Mackau, captain of a store-ship—Le Golo— **and** the interest and zealous care manifested by that officer **were** rewarded by the comparatively slight loss of only twenty-three fishes during the entire voyage to the West Indies; and when **it is** recalled that a slight blow, an **abra-** sion of the sides, or loss of a scale may cause death, and the difficulty of adjusting the supply of fresh water, &c., to their necessities **is** taken into consideration, the small per- centage of **the lost must** be considered as remarkable. **Of the seventy-seven** which remained alive, twenty-six **were** distributed **to the** islands of Martinique **and** Guade- loupe severally, and twenty-five to the colony of Cayenne. The fortunes of the strangers in their new places of abode were various. Cuvier and Valenciennes, in the seventh **volume** of their "Histoire Naturelle des Poissons," pub- **lished in** 1831, acknowledge the reception of one of the fishes originally taken from Isle-de-France to Cayenne. The belief that their acclimatization in America had suc-

ceeded has even found utterance in the statement as a fact
which has obtained currency in several publications. Although the fishes introduced continued to live, none seemed
to be fruitful in their new quarters, and there is no published evidence that any individuals of the species are now
living in America. We have the fullest and most authen-
tic details concerning its fate in Martinique.

The little fishes, on their arrival at Martinique, were
placed in a large basin of fresh water; the largest of them
was only about three French inches long. Some months
after, they were transferred to a small pond in the botanic
garden of Saint Pierre; all were still alive and healthy,
and had attained a length of from ten to twelve inches.
Their subsequent increase was, however, much less rapid,
and nearly six years were required to little more than
double that length, for in 1827 the largest had only gained
a length of from twenty-four to twenty-seven inches. The
subsequent rate of increase was still less rapid, as might
naturally be supposed; and the last survivor of the original
twenty-six, which was served on the table in 1846, twenty-
seven years after its arrival at Martinique, measured about
a metre or somewhat more than thirty-nine inches in
length. None of these fishes had been able to propagate
their race in the island during all this time. Five years
after their introduction, a formal announcement was, indeed, made that numerous young gourami had made their
appearance in two broods, at intervals of only six months,
but it was soon discovered that the supposed young gourami
were native fishes that had gained entrance into the preserves of the gourami. The sudden revulsion from the
hope and high expectations to which the apparent success
had given rise, to chagrin and despair, unhappily reacted
on the poor fishes, and was doubtless enhanced by the ridi-
cule which the exposure of the nature of the discovery

entailed on the historian of that discovery, and which en-
gendered a proverbial expression in the island. The prospect of propagating the gourami appearing hopeless, one
after another was caught and served up on the table of the
governor when a distinguished guest was to be entertained,
and thus was the last disposed of in 1846. Although
equally full details have not been published concerning
those introduced into Guadeloupe and Cayenne, no greater
success appears to have rewarded the attempts to propagate the species. As to the latter, it has recently been
stated that the fish known as connani is the same as the
gourami, and occurs abundantly in the rivers of Guiana,
but the connani is evidently an entirely different fish, and
even a member of a very distinct family.

Repeated attempts have been made in recent years to
introduce the gourami into France, Algiers, and Egypt,
but the fishes have either died on their way to their respective destinations, or have survived for but a short time
their introduction into the new waters; a sudden diminution of the temperature has proved disastrous in its results
to them, and the greatest care and precaution are necessary
to protect them from the changes of the weather. The
last attempt to introduce the gourami into France which
has come to the knowledge of the compiler was made in
the spring of 1865. Nineteen young fishes, in a glass
vase, were consigned to the steamer running between
Mauritius and Suez, which left the former place on the
20th of March. All survived the perils of the voyage as
far as Alexandria; but on the route from that place to
Marseilles, where a comparatively low and unequal temperature prevailed, eight of them died. Of the eleven that
arrived in safety, one other died the following night; but
the fate of the rest has not been recorded in the French
periodicals yet received at Washington.

Eleven young gouramis were also safely transported, in the autumn of 1864, from the island of Mauritius to Algeria, but their fate is likewise unknown. Attempts have been made to introduce the species into Egypt; but the results, so far as known, have not proved favorable.

The interest excited in the gourami, and the attempts to acclimatize it, have not been confined to the French. The English settlers of Australia and Tasmania have endeavored to introduce the species into their waters, and individuals have survived the voyage to those distant countries. At Victoria, Melbourne, and Hobartstown, there are acclimatization societies which have undertaken the introduction, into their respective districts, of desirable plants and animals; and of the fishes, the gourami has been one of the most sought for. Individuals of that species were secured for Victoria, through the exertions of a merchant of the town, but the history of the undertaking is unknown. At Melbourne, after unsuccessful efforts, the Society of Acclimatization finally received, from Mauritius, eighteen living fish, out of a total of thirty that were embarked for that place. No accessible record exists of its introduction into Tasmania.

The impracticability of naturalizing it in cold *countries.* —Such is the history of the more prominent attempts to introduce the gourami into foreign waters. The narrative will readily demonstrate that its acclimatization in even warm temperate countries is by no means easy; and the natural inference, resulting from a study of the fate of those efforts, is that it will be useless to attempt its domiciliation in countries where the temperature in winter is sufficiently low to allow ice to form on the streams. If, therefore, it is desired to introduce the fish in the American waters, the attempt must be made in the Southern States, and in warm or protected pools or ponds. It will be doubtful whether it can be propagated even there at first, and the habits of the species must be still more closely studied in order to ascertain why it should have proven sterile in the West Indian islands and Cayenne. It cannot have been on account of want of sufficient heat, for the mean temperature is not very different from that of Mauritius; nor can it be due to the difference in time of the seasons, for the species has been successfully acclimatized in China, which is north of the tropics, as well as in Mauritius and Reunion. The cause of sterility is, therefore, at present inexplicable; but when it is known, it may perhaps be counteracted. It would appear to be extremely doubtful whether the species can be introduced and reared in France; but yet it must be remembered that so eminently experienced and scientific a man as M. Coste, the academician, has pronounced the opinion that it can be effected, and he has published instructions to guide those to whom carriage of specimens may be intrusted. Possibly by persistence of effort, and by selection of hardy individuals for stock, success may eventually be attained; and if such can be had for France, there seems to be no reason why like fortune should not be expected in the United States, as far north as the latitude of Virginia. Doubtless, the fish would be a very valuable acquisition if it could be reared, and the more so as it is herbivorous, while the most esteemed fishes, found in the more temperate regions of the United States, are more or less carnivorous.

Rules for transportation and introduction.—As to the introduction, it would, probably, be more readily effected by the transportation of nests with the ova, than by that of the fishes themselves, and such a course would at least require less care and attention, and would have the additional advantage of furnishing so many more individuals to select from. If, for any reasons, it is preferred to experiment with the young, the smallest should be chosen, and they should be placed in wooden or earthenware vessels; the latter would be preferable, and those having a capacity of from ten to fifteen gallons would perhaps be best, but tubs or casks, when perfectly clean, may be used. The receptacle, whatever it may be, should be suspended, in order to avoid the disturbance of its contents by the incessant rolling of the vessel, such motion being prejudicial to the welfare of the fishes. The fishes should also be fed, and a supply of suitable plants should, therefore, accompany them. I may conclude with a translation of the specific instructions of M. Coste, from whom, indeed, I have derived the hints above offered :—

" 1. Very young fishes should be selected.

" 2. These fishes should be distributed among several receptacles.

" 3. Care should be taken not to crowd too many together in one receptacle.

" 4. The water should be renewed partially or entirely whenever it becomes necessary

" 5. It should also be aerated from time to time.

" 6. The fishes should be fed whenever they shall seem to require it.

" 7. The remains from the food which has been given to the fishes should be carefully taken up from the bottom of the receptacle, and removed within eight hours after feeding; the dejections and other impurities which would injure the water should also be removed.

" 8. Finally, the several receptacles should be kept in different places, and under various conditions."

VII.

COLD SPRING TROUT-PONDS.

The following account of these ponds, and matters connected with them, has been written out by the proprietor, Rev. Livingston Stone, at my own request, for this book. It was not until I had completed the chapters on trout-breeding, that I received any communication from Mr. Stone. Having occasion to write him in regard to the salmon ova placed under his charge by the New Hampshire Fish Commission, I found from his letters in reply, that his establishment was more extensive, and embraced the cultivation of a greater variety, than I had supposed. It will be seen that he fully endorses in its many bearings, all that I have said as to the importance of fish culture. His remarks on the necessity, when one rears them in large numbers, of having young trout in a defined space where they can be fed and attended to, in substance, correspond with the directions I have given. Though neither of us was aware of the other having engaged in this line of business, we have from similar experience and experiments, arrived at the same conclusions on the most important points connected with it. Mr. Stone's rearing-box, a model of which he sent me a few weeks since, is the most complete contrivance of the kind I have seen, and is particularly adapted to the wants of those who wish to raise a few thousand young trout. With the accompanying directions, the proper requisites, and with ordinary care, one can scarcely go wrong.

The Cold Spring Trout Ponds are situated in Charlestown, N. H., which is a town on the Connecticut river, about 40 miles north of the Massachusetts line. The ponds and hatching-works are built on two streams, the smaller of which, with a hatching capacity of about five millions, is used chiefly for hatching purposes. On the larger stream are the spawning-beds and the ponds for the breeding trout. The hatching-houses are located at the head of the smaller stream, just where the springs issue from the ground. The springs are peculiarly well adapted to their purpose, being very large and of even temperature, standing at about 47° Fahrenheit from the first of December to the first of May. As is the case with other springs running at a considerable depth below the surface, they are a trifle warmer on the first of December than on the first of May. The success which has been met with in these hatching-works is of the most encouraging kind. In some of the most favorably situated boxes, containing trout spawn, the loss was almost nothing, hardly three per cent., while in the salmon beds it was even less, being under one per cent.

The whole amount hatched this season was between one hundred and fifty thousand, and two hundred thousand trout, and ninety-nine per cent. of the impregnated salmon eggs deposited here by the New Hampshire Commissioners. The water, however, on this stream is rather too cold for growing trout well, so after they are hatched and begin to feed, they are taken down to the larger stream, also fed by perennial springs, but warmer in the summer, where they are kept in rearing-boxes until winter. There is now a large stock of breeders on this stream, which will be increased by the next spawning season to thirty thousand, some of them varying from a half a pound in weight, to a

23

pound and upwards. It is expected that a very large supply of spawn will be taken from them this fall.

There is connected with the Cold Spring Ponds, a farm of five hundred or six hundred acres, situate on a spur of Monadnock Mountain, sixteen hundred feet above the level of the sea. Through this farm, runs one of the finest streams for growing trout that can be found in New England. It is the outlet of Monadnock Lake; famous for the extraordinary clearness of its waters, and the superior size and quality of its trout, and not being exposed to freshets, but supplied wholly by springs, it never rises nor falls the year round. This last circumstance makes the stream a safe one for trout growing, while its great size makes it capable of sustaining an almost unlimited stock of fish. The object of having this place connected with the Cold Spring Ponds at Charlestown, is to try the experiment on a large scale of raising trout as an article of food. All the conditions here are favorable to the experiment, and no pains will be spared to give it a fair trial. If trout cannot be raised here successfully on a large scale, it seems safe to say that they cannot be raised anywhere successfully. There is a small stock of fifty thousand trout on the stream at present, which it is hoped will be increased by an addition each spring of a quarter of a million and upwards. They will be kept till the first of December in rearing-boxes, when they will be transferred to ponds built for them. More than usual interest is felt in this branch of the establishment, from the fact that no attempt to raise trout in large numbers from the eggs, has ever yet succeeded. Here let us say a word about the use of a rearing-box in growing trout. It is the firm conviction of the writer, that a rearing-box is indispensable to the culture of trout in large numbers. As all know, who have had any experience in raising trout—when the young fry are thrown promiscuously into a pond, there is an inexplicable but constant waste going on all the time, and the greater the number of fish, compared with the size of the pond, the greater the waste becomes. Then, again, the streams which are generally **used** for growing trout are too small to supply *natural* food to any large number of fish, while **at the same time the ponds built on them, are too large to** allow of systematic artificial feeding. The consequence is that the young trout above a certain numerical limit die of starvation. It is therefore very desirable—indispensable we may say—to confine them where the waste just mentioned may be prevented or at least observed and accounted for, and where they can be held well in **hand,** for the purposes of artificial feeding. **It** is with these objects in view that the **rearing-box is constructed,** and it is thought that **it will revolutionize the system of trout** raising, as from **60 to** 80 per cent. of young fry can now be raised, even **when** millions are experimented with, while by the old method of pond growing, it was difficult to rear any considerable percentage in so limited a number even as ten thousand. The rearing-box now in use at the Cold Spring Ponds, seems to combine all the requisite points, and **is** recommended to all, who prefer to adopt this method **of** rearing trout or salmon.

Another branch of the Cold Spring Ponds is the black bass department. The stock of black bass breeders at the ponds is not extensive, but large numbers of this fish have been caught, and are now confined in **ponds in the state** of New York, and in the **northern part of** Vermont, for use during the spawning **season, which contrary to the usual statements in books, is for that latitude,** during the **month of June, instead of April and May.*** From these

---

* **In the chapter** on naturalization, **I** mentioned **the** size of bass **at a year old in a pond** near Newburgh, **and remarked** also that I

spawners a large number of ova will be taken, and transferred to the beds at Charlestown to be hatched; but as
bass hatching has not yet been reduced to a science like
trout and salmon hatching, no such results are expected as
have been obtained with these latter named fish. The
hatching-beds for the bass are built on the lower stream
of the Cold Spring Ponds, the other being too cold in the
summer to answer the purpose.

There is still another branch of this fish-breeding establishment, and without doubt the most important one, viz.;
the salmon breeding ponds on the Miramichi river in New
Brunswick. Here a salmon fishery has been secured, and
everything put under way, for carrying on large salmon-
breeding works, on the same principle but on a larger scale
as the trout-breeding ponds at Charlestown. A large
quantity of salmon ova and young salmon will be taken
here this fall, and it is hoped that those who are interested
in restocking the American rivers with salmon, will not be
slow to avail themselves of this opportunity of obtaining
the ova or young fish.

It is very gratifying to see the daily increasing interest
in the community, in having our barren and profitless
streams and ponds replenished with fish. People seem to
be waking up to a sense of the value of water, as a food-
producing agent, and all are beginning to understand, that
in our lakes and rivers are to be found a source of revenue,
too promising to be neglected. Indeed a fish-raising fever

---

saw numerous fry of this season near the margin of the pond. These
young fish were not less than an inch long on the 12th of June, and
consequently must have come from spawn deposited the latter part
of April or in May. I do not mention this fact in opposition to the
above remark, that bass spawn in June in New Hampshire; a few
degrees of latitude will make a great difference in the time of fish
that spawn in the spring or early summer.—T. N.

is springing up in this country, and people are as eager to procure fish to rear, as ever they were to obtain fancy stock in sheep, or horses, or poultry. This fever will have its rise, culmination and **decline without doubt** like others similar, but **unless the signs of the present are very delusive**, its *results* **will be of a vastly more important** and substantial.

Suppose for instance that the original conditions favorable to the existence of salmon and shad, were restored in **a river** like the Hudson. Who can estimate the immense value which that river would assume in three or four years? Millions of dollars would hardly buy the millions of fish that could be taken from its waters.

There is nothing **to prevent these** original conditions being **restored in many at least of our rivers.** The food of **the salmon and shad is** found in the sea. Here they get their **growth and vigor, and until** the illimitable stores of the sea begin to fail in their supply of food, there will exist no necessary obstacles to the restoration of their former fruitfulness to our great rivers. It is the same in our lakes and ponds. Where a mere bagatelle of sunfish, and pouts,* and small perch are now caught, thousands of dollars worth of black **bass** might be reared. It **is hoped that all who** have the time and opportunity **will spare no pains to do** their part in replenishing the waters which lie within their reach. The fish-raising fever may have a similar run to **many others, but it is one** which every one should encourage, inasmuch as in its consequences, **it will** react in the most beneficial manner upon all members of the community, **both rich** and poor, but especially upon the poor.

The great desideratum which is now sought, is, to bring fish **culture out of** the province of mere fancy work, where

---

* Catfish.

23 *

it is only the amusement and recreation of a few wealthy
men, and to make it an every-day practical thing with every
one who has the water facilities for engaging in it. What
we want, is, to have poor men earn their living or a part
of their living by fish culture.   If this end can be reached,
then the new fish-raising movement, is worthy the attention
and encouragement of every public-spirited man.

All that is needed to effect this end, in the opinion of
the writer, is, care, study, and perseverance in the work.
Nature supplies, in the countless numbers of ova in fish,
boundless resources to start from.   All that man has to do,
is to provide the conditions requisite to avail himself of
nature's vast supplies.   It seems as if he might do this, as
yet no insuperable obstacle has presented itself.   Everything conspires to confirm the most ardent faith in favorable results.   Let every one who is interested in this movement give what time and effort he can spare, and in less
time than we suppose, a complete revolution may be effected
in our American waters, and our barren rivers and profitless ponds be made the repositories of great wealth.

The Salmon for the Connecticut River.—The salmon
spawn sent to the Cold Spring Trout Ponds by the N. H.
Commissioners in the fall of 1867 to be hatched for the
Connecticut river, arrived at their destination on the evening of the 22d of November.   They were taken in the
Miramichi river, on the 10th, 18th and 22d of October, by
Dr. Fletcher, of Concord, N. H., by whom they were carefully packed in wet moss, enclosed in champagne baskets.
On their arrival at Charlestown they were unpacked as
speedily as possible, and after being thoroughly separated
from the moss, were deposited in the hatching-beds prepared for them.   Large, round, plump, and of a beautiful
salmon color, they looked very prettily resting on the clean
gravel, in the clear running water.   But a·more gratifying

sight still, was the egg by itself, when held up to the light
and examined; for there within the thin transparent shell,
could be seen the curled body of the young embryo, and
the two distinct black specks which were to be its eyes.
It turned out, however, that only about twenty-five per cent.
of the ova were impregnated. This, however, experience
has shown to be as large a percentage as could be expected
from fish caught with a spear, as Dr. Fletcher was obliged
to take them. The unimpregnated eggs gradually became
opaque and were removed from the beds, although some
remained unturned long after the good eggs were hatched,
and could be clearly seen then, as all along previously, to
be perfectly empty. The impregnated eggs did remarkably
well; almost all of them lived, and hatched considerably
over ninety-nine per cent. The newly hatched salmon
were very lively, and the loss by death, while the yolk
sac remained, was very small, even less than when in the
egg state. After the sac disappeared there was a slight
mortality among the young fish for a few days. Since
then they have been very healthy, and are now doing finely.
They were transferred, a short time after becoming fully
formed fish, from the hatching-beds to the rearing-box of
the Cold Spring Ponds, where they are still kept.

It is the plan of the commissioners to have them retained
and reared artificially, until they are ready to go to the sea,
which will be next spring for one-half of them, and the
succeeding spring for the other half.

The number which was obtained this year for the Connecticut river, is wholly inadequate to the requirements of
a river of such magnitude, and the movement made this
year for stocking it with salmon, is to be regarded as
experimental merely. The few thousand smolts that come
from this batch of eggs will hardly be heard from again
in so large a river, but it is hoped that hereafter when the

plans for the purpose become more matured, the young salmon will be put in the river by the hundred thousand instead of by the thousand. Then we shall without doubt have returns, which well correspond in some more adequate measure to the great opportunities which are presented to us.*

VIII.

CLOVE SPRING TROUT PONDS.

Mr. Christie takes his supply from two springs of unvarying temperature, discharging seven hundred gallons a minute. They are situated on the brow of a pretty hill, shaded by fine old oaks and wide-spreading sugar maples, about twenty-five feet above the level of the meadow below. Although flowing through strata of limestone, the water is of the kind termed "soft." Before the door of the dwelling-house he is erecting in the grove, and on the slope of the hill, stretch the two larger ponds parallel with each other, and divided by embankments ten feet wide. The upper, which he calls pond No. 2, is about two hundred and twenty-five feet long by twenty wide, the depth averaging something over four feet. The lower, which is pond No. 3, is of the same length, thirty feet wide, and varying in depth from five to twelve feet. Each pond has an outlet in the bottom to draw it off, should it be necessary to do so at any future time.

---

* A short time after the salmon began to be hatched at the Cold Spring Ponds, they received a visit from Theodore Lyman, Esq., the secretary of the New England commissioners, who carried specimens of the embryos of both eggs and young fry to Prof. Agassiz, by whom very accurate drawings were taken of the embryos in different stages of development. The eggs and young fish themselves were preserved in alcohol, and can now be seen on the shelves of the Museum of Comparative Zoology at Cambridge.

The smaller of the two springs which is five feet higher up the hill than the larger, is led off to one side to supply the hatching-house and nursery. After which the water unites with that from the large spring, and flows through two rearing-races into pond No. 1, and then through spawning-races into ponds No. 2 and No. 3. The young trout are kept from the time they leave the nursery and rearing-races until they are about twenty-one months old in pond No. 1. After this age they are to occupy pond No. 2 for a year, and then pond No. 3, from which they are to be taken for market.

The hatching-house, forty-four feet long and sixteen feet wide, occupies, in part, an excavation made in the side of the hill, and extends out on a sloping lawn.

The fall from the upper spring is sufficient to allow of the hatching-troughs being elevated three feet above the level of the floor. Thereby saving a great deal of laborious stooping during the hatching-season. The nurseries or rearing-troughs are also elevated, and discharge by miniature fish-ways into the rearing-races supplying pond No. 1, which extends on the lawn between the hatching-house and No. 2. The hatching-house is planned for eight troughs, each thirty-two feet long, in case he should require as many. Each trough being divided into twenty nests, and each nest holding four or five thousand eggs, he will be able, if he should find sale for them, to lay down from six to eight hundred thousand eggs every season.

In the meadow below and in full view from his dwelling-house, Mr. Christie will have a pond or miniature lake of six or eight acres, into which he will discharge all his trout from pond No. 3 that may be unsold at the end of each season, as well as the young fish he may not find sale for. Here, by the time the pond is stocked there will be a great deal of natural food. He will introduce chub, shiners, killies and other harmless species, to increase the amount of food. This pond he will keep as a preserve for angling.

The hatching-house and ponds are in accordance with plans furnished by the writer; the former having been enlarged and improved in some of its details by the owner.

Mr. Christie commenced his ponds in the summer of 1867; not being completed in time, he erected a temporary hatching-house last fall, and succeeded, with the assistance of the writer, beyond his anticipations; having no place for his young fish, he sold them in the neighborhood, and supplied persons at a distance with eggs. Out of eight thousand sold to Mr. Comfort, on the Norristown railroad, only seven or eight imperfect eggs were found on delivery. He has a goodly supply at present, and by the spawning-season, has a fair prospect of increasing his number of brood-trout to three thousand. He has offers from persons in his neighborhood, who have facility for rearing trout, but none for hatching them, to take his surplus fry and grow them for market, each party to participate in the profits. His address is P. H. Christie, Clove, Dutchess county, New York.

IX.

CULTIVATION OF FUR-BEARING ANIMALS.

Since fish culture has been introduced in this country, many persons have become convinced that the high price which the finer furs command, will justify the domestication of animals from which they are taken. A fine mink skin, for instance, will bring from six to ten dollars when sold to the furrier. As this newer branch of industry is attracting some attention, I may appropriately give the following from a Montreal paper.

BREEDING THE MINK.

CASADAGA, Chautauqua Co., N. Y., Jan. 21.

"I have just availed myself of an opportunity to fulfil your desire that I should visit the 'Minkery' at this place, concerning which a few brief paragraphs have floated through the newspapers, and give to the readers of the "Express" some description of the very novel and interesting experiment undertaken by Messrs. Phillips & Woodcock, in breeding and domesticating the Mink. I found their 'peculiar institution' as curious as I had been led to expect, and as well worth an examination. It possesses not only the interest which naturalists would find in it, from the remarkable opportunity it affords for studying the habits of a singular and little known animal, but it represents one of the beginnings of a new branch of animal propagation and domestic culture, which is destined, I have no doubt at all, to assume great importance hereafter. When we consider, on the one hand, how constantly a demand for the finer furs is increasing from year to year, while the supply still more rapidly diminishes, as the animals furnishing such furs are exterminated in their wild state by the encroachment of civilization upon their haunts, we can see very well that the question whether these fur-bearing animals are capable of domestic propagation or not is a serious one, and that to determine by experiment that they are, is to found a description of business which can hardly fail to grow extensive and important. If the wealthy society of northern climates has no recourse but to the trapper for its furs, it will soon have to dispense with that elegant luxury; for the wild domain of nature is being so rapidly narrowed on both continents, that the trapper will, at no distant day, have his hunting field limited to the polar circle.

"But here, at this juncture, when the prospect of an

exhausted fur trade begins to be made pressing **by** enormous prices, comes up the idea of these gentlemen in this region of country who have undertaken, **with thoroughly** Yankee shrewdness, to propagate one of the most valuable **of the** fur-bearing animals, the mink, in a state of semi-domestication or confinement; and the fact that their experiment is so far promising nothing but successful results, is a fact to be announced as one of public interest and importance.

"Messrs. Phillips & Woodcock, whose 'Minkery' I **have** visited, are **not, I believe,** the pioneers of the business, but entered upon it with some **guidance from** the experience of others who, during late years, have been testing the domestication of the mink. They commenced **their under-**taking in December, 1866, with seven pairs of spring 'kittens,' as they call them, from which they expected no increase the following spring—last year. They were agreeably disappointed, however, by obtaining young from six of the females, altogether to the number of twenty-six. **The product was** from one to seven each, showing a remarkable variation. It is said by those experienced that the prolificness of the mink at the age at which this increase was obtained, may be considered as its minimum, as it is common for them in later periods to bear from six to nine annually; so that the seven original pairs may be expected to largely increase their progeny next spring, **while the young 'kittens' of last** spring will at the same **time become fruitful. Another year, therefore, is likely to multiply the** present stock of the breeders several times.

"The 'Minkery,' designed to accommodate one hundred minks for breeding, consists, first, of an enclosure about forty feet square, made by digging a trench one foot deep, laying a plank at the bottom, and from the outer edge starting the wall, which consists of boards four feet high, with a board to cap the top, projecting inward eight or ten inches to

prevent their climbing over. Within this enclosure is a
building fourteen by twenty-four, supplied with running
water, from which the mink catch living fish, that are often
furnished, with the greatest delight. The building is constructed with an alley three feet wide around its entire circumference. Within, are two rows of cells four feet deep,
and from two and two and a half wide, each having a door
ventilated at the top and bottom with wire screens, as is
also the outer wall opposite the cell. There is also at the
front entrance what the proprietors call the ante-rooms,
four by four feet, which must be fastened within every time
the building is entered to prevent the escape of the imprisoned animals. On entering the main hall, which the
minks have access to (when not rearing their young), they
present a very playful group. The person feeding them is
often mounted for their food, and their tenacity of hold is
so strong that they may be drawn about or lifted without
releasing their hold upon the food. The nest of the female
is very peculiarly constructed of grass, leaves, or straw,
with a lining of her own fur so firmly compacted together
as to be with difficulty torn in pieces. The aperture leading to the nest is a round opening just sufficient to admit
the dam, and is provided with a deflected curtain, which
covers the entrance and effectually secures her against all
invasion when she is within. About the middle of March
the females are separated from the males until the young
are reared. The necessity of this arises from the fact that
the male seems inclined to brood the young almost as
much as the dam, when both are permitted to remain
together.

"The expense of feeding the animals is almost nominal,
being supplied pretty much entirely from the usual offal of
the farm-yard, with occasional woodchucks and game in
general. They eat this food with equal avidity after

24

decomposition has taken place, devouring every particle of flesh, cartilages, and the softer bones. The flesh and bones entire of the woodchuck are consumed often at a single meal. While the expense of keeping is thus trivial, the profitable yield of the animal is immense, it being considered a moderate estimate to claim that one mink with her increase will equal the avails of a cow. Should this calculation hold good when the propagation of the mink is carried to a large scale, the business will become one of the most profitable in the world.

" So far, the experience of these gentlemen with the undomesticated mink has not been satisfactory, as their shyness cannot be overcome, and they have never obtained any increase from the animals in their wild state. They had to be taken when young and domesticated.

" Casadaga, the scene of this novel experiment, is a pretty village very pleasantly situated upon the shore of Casadaga Lake, which is three miles long, abounding with fish, and its waters supplied entirely by springs. It is the very dividing ridge of waters between the great courses of the north and south. The town will be reached one year hence, probably, by the Dunkirk, Warren, and Pittsburgh Railroad, now distant ten miles from Dunkirk. It has a population of a few hundred, does some manufacturing, has two dry-goods stores, two groceries, and good fishing, as many a Buffalonian can attest."

X.

AMERICAN FISH FOR ENGLISH WATERS.

In a chapter on the naturalization of fishes, I have alluded to a suggestion which I made to Mr. Francis, concerning the advantages of acclimating the smaller species of catfish in the waste waters of England. As it may be a matter of interest to some persons to know what other fishes are recommended, I give my letter as published in " The Field" with some few corrections, as well as Mr. Francis's very sensible remarks prefacing it. I also give some extracts from Mr. Francis's letter in reply to mine, which I regret to say, does not show that the acclimation of fresh water species is making the progress we had hoped for.

Sir,—The accompanying letter from a gentleman in the United States contains so much which cannot fail to be exceedingly interesting to a large portion of the readers of " The Field," that I have no hesitation in making it public, merely suppressing the name of the writer. The question of whether salmon can propagate when cut off from the sea receives here a very valuable reply; for although we cannot of course be certain that the fish noted by T. N. really were true salmon originally, there is a great air of probability in the surmise; and it seems difficult to understand what particular effect upon the constitution or organs of generation of fishes the salt water can have, that any particular fish which breeds in fresh water should be incapacitated from procreation by the want of a trip to the sea. My own theory is, that it is simply the want of that profuse nourishment which the sea affords which is felt by the fish ; and until the experiment suggested by me some time since, of confining some kelts* and feeding them abundantly, is tried with a view to see how far the fish can be restored to condition without a visit to the salt water, we can form but a mere conjectural opinion on the subject, which is of little value. No doubt the fish noted by T. N. here, are the

* This term is applied to salmon which have recently spawned.—
T. N.

same as those mentioned a few weeks since by your correspondent " A Wandering Naturalist," who speaks of a fish which he calls "the silvery salmon trout" of the Schoodic Lakes and the St. Croix.

As regards the introduction of American fish, there are undoubtedly many which would be of great value to us; and, if we had any piscatorial society in this country, immense benefits might be conferred upon our rivers and lakes by means of it. One or two attempts have been made . to introduce American fish, but they have failed, for the want of the commonest care. Here is an account, from another correspondent of mine in the States, of the failure of an attempt to bring over the bass:

" ——met with a misfortune before he left here. He got a letter of introduction to a person in ——, who had black bass for sale, and he employed mechanics, who constructed a water tank* for transporting his fish in, and started after the bass. The gentleman who owns the bass ponds entertained him hospitably, made his men draw a pond for bass, and *presented* the bass to ——, who started with them for this city. After three hours' travel by rail the fish appeared sound and healthy; and, being then on board a steamer which would reach here the next morning, he did not think it necessary to change the water, add more, or vivify it by an air pump. The result was, that when he arrived here the next morning his fish were all dead, and his water tank, which cost forty dollars, a dead . loss. My chagrin or regret hardly prevented me from characterizing the affair as it deserved. But, ——'s *faux pas* notwithstanding, I can send back bass to England."

Comment upon such a wretched failure is scarcely necessary. The worst of these failures is, that they deter others from attempting again a thing which, after all, with the

---

* Fish with sharp spines should have twice as much room in transporting them as soft finned fish, as they are apt to wound each other if too closely confined.—T. N.

commonest care, may be comparatively easy. The stocking of the Potomac with salmon bass is an instance, on the other side, of what a little shrewdness and readiness in resource may do.

Many of these American fishes, as the bass, shad, &c., would be particularly valuable to us as estuary fish, and there are very few of our rivers which they would not suit; and, after being naturalized in one or two, they would spread to others of their own accord. Unfortunately, however, if they get on but slowly in the progress of pisciculture in the United States, we do not get on at all. In fact, if we are doing anything, we are going back. This is most unfortunate, as there really is a splendid field of operations in this country, if there were any means of directing, assisting, and encouraging those operations.

FRANCIS FRANCIS.

Dear Sir,—In the second edition of your valuable work on fish culture, page 21, you speak of a species of salmon above the Falls of Niagara, in the great lakes, visiting the vicinity of Salt Springs, &c. I refer you to the passage.

In accordance with the wish you express, I would say there are no salmon above the falls alluded to; that they were never known there. The only species of salmo attaining the size of the salmon are *Salmo naymacush*, and another lately detected by Professor Agassiz—I forget the scientific name just now, but previously it was confounded with *S. naymacush*. Both of these species grow to the weight of 80lb., and have been known larger. They are inferior fish, both in beauty and flavor, compared with the anadromous salmon. In habits, and in fact in appearance, they are very like your *Salmo ferox* of Scotland.

Now as to a salmon we have, which *does not go to sea*. It is found in the Schoodic Lakes, which are drained by

24 *

and connect with the St. Croix, which river divides the state of Maine from the British province of New Brunswich. Agassiz says there is no doubt of there being land-locked salmon, having all the specific characteristics of *Salmo salar*. It is supposed that in past centuries, perhaps ages ago, some obstruction was interposed, and, not being able to go to sea, they eventually propagated their species, and remained, producing dwarf salmon ; and, though having free access to the ocean since, have been so modified as to lose their anadromous instinct, and do not attempt to migrate. They are much like grilse in the sport they afford, leap often and high when hooked, and not less plucky for their size, which averages about 1½lb., though sometimes they attain 4lb. or 5lb., and in rare cases 7lb. Great catches are made every summer by anglers on both sides of the border. Capt. C., R. A., stationed at Fredericktown, N. B., is very successful in taking them. The sport is only with the fly, of course, large trout flies being generally used. This fish would do splendidly in your Scottish rivers and lakes, particularly where the latter are connected by the former.

In reading your account of the introduction of *Silurus glanis* into England, the thought occurred to me that the smaller species of our catfish, of which there are two, the white and yellow, would be a great acquisition to your sluggish and fat waters. They are exceeding fine pan fish, the heads being taken off when so cooked, and they make an excellent stew with the heads on. In the former case they are skinned as eels ; in the latter only scraped and cleansed, the skin and head remaining, contributing to the gluten, which adds to the richness of the stew. There are some gigantic species of this fish in streams of the Mississippi valley, but they are coarse, tough, and distasteful. They are exceedingly hardy, and occupy such habitat as eels generally do. They can hardly be called predacious, but herbiverous, as carp are, and therefore not destructive to the fry of finer species. Although fond of muddy streams and still waters, they will thrive in any water, and would perhaps **improve on** the condition of the Thames below **London, which is so** detrimental to other fish. They are found all spring, summer, and autumn, **in** our Philadelphia market, tied in bunches, unhided and decapitated, **and** hawked about the streets by fish women. The texture of the meat is something like trout, and they are next to **that** fish in excellence for the pan.

Another fish I have for some time thought of bringing to your notice—you have made slight allusion to it—the black bass. **There are two species :** *Grystes nigricans*, **the** lake bass ; **and** *Grystes salmoides*, **the bass of the western** and southern waters (by west I mean west of the Allegheny **mountains**). They are predacious rascals, though, and would play havoc with salmon fry, and therefore should not be introduced into such streams ; the *G. nigricans*, however, would seldom if ever go out of the lakes, especially into such water as salmon spawn in, though the other species might.

Both of these species are very easily naturalized in any new habitat. Many of our lakelets, ponds, and millponds **have become productive** of *G. nigricans*. The other fish, *G. salmoides*, has been introduced into the Potomac, and become abundant there. Three rods have made a catch in a day of 326lb. This fish was unknown in the Potomac until about fourteen years since, when an engineer on the Baltimore and Ohio railroad, as he was about starting east-**ward, put twenty** of them into a bag-net and soused them into the water tank of the locomotive. When he arrived at Cumberland, a town on the eastern side of the moun-tains, he let the fish loose into the Potomac, a diminutive stream there, and the consequence is they have multiplied in all the tributaries of that river (and now afford fine sport, as they rise beautifully at the fly, and are excellent eating) as far down as the Great Falls, about twenty-five miles above Washington. Not being anadromous, they show no disposition to shoot the falls and make their escape to tide water.

I would say further of the catfish, that any mercantile house at Philadelphia or Baltimore, in connection with London or Liverpool, could easily procure a few score of them and send them over. They are so hardy that the steward of a steamer or sailing vessel, for a small fee, would take charge of them, and land them with little or no loss in numbers.

In conclusion of this letter, I must thank you for the instruction I have derived from your book on fish culture, as well as that on angling; and, further, would ask the favor of your sending me any further information in a printed form that has appeared on the stocking of salmon rivers in Great Britain, the progress of the Thames Angling Preservation Society, &c. We are making but slow progress in pisciculture here, but are beginning to open our eyes to its advantages in bringing back salmon and shad to the rivers from which we have banished them, and are doing something at least to this end.

By the way, if you could introduce our shad into your rivers, it would be a great acquisition; its average size is 3½lbs. to 4lbs., and it grows to 7lbs. All of your countrymen who have eaten of it here can testify as to its juicy, delicate flavor. It also smokes and salts down well. Further in its favor, it is a sea fish, paying only one annual visit to our rivers, and that for the purpose of spawning; deriving all its growth from its feeding-grounds at sea, like the salmon, but, unlike that fish, increasing in fresh water, up to the time of its spawning, in both flesh and flavor. No food, however, has been at any time found in its stomach after entering our rivers. There may be one obstacle, however, to its introduction into European rivers; this is, that its spawn hatches out in the incredibly short time of fifty-two hours. It was so proved on the Connecticut river last summer, when forty millions of young shad were produced by artificial impregnation and incubation, and turned loose in that river. The young shad migrates to sea the first summer. **T. N.**

Francis Francis, Esq., Twickenham.

___

The following is Mr. Francis's letter on receipt of the author's.

THE FURS, Twickenham, Middlesex.

DEAR SIR,—Very many thanks for your most interesting letter, which was so interesting to me that I took the liberty of publishing it in "The Field," and herewith I send you a copy of the paper with a few remarks of my own introductory. I hope you will not think I have taken an undue liberty; but I thought as I did not publish the name, that I might do so. Singularly enough, the publication of it with my remarks has turned up a prospect of something useful resulting. For the Earl of Breadalbane, who is an old acquaintance of mine, wrote to me this morning upon the subject, and said if I would start a piscicultural society he would make a commencement, and put his name down for £100 and a yearly subscription of £10 or £20 as the case might require. Since the acclimatization society broke up my fish cultural establishment, we have been at a standstill. Indeed, we have been going back, and nothing practical has been done in pisciculture or even attempted.

*   *   *   *   *   *   *   *   *

A great fuss has been made about stocking the Thames with salmon. Hundreds of pounds have been spent, and

hundreds of thousands of fry have been wasted. For in
its present state no salmon fry can pass through the London
filth to the sea. I told them that it was impossible from
the first. Mr. Ffennel, our late inspector, and every person
really acquainted with the salmon, said the same thing.
Yet, have they gone on with this insane experiment for six
or seven years in succession, and never a single grilse has
been seen above London, nor will any be seen until the
sewerage, which is terribly poisoned with gas, refuse, and
many other matters fatal to fish, can be disposed of, when
the thing may be practicable. As regards the young trout
put into the river, they are picked up by the perch and pike
to a large extent, and those that are left, as they rise freely
to the fly, are caught in a considerable number before they
get to a pound weight, so that very few ever increase to benefit in any way the stock of the river. I greatly fear that the
whole thing is little better than a complete failure. Last
season almost the whole of the fry were stolen by one of
the men about them, and sold surreptitiously, as they are
worth money. There is really no piscicultural news at all
beyond this. I wish there was—and such being the state
of things, I am sorely tempted to try my hand again by
Lord Breadalbane's offer, if it were not for the immense
amount of trouble and expense which such work entails
without any prospect of paying even in the long run. Lord
B. was much struck with your remarks on the catfish,* &c.,

---

* It will be seen on page 216 how these fish can be transported in
wet cloths; last spring a few of them were quite lively when shaken
from a blanket after the wagon had returned to the city, when they
had been out of water for twelve hours. I have no doubt that with
some care they could be sent to England by steamer in the same
way. Keeping the cloths saturated with water not over ten degrees
above freezing point, and a daily examination to take out any that
might die, I think would insure the transportation of at least half
of them. The experiment would cost but a trifle.

TROUTDALE HATCHING-TROUGHS.

so probably I may have to trouble you again for further information.

XI.

DR. J. H. SLACK'S TROUT-BREEDING ESTABLISHMENT.

The three illustrations, "Trout Dale Spring," "Trout Dale Hatching-house," and "Trout Dale Fish Ponds," appeared originally in the June number of "Harper's Weekly." The publishers of this book purchased the plates, which, with some little alteration have been made to contribute to the ornate appearance of this appendix.

This establishment is in Warren county, New Jersey, near the Musconetcong creek, about a mile and a half from Valley station, on the Central Railroad of New Jersey. It is nine miles east of the town of Easton, Pennsylvania, and sixty-five miles west of New York. It was commenced by the writer in May 1866, and sold in an uncompleted condition to Dr. J. H. Slack, in September 1867.

The spring discharges something over a thousand gallons per minute; which is about one-third the flow of the Ingham spring, where the writer is about to construct another trout factory. The water is uniformly at 50° winter and summer.

The hatching-house is in accordance with the plan in the third chapter of this book. So, also, are the ponds (which lay parallel to each other in front of the hatching-house) such in their proportions, as I have recommended. Dr. Slack's success, as well as that of others who engage in the business, will depend much on that careful attention to details which I have so strongly urged.

XII.

STEPHEN H. AINSWORTH'S NEW HATCHING-RACE, FOR NATURAL PROPAGATION.

On a preceding page I have alluded to the loss of ova which the trout culturist sustains by fish spawning in the race at night, or between the stated times of driving them down into the trap for the purpose of manipulating them. Persons who are not thoroughly acquainted with the indications of ripeness of trout, also take many immature eggs, and from lack of experience do not fecundate all they obtain. To obviate such loss, Mr. Ainsworth has invented the hatching-race described below. It is unnecessary to say that he would submit no plan without giving it much deliberate thought; that he is thoroughly practical, as can be judged from his success in matters belonging to his several avocations: *i. e.* nurseryman, farmer, and stock-raiser. The description of the hatching-race are his own words.

"First build the race three or four feet wide, the sides of plank, and bottom of plank or stone nicely paved, so as to have the bottom perfectly clean at all times. Cover the whole bottom of the race with wire screens of zinc or of iron painted, about ten or twelve wires to the inch, so as to hold all the spawn that falls on them. Place these screens on half inch strips of wood so as to hold them and the spawn half an inch above the pavement. Nail these screens on to a one inch frame, and place them side by side the whole length of the race; which may be from ten to fifty feet long, according to the number of spawning trout.

"Then make another set of wire screens, of about three wires to the inch, so that the spawn will **fall through with** ease, and nail these on to a frame one by two inches. Have handles on all of them, so as to take them up easily. Place these over the fine ones, which will give a space of one inch between the top and bottom screens. Now sift gravel through a sieve **of two wires to the inch, so as to be** sure to get out all the gravel that would **pass** through the **upper** screen. Wash this coarse gravel clean, **and** put it about two inches thick on the upper screens. Then make small nests, within every foot or eighteen inches of each other, by digging nearly down **to the wire of the upper** screen.

"The female trout will whip the gravel in these nests clear down to the wire and deposit their spawn, which will mostly fall through to the lower screen, and be plainly in sight. The male will eject his milt as usual upon them, with the whip of his tail to agitate the water, and thus **impregnate** them all. The female will now cover them **up, and likely** sift all the spawn that has lodged **in the gravel,** through the upper screen on to the lower one, and thus in time deposit all her spawn in perfection and perfectly impregnated.

"The water should be from ten to twelve inches deep over the gravel in the race, with a gentle current. Should any spawn remain in the gravel, they will be **very** likely **to fall down by raising the upper** screens up **and down a few** times in the water, or with a little sifting at **most, so that** nearly all will find their way **on to the under** screen. **I** would take out all the screens **in from one to six days, and** place the spawn in my form **of hatching box.**

"**Firstly, this** method will **always ensure** perfect impregnation;

"Secondly, it **will** save three-fourths of the time at least;

25   T

"Thirdly, it will save all the parent trout in health, whereas, in artificial impregnation it kills some by constant handling;

"Fourthly, the young will be more perfect, stronger, and healthier, from the perfectly mature spawn;

"Fifthly, the trout cannot get at the spawn to eat them;

"Sixthly, it saves a world of care and watching.

"These screens can be placed in any stream, and the spawn is taken in perfection. They will handle best the width of the wire cloth, and the length the width of the race, with handles at the ends."

XIII.

CRUSTACEA.

The following extracts from "The Harvest of the Sea," will give some idea of the immense number of Crustacea consumed by the people of London, as well as an insight of the natural history of some of the members of this class of animals. I am not aware of any statistical information having been furnished of the amount of this kind of food, in the United States, but the number of lobsters consumed east of New-York must be immense.

Crabs are more commonly eaten south of that city along the whole extent of our coast, and are generally considered a delicacy, soft crabs particularly so. Crabs are found in immense numbers in the shoal waters of the southern sea-board states. In some of the creeks on the Chesapeake Bay, I have seen them so numerous that some thousands might have been counted on the area of a single rod of the

TROUTDALE FISH-PONDS.

bottom. There is no doubt, that where they are so abundant, enclosures might be made of hurdles, and hard crabs collected and kept until the time of shedding. Soft crabs, as they would then be, command a high price in our city markets, varying from seventy-five cents to a dollar and a half per dozen.

Shell-fish is the popular name bestowed by unscientific persons on the crustacea and mollusca, and no other designation could so well cover the multitudinous variety of forms which are embraced in these extensive divisions of the animal kingdom. Fanciful disquisitions on shell-fish and on marine zoology have been intruded on the public of late till they have become somewhat tiresome ; but as our knowledge of the natural history of all kinds of sea animals, and particularly of oysters, lobsters, crabs, etc., is decidedly on the increase, there is yet room for all that I have to say on the subject of these dainties ; and there are still unexplored wonders of animal life in the fathomless sea that deserve the deepest study.

The economic and productive phases of our shell-fish fisheries have never yet, in my opinion, been sufficiently discussed, and when I state that the power of multiplication possessed by all kinds of crustacea and mollusca is even greater, if that be possible, than that possessed by finned fishes, it will be obvious that there is much in their natural history that must prove interesting even to the most general reader. Each oyster, as we have seen, gives birth to almost incredible quantities of young. Lobsters also have an amazing fecundity, and yield an immense number of eggs— each female producing from twelve to twenty thousand in a season ; and the crab is likewise most prolific. I lately purchased a crab weighing within an ounce of two pounds,

and it contained a mass of minute eggs equal in size to a
man's hand; these were so minute that a very small portion of them, picked off with the point of a pin, when
placed on a bit of glass, and counted by the aid of a power-
ful microscope, numbered over sixty, each appearing of the
size of a red currant, and not at all unlike that fruit: so
far as I could guess the eggs were not nearly ripe. I also
examined about the same time a quantity of shrimp eggs;
and it is curious that, while there are the cock and hen
lobster, I never saw any difference in the sex of the
shrimps: all that I handled, amounting to hundreds, were
females, and all of them were laden with spawn, the eggs
being so minute as to resemble grains of the finest sand.

Although the crustacean family counts its varieties by
thousands, and contains members of all sizes, from minute
animalculæ to gigantic American crabs and lobsters, and
ranges from the simplest to the most complex forms, yet
the edible varieties are not at all numerous. The largest
of these are the lobster (*Astacus marinus*) and the crab
(*Cancer pagurus*); and river and sea cray-fish may also be
seen in considerable quantities in London shell-fish shops;
and as for common shrimps (*Crangon vulgaris*) and prawns
(*Palæmon serratis*), they are eaten in myriads. The violet
or marching crab of the West Indies, and the robber crab
common to the islands of the Pacific, are also esteemed as
great delicacies of the table, but are unknown in this
country except by reputation.

*   *   *   *   *   *   *   *   *

Mr. *Cancer pagurus* is watched as he bustles out for his
evening promenade, and, on being deftly pitched upon his
back by means of a pole, he indignantly seizes upon it with
all his might, and the stick being shaken a little has the
desirable effect of causing Mr. Crab to cling thereto with
great tenacity, which is, of course, the very thing desired

by the grinning "human" at the other end, as whenever he
feels his prey secure he dexterously hauls him on board,
unhooks the crusty gentleman with a jerk, and adds him to
the accumulating heap at the bottom of the old boat. The
monkeys in the West Indies are, however, still more ingenious than the "fisher loons" of Arran or Skye. Those
wise animals, when they take a notion of dining on a crab,
proceed to the rocks, and slyly insinuating their tail into
one of the holes where the crustacea take refuge, that
appendage is at once seized upon by the crab, who is thereby
drawn from his hiding-place, and, being speedily dashed to
pieces on the hard stone, affords a fine feast to his captor.

* * * * * * * * *

The west and north-west coasts of Ireland abound with
fine lobsters, and welled vessels bring thence supplies for
the London market, and it is said that a supply of 10,000 a
week can easily be obtained. Immense quantities are also
procured on the west coast of Scotland. A year or two ago
I saw on board the *Islesman* steamboat at Greenock a cargo
of 30,000 lobsters, obtained chiefly on the coasts of Lewis
and Skye. The value of these to the captors would be
upwards of £1000, and in the English fishmarkets the lot
would bring at least four times that sum. As showing how
enormous the food wealth of the sea still is, notwithstanding
the quantity taken out of it, I may cite here a few brief
particulars of a little experiment of a charitable nature
which was tried by a gentleman who took a warm interest
in the Highland fishermen, and the results of which he
himself lately made public. Commiserating the wretched-
ness which he had witnessed among many, who, although
anxious to labor, were unable to procure work, and at the
same time feeling that the usual method of assisting them
was based on a mistaken principle, this gentleman under-
took the establishment of a fishery upon a small scale at

25 *

his own expense. He therefore expended a sum of £600, with which he procured eight boats, completely equipped, and a small smack of sixteen tons. The crews, consisting of thirty men, he furnished with all the necessary fishing materials, paying the men weekly wages ranging from nine to thirteen shillings, part of the sum being in meal. The result of this experiment was, that these eight boats sent to the London market in a few months as many lobsters as reimbursed the original cost of the fishing plant. The men and their families were thus rescued from a state of semi-starvation, and are now living in comfort, with plenty surrounding their dwellings; and have, besides, the satisfaction of knowing that their present independent condition has been achieved principally by means of their own well-sustained industry.

A very large share of our lobsters is derived from Norway, as many as 30,000 sometimes arriving from the fjords in a single day. The Norway lobsters are much esteemed, and we pay the Norwegians something like £20,000 a year for this one article of commerce. They are brought over in welled steam-vessels, and are kept in the wooden reservoirs already alluded to, some of which may be seen at Hole Haven, on the Essex side of the Thames. Once upon a time, some forty years ago, one of these wooden lobster-stores was run into by a Russian frigate, whereby some 20,000 lobsters were set adrift to sprawl in the muddy waters of the Thames. In order that the great mass of animals confined in these places may be kept upon their best behavior, a species of cruelty has to be perpetrated to prevent their tearing each other to pieces : the great claw is, therefore, rendered paralytic by means of a wooden peg being driven into a lower joint.

I have no intention of describing the whole members of the crustacea; they are much too numerous to admit of that, ranging as they do from the comparatively giant-like crab and lobster down to the millions of minute insects which at some places confer a phosphorescent appearance on the waters of the sea. My limits will necessarily confine me to a few of the principal members of the family—the edible crustacea, in fact; and these I shall endeavor to speak about in such plain language as I think my readers will understand, leaving out as much of the fashionable " scientific slang" as I possibly can.

The more we study the varied crustacea of the British shores, the more we are struck with their wonderful formation, and the peculiar habits of their members. I once heard a clergyman at a lecture describe a lobster in brief but fitting terms as a standing romance of the sea—an animal whose clothing is a shell, which it casts away once a year in order that it may put on a larger suit—an animal whose flesh is in its tail and legs, and whose hair is in the inside of its breast, whose stomach is in its head, and which is changed every year for a new one, and which new one begins its life by devouring the old! an animal which carries its eggs within its body till they become fruitful, and then carries them outwardly under its tail; an animal which can throw off its legs when they become troublesome, and can in a brief time replace them with others; and lastly, an animal with very sharp eyes placed in movable horns. The picture is not at all overdrawn. It is a wondrous creature this lobster, and I may be allowed a brief space in which to describe the curious provision of nature which allows for an increase of growth, or provides for the renewal of a broken limb, and which applies generally to the edible crustacea.

The habits of the principal crustacea are now pretty well understood, and their mode of growth is so peculiar as to render a close inspection of their habits a most interesting study. As has been stated, a good-sized lobster will yield about 20,000 eggs, and these are hatched, being so nearly ripe before they are abandoned by the mother, with great rapidity—it is said in forty-eight hours—and grow quickly, although the young lobster passes through many changes before it is fit to be presented at table. During the early periods of growth it casts its shell frequently. This wonderful provision for an increase of size in the lobster has been minutely studied during its period of moulting. Mr. Jonathan Couch says the additional size which is gained at each period of exuviation is perfectly surprising, and it is wonderful to see the complete covering of the animal cast off like a suit of old clothes, while it hides, naked and soft, in a convenient hole, awaiting the growth of its new crust. In fact, it is difficult to believe that the great soft animal ever inhabited the cast-off habitation which is lying beside it, because the lobster looks, and really is, so much larger. The lobster, crab, etc., change their shells about every six weeks during the first year of their age, every two months during the second year, and then the changing of the shell becomes less frequent, being reduced to four times a year. It is supposed that this animal becomes reproductive at the age of five years.

    *   *   *   *   *   *   *   *

When the female crustacea retire in order to undergo their exuviation they are watched, or rather guarded, by the males; and if one male be taken away, in a short time another will be found to have taken his place. I do not think there is any particular season for moulting; the period differs in different places, according to the temperature of the water and other circumstances, so that we might have shell-fish (and white-fish too) all the year round were a little attention paid to the different seasons of exuviation and egg-laying.

The mode in which a hen lobster lays her eggs is curious : she lodges a quantity of them under her tail, and bears them about for a considerable period ; indeed, till they are so nearly hatched as only to require a very brief time to mature them.* When the eggs are first exuded from the ovary they are very small, but before they are committed to the sand or water they increase considerably in size, and become as large as good sized shot. Lobsters may be found with eggs, or " in berry" as it is called, all the year round ; and when the hen is in process of depositing her eggs she is not good for food, the flesh being poor, watery, and destitute of flavor.

XIV.

SALMON HATCHING ESTABLISHMENT ON THE
MIRAMICHI.

Just before going to press, I have received the following additional information from Rev. Livingston Stone concerning this project. It will be seen from his remarks, that all the difficulties which have heretofore existed in the transportation of salmon ova to the United States, are soon to be surmounted. All of the Atlantic states north of the Chesapeake bay may therefore have an opportunity, at but small expense, of restoring exhausted rivers, and trying the experiment of naturalizing salmon in those which were not its natural habitat.

" The salmon breeding establishment on the Miramichi was started by myself, and is owned nominally by myself,

---

* Lobsters collect in large numbers through the summer in shallow water along the sandy shores of the bay of Chaleurs, to deposit their eggs. Such a place is called by the habitans "a lobster camp."

although others will be interested in it to some extent.
The object of it is, to supply salmon spawn and young salmon for stocking the American rivers. The present plan
is to collect just before the spawning season, as many live
salmon as possible, in a large enclosure provided with artificial spawning-beds, and to take the spawn from the parent
fish, after the manner that trout spawn are taken.

"The eggs will be kept at the Miramichi until old
enough for transportation, when they will be brought to
headquarters at Charlestown, and placed in the hatching-
beds, there to be hatched.

"There are at present thirty-two troughs, each twenty
feet in length, prepared to receive the salmon ova, with
provision for more if needed. These hatching-troughs are
in a building made for the purpose, sixty feet by twenty-
seven wide. The troughs will be able to receive 2000 ova
to the foot. The spawn will be ready to transport from the
Miramichi about twenty days after being taken, and will be
ready for the second transportation any time after that."

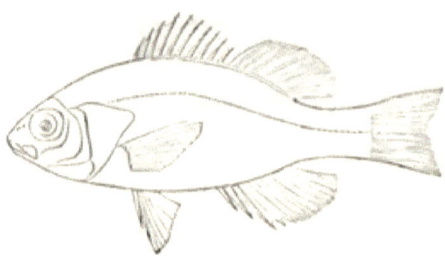

INDEX.

26

THE END.

ERRATA.

The plate facing page 141, is taken from the first Report of the Massachusetts Fish Commissioners, and represents the successive growth of the young shad from the age of two or three weeks, until the time of migration to sea late in the summer, or in early autumn.

Page 48, line 17, for "beyond to the middle," read "beyond the middle."

www.ingramcontent.com/pod-product-compliance
Lightning Source LLC
Chambersburg PA
CBHW060514030726

47498CB00004B/941